Youth Development and Physical Activity

Linking Universities and Communities

Don Hellison, PhD
University of Illinois at Chicago
Nick Cutforth, PhD
University of Denver
James Kallusky, EdD
California State University, Los Angeles
Tom Martinek, EdD
University of North Carolina at Greensboro
Melissa Parker, PhD
Jim Stiehl, PhD
University of Northern Colorado

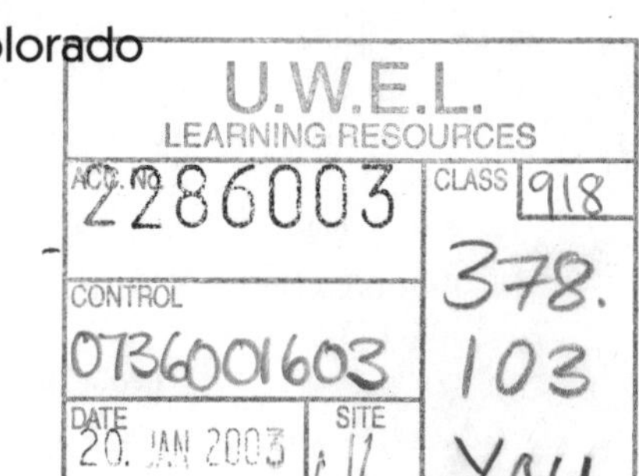

Human Kinetics

Library of Congress Cataloging-in-Publication Data

Youth development and physical activity : linking universities and communities / Don Hellison ... [et al.].

p. cm.

Includes bibliographical references and index.

ISBN 0-7360-0160-3

1. Physical education of socially handicapped youth--United States. 2. Community and school--United States. 3. Student service--United States. I. Hellison, Donald R., 1938-

GV444 .Y68 2000

378.1'03--dc21

00-031926

ISBN 0-7360-0160-3

Acquisitions Editor: Scott Wikgren; **Managing Editor:** Amy Flaig; **Assistant Editors:** Derek Campbell, Mark Zulauf; **Copyeditor:** Julie Anderson; **Proofreader:** Jim Burns; **Indexer:** Betty Frizzéll; **Graphic Designer:** Robert Reuther; **Graphic Artist:** Dawn Sills; **Cover Designer:** Fred Starbird; **Art Manager:** Craig Newsom; **Illustrator:** Accurate Art; **Printer:** Versa Press

Printed in the United States of America

10 9 8 7 6 5 4 3 2 1

Human Kinetics
Web site: http://www.humankinetics.com

United States: Human Kinetics, P.O. Box 5076, Champaign, IL 61825-5076
800-747-4457
e-mail: humank@hkusa.com

Canada: Human Kinetics, 475 Devonshire Road Unit 100, Windsor, ON N8Y 2L5
800-465-7301 (in Canada only)
e-mail: humank@hkcanada.com

Europe: Human Kinetics, P.O. Box IW14, Leeds LS16 6TR, United Kingdom
+44 (0)113-278 1708
e-mail: humank@hkeurope.com

Australia: Human Kinetics, 57A Price Avenue, Lower Mitcham, South Australia 5062
(08) 82771555
e-mail: liahka@senet.com.au

New Zealand: Human Kinetics, P.O. Box 105-231, Auckland Central
09-309-1890
e-mail: humank@hknewz.com

Contents

Foreword

Joe Kahne, PhD, Mills College, Oakland, California

Athletics occupies a privileged place in our culture. Interest in sports spans age, social class, religion, race, and gender. Second perhaps only to the weather, sports provide a topic of shared concern. In providing a strategy for channeling children's and adolescents' interests in athletic activities in highly productive directions both during and after school, this book makes a fundamentally important contribution.

Unfortunately, team sports and related athletic programming often fail to fully tap their developmental potential. Frequently, such programming provides youth with safe, structured, and enjoyable diversions. Given that unstructured time after school is often "high-risk" time for youth, such programming is both logical and desirable. When assessed from the standpoint of a youth development agenda, however, much athletic programming comes up short. Indeed, several large quantitative studies have found that the benefits (academic success, status attainment, and future civic involvement) associated with other forms of extracurricular activity do not hold for athletics.

In response to this dilemma, the authors provide a two-pronged approach. First, they detail a strategy for embedding a youth development agenda into physical education curriculum. Their strategy focuses on youth capacities. It builds on the opportunities for competence and intrinsic motivation afforded by physical activity programs to promote both personal and social responsibility. Their responsibility model is structured to provide opportunities for leadership, for feedback, for self-regulation, and for personal support. As a result, participants develop more than athletic capacities—they develop into more responsible and capable individuals.

Roughly a year ago, I had the opportunity to look closely at this approach. I was studying the degree to which the after-school opportunities in a particular Chicago neighborhood promoted a youth development agenda. Consistent with studies previously noted, I found that youth enjoyed after-school sports programming, but that such curriculum provided fewer supports for youth development than other after-school curriculum. I was aware that Don Hellison employed a nontraditional physical activity curriculum focused on youth development, and I asked if I could include it in my study.

Don worked with very similar youth in a similar neighborhood, but his results were quite different. The level of support for youth development reported by students who participated in this athletic program was significantly greater than that identified by students participating in traditional athletic after-school activities. Students benefited from the focus on responsibility and from opportunities for leadership, reflection, feedback, and personal support.

But this book is about more than broadening the focus of physical education curriculum. It makes a second substantial contribution by highlighting the potential benefits of strengthening ties between schools and universities. In this case, the authors' motivation stems from their desire to provide youth with high-quality programming while developing the next generation of physical educators. The implications of what they are doing extend far beyond physical education. The kinds of links they are making between the university and the community could profoundly and positively alter the education of teachers, social workers, and others in the service sector. Moreover, the stance they assume—their willingness to become directly involved with underserved populations—provides a blueprint for those hoping that universities will provide greater direct support for their communities.

Although motivated by the very real successes they experience in their work, the authors are not blind romantics. They recognize that transforming teacher practices is a difficult process. In many reports it requires a cultural shift. They are also well aware that they are not the first to try to strengthen links between universities and communities. Universities face multiple pressures and must respond to multiple priorities; the road toward changing university practices will be bumpy at best.

Although the challenge that confronts those with these commitments is substantial, we are very lucky to have this book. It provides a place from which we can begin.

Preface

Don Hellison

"Society has needs and problems; universities have disciplines and departments." (Lawson, 1997, p. 20)

A fresh breeze is blowing in American higher education, threatening to ruffle the ivory tower image of many colleges and universities. This breeze is university–community collaboration, which has recently emerged as an agenda item for discussion, debate, and, in some schools, action. Historically, most universities have tended to ignore the communities in which they live, other than to offer an education to those residents who qualified and could afford it. Of course, faculty have wandered into the community from time to time to supervise student teachers, collect data, or make a speech at some public affair, but for the most part "town and gown" have remained separate worlds. This is changing. University faculty, often encouraged by their deans and provosts, are finding ways of using their talents to benefit local communities. University students are also becoming involved, sometimes by tackling real-world problems and needs as part of their university education, sometimes as a result of genuine outreach activities in professional preparation programs such as teacher education.

Service Learning

The linkage of student involvement in the community to university coursework is now being called service learning, especially if it is accompanied by structured critical reflection. Many universities, and in at least one case a large multicampus state university system, are encouraging faculty to include service learning in their courses. Service learning often focuses on the benefits derived by the participating university student, but our experiences suggest that service learning can also contribute to the community, if it is structured to do so. In addition, applied research conducted by university students can be a form of service learning if such research contributes to community development.

Underserved Youth

University–community collaboration is very timely, because communities small and large struggle with a number of seemingly intractable issues. Many of these issues involve today's youth. Read any newspaper and you will find reports of youth violence, drugs, gangs, teen pregnancy, and the like. These phenomena are no longer inner-city problems; they are occurring among White kids in affluent suburbs and in small towns, as well as in the poorest metropolitan neighborhoods. Poverty is of course one factor associated with these problems, but the presence of these problems across social and economic boundaries indicates the range and complexity of causal factors. In many neighborhoods, schools and social agencies are underfunded, in need of reform, or in scarce supply. In other communities, services seem more abundant, but kids' needs are still not being met.

Too often, youth are blamed for possessing bad attitudes and inappropriate or even reprehensible behaviors, a perspective frequently built into program policies. We use the term *underserved youth* to emphasize services that these kids need to build on their strengths and develop to their full potential. Rather than focusing on their problems, rather than trying to keep them off the street or lock them up, we want to help them become who they are capable of becoming. More focused programs such as conflict resolution are popular and numerous, but holistic strength-based programs such as those we have in mind are scarce, despite the Carnegie Council on Adolescent Development's report of the attraction of youth to these kinds of programs. A holistic, strength-based approach capitalizes on the potential but mostly untapped contributions of community physical activity programs to the physical, emotional, social, and spiritual health of children and youth.

The Role of Physical Education in Higher Education

The field of physical education in higher education (i.e., kinesiology, exercise and sport science, etc.) has lagged behind other departments and disciplines in its community involvement, especially regarding underserved youth. This is so despite the rich opportunities for contributing to these kids' lives via outreach and applied research by faculty and students in sport pedagogy, coaching education, sport psychology, sport sociology, sport management, and so on.

For example, student internships such as those in teacher education tend to be professional training grounds rather than service learning experiences that emphasize helping needy youth. Social conscience as a curricular theme appears to be confined for the most part to course lectures, for example, in sport sociology, rather than being connected to community involvement. To address the difficult attitude and behavior problems of today's kids, teacher education often uses classroom management strategies aimed at controlling and motivating students, a strategy that falls far short of helping students to address the social problems they face and sidesteps the need for more holistic, strength-based programs.

These examples do not begin to reflect the depth of indifference to community service and applied research in many physical education in higher education departments. The primary emphasis, for a variety of reasons, is on the continual buildup of specialized bodies of subdisciplinary knowledge (e.g., exercise physiology, sport psychology, sport pedagogy), preferably externally funded by the federal government or a large foundation. Our vision of a more holistic, practice-based, community-informed vision of youth work, service, and research obviously conflicts with current perspectives and practices.

Youth Development

Physical education in higher education's involvement in the community may be enhanced by the emerging field of community youth development. Traditionally, physical education departments offer a teacher education program aimed at educating students for careers as public school teachers (and, sometimes, coaches). They also may offer a degree in community physical education or some similar term, but in many cases little leadership exists to provide meaningful courses and experiences leading to careers in social agencies, such as the YMCA, Boys and Girls Clubs, and park districts, despite the historical precedent set by George Williams College (with the YMCA) and a few other institutions. These kinds of organizations provide many of the extended day programs for kids, programs that are more often than not physical activity-based. Moreover, physical activity programs that claim to address the social ills of underserved youth—for example, the Chicago Housing Authority's Midnight Basketball (also in other cities, usually sponsored by some city agency), the NCAA-sponsored National Youth Sport Program, Nike's P.L.A.Y. program, and Illinois politician Jesse White's Tumblers—are increasing in number and have attracted substantial media and political attention and debate.

Community youth development is an emerging field of its own, in part because the demand for trained youth development professionals is estimated to increase by 45 percent by the year 2002! Youth development now has its own professional journal, *CYD Journal: Community Youth Development* (formerly *New Designs for Youth Development*), and national organizations such as the National Network for Youth and American Humanics. The DeWitt-Wallace/Reader's Digest Fund recently demonstrated interest in this emerging field by funding a four-year study to evaluate the quality of youth development work in the United States.

Right now, youth development is without a home in most universities. Schools (colleges, departments) of social work don't really focus on youth development nor do schools of education. Departments of recreation and/or leisure studies as well as programs in therapeutic recreation have shown some interest, but physical education in higher education, with its historic commitment to sport and exercise pedagogy, psychology, sociology, and administration, could step into the breach, thereby expanding opportunities for the employment of graduates, service learning experiences in the community, and applied research focused on physical activity programs for underserved youth. Wherever physical activity programs for underserved youth exist or can be created becomes a potential setting for involvement of faculty and students, as well as possible employment before or after graduation. This broad conceptualization includes schools but does not exclude other settings.

Our Commitment

The six authors of this book, however, are very much interested in youth development and have a combined 70 years of direct experience with, and the development and evaluation of programs for, underserved youth. Despite the various paths our careers as physical education professors have taken, all of us have arrived one way or another at the same place: We are committed to trying to help kids in underserved neighborhoods in our communities, with whatever spinoffs occur from this activity. For some of us, this means working in the inner-city; for others the focus is sons and daughters of migrant workers or kids who are in alternative schools or who have been expelled from school. Some of our colleagues have used our ideas with more affluent youth, whom, they say, also need help. In all cases, this work is based on a holistic, strength-based youth development approach that uses physical activity to teach kids to take responsibility for their own well-being and for being sensitive and responsive to the well-being of others. This approach has acquired a variety of names over the years, for example, TPSR (Teaching Personal and Social Responsibility), but is most commonly called simply the responsibility model. (See chapter 3 for a description of this approach.)

Central to our commitment to provide youth development programs in our underserved communities is our own participation in teaching underserved kids. In addition, we have gotten our university students involved, thereby linking university professional preparation programs and service learning experiences to these community youth programs. Attempting this linkage has, in turn, required either some reconceptualization of existing university programs or the development of new ones, for example, the expansion beyond traditional teacher education programs. It has also meant finding ways to learn whether our work is making a positive impact and how to develop better models from which to proceed, as well as identifying appropriate means for sharing the processes and outcomes with others. This book is our most complete attempt to do so.

About This Book

In this book, you will find our motives for swimming against the tide of tradition; our struggles to gain the trust of our community counterparts; the approaches to youth development, community programs, and professional preparation/service learning programs that we have found most useful for our work; and how we have evaluated the processes and outcomes of our programs. You will also "hear" the voices of kids in our programs and of university students who teach in, and provide leadership for, these programs. We have tried to do all of this in a reader-friendly style, sprinkled liberally with stories to illustrate our ideas-in-practice. Most chapters offer specific "how to" guidelines in such areas as getting started, developing and implementing different kinds of programs, and evaluating the processes and outcomes of these programs in action.

The ultimate purpose of this book is to improve the lives of underserved youth, but to accomplish this, several changes need to occur. For one, youth programs need to be better. For another, youth programs need to be more plentiful. This book contributes to both of these needs in two ways: (1) by describing a model for program development and evaluation along with specific examples of this model in action in a variety of settings with a variety of physical activities, and (2) by arguing for an engaged university that will not only prepare future youth development professionals but also provide its local community with service-based teaching and research-based program development.

If you are a university student interested in working with kids, this book will help you do just that. If you are interested in reaching out to kids while you are a student, this book will help show you the way. If you are interested in studying physical activity programs for youth, this book will give you concrete examples of the interaction of research and practice plus guidelines to help you evaluate current programs and develop new ones. If you are a practicing youth professional, we hope that this book contains some helpful ideas for your practice. If you are a university professor, this book advocates that you become a catalyst for a more engaged university, with more opportunities for students to participate in community-based service learning, professional preparation, and applied research.

Acknowledgments

This book is the result of a partnership developed among the authors as the result of support from the Great Cities Institute and the Center for Urban Educational Research and Development (CUERD), both based at the University of Illinois at Chicago. The Great Cities Institute provided Don Hellison with a year of released time from teaching duties as well as space and clerical assistance for the specific purpose of forming, strengthening, and expanding the partnership. CUERD sponsored an initial partnership conference in Chicago in 1998. The Provost's Office at the University of Denver sponsored the second partnership conference in 1998, and the School of Health and Human Performance, University of North Carolina, Greensboro, sponsored the third partnership conference in 1999.

Special thanks to Dave Walsh (University of Illinois at Chicago), Julie Trujillo (University of Northern Colorado), and Tammy Schilling (University of North Carolina at Greensboro) who contributed to chapters 7, 8, and 12, respectively.

The authors express their appreciation to Susan Dunlap (University of Denver) for her editorial assistance.

Finally, this book would not have been possible without the advocacy and support of Scott Wikgren at Human Kinetics.

PART I

Realities and Visions

Part I provides the context for this book by describing life for underserved youth in terms of what is and what could be. In chapter 1, Jim Stiehl describes kids' realities and paints a bleak picture of the challenges facing today's young people. In chapter 2, Missy Parker calls on us to serve these young people. She outlines several essential components that must be present if physical activity programs are to help young people to navigate their life circumstances.

Chapter 1

The Way It Is

Jim Stiehl

Kids want teachers and program leaders "who take an interest in them, and get to know them, and who don't judge them too harshly before they find out what they really can do. . . . I want a chance to work with people willing to do whatever it takes to educate children. . . . Of course it's going to be hard. Of course. But too many in this country have the belief that if it's too hard, we should just stop. That we should throw people away. You throw away ideas, maybe, but you don't just toss out a whole generation of kids. It's a struggle. But it has to be done. (Charlene Jordon, cited in Rose, 1995, pp. 201-203)

Through the steam from a coffee mug held over the morning paper, I read the following side-by-side headlines: "Youths Volunteer to Make a Difference" and "Youth Crime on the Rise." The first article outlined how various groups of young people were creating and voluntarily running a childcare center, hoping to start a mentoring program led by students, and dissolving stereotypes that adults have of young people. The second article included the following quotes. From a school administrator: "He had a smile that would light up a room. He wasn't a troublemaker, he wasn't on the honor roll, and he didn't spend a lot of time in my office. We need to keep in mind that it's very possible for good kids to become victims of bad situations." From his dad: "He was my partner, and I loved the boy with a passion only God knows, and I'm going to miss him dearly."

We suspect that as other readers scanned these two articles, the collective *why* was spoken once more. Why are some kids headed in a favorable direction, and others not? Why are so many victims and so many suspects so young? Why is America littered with alienated families, troubled and troubling kids, and violence in the streets? Who or what is to blame? Why do some still react to this news with wonder, sadness, anger, and even shock, and, perhaps too frightening to ask, why have others become numb to it all?

Nobody knows the answers to these questions. There are only theories as to the causes of such circumstances and our reactions to them. Causes range from MTV and video games to shoot 'em up movies and television shows, from malls and materialism to misguided policies and policymakers, from deadbeat dads and working moms to broken homes and plundered schools. It depends on whom you ask. Reasons for numbness to the news include bombardment by media sensationalism, acceptance of certain myths about teenagers (they are selfish, lazy, and undisciplined; they do not care about the planet; they are an island in our society), and a sense of inadequacy and resignation (this is someone else's problem and, besides, what could I possibly do about it?). Worst of all is apathy, which Kurt Hahn (creator of Outward Bound and other experiential-based programs) attempted to "outflank, in kids' 'loudish years,' with activities and physical endeavor" because of his concern for their "lack of participation . . . and irresolute sense of purpose" (Jeneid, 1967, p. 2). Apathy, resignation, perceived powerlessness, and even fear are all barriers to possible intervention. The barriers often begin to melt, however, when the problems become personalized.

Vignettes From Underserved Youth

The purpose of the following vignettes is twofold: to underscore some of the conditions frequently associated with underserved youth, and to provide snapshots into the lives of some kids we work with. Following the vignettes are descriptions of some circumstances that led to their struggles.

Tonya

Tonya is 14 years old. At night, she takes her teddy bear to bed and tries to fall asleep under her grandma's quilt. Her sleep is restless and is frequently burdened with images of something she does not fully understand. Tonya is a child, and soon she will have a child of her own. The images in her sleep are about a "friend" who told her nice things ("you are my favorite"), groped with her on soiled sheets, and then left her under a sign that buzzed and blinked "No Vacancy."

Her cries at night are unlike most children's cries. They are not about being afraid of the dark. These cries have a raw, naked sound that seems to start from deep inside and move out—confused, naive, frightening cries. To hear them is terrifying.

Not that long ago, hers was the heart of a child, afraid of very little and open to the suggestions of each day. Then she was robbed in broad daylight. Not only were her hopes and dreams pilfered but perhaps her capacity to dream as well. What were those dreams? Maybe simply playing with friends; laughing, running, falling down. Maybe imagining herself a princess listening to kind words and gentle promises whispered by a handsome prince, or being kissed by her daddy.

These days, laughter, promises, and kisses are not the same to Tonya. She carries many things: a short-term hurt with a long-term heal; fire in her belly and shame in her eyes; and a dread that soon she will be confronted head-on with a responsibility, a total responsibility. Who will prepare her? Who will help her either to run away or to figure out how not to run? And if she stays, who will help her figure out how to make that choice rich?

It's a tricky business.

Hector

Hector's friends don't go out after dark anymore. Just the other night a man was dragged from his car, knifed repeatedly for the few dollars in his wallet, and left bleeding in the gutter. It wasn't always that way. Hector has fond memories of Greg, his only pal. Because, given Hector's "condition," it wasn't wise for him to be home alone, Greg could always be counted on to remain at his side until Hector's mother came home from work. Playing together provided Hector with companionship. It also helped to offset the taunts of agemates who ridiculed him as "missing an oar" or as being "a few fries short of a happy meal."

Nowadays, Greg won't be seen playing with Hector, especially after dusk. The neighborhood has become increasingly harsh and brutal. And besides, Hector mostly stays inside with his mom because of her brain tumor. She needs what little care Hector can provide. His dad might have helped, but he ran out shortly before the insurance did. So Hector stays inside, not prepared to care for a dying mom, afraid to be alone, and scared of the dark waters swallowing her—and him.

These things take their toll.

Rat

Rat is a fighter of sorts. His brown skin and red eyes personify the brown and red desert that he once called home. At age 12 he fled with his mother to Los Angeles. He carried with him scars and anger, the product of frequent beatings by a cruel father whose system was toxified regularly and irreparably. New to the streets of a large city, Rat confronted an atmosphere of hostility, hatred, and suspicion. Today, a hardened 14-year-old, Rat is skilled at con games and jive. He tends to exaggerate his war stories, often refers to others as "chickens," and is proud of his arrest record (20 arrests in less than two years, mostly for petty theft—not, as he claims, for "cutting and stabbing").

He also boasts of the system's inability to keep him locked up for long, unaware of his own long-standing spiritual and psychological imprisonment. Rat lives without a future, has no genuine friends, is locked in a cage. He is a fighter of sorts: intelligent, but unable to distinguish actual opponents from imagined ones, and with no one in his corner. A tough kid living a tough life.

Eddie

I hadn't heard from Eddie for a while and was glad to see him again. He approached me and, using the current greeting of choice among teens, said, "What up, dog?" I smiled and asked where he'd been lately. Because no self-respecting teenage guy cruises girls at the mall anymore, he simply said that he was a "player out mackin'!" Perpetually angry that too few people ever give him his "props," he was happy to accept the challenge of a quick game of one-on-one basketball. He said he's always "down with" basketball, the only activity he considers "phat."

Though young themselves when the term "propers" (respect) first was in vogue (from Aretha Franklin's 1967 hit, "Respect": "give me my propers, when I get home"), Eddie's parents are not inclined toward the latest slang (they're not "down" with the new language of the streets). Eddie's dad is a teacher and his mom sells real estate, so proper grammar is necessary to their livelihoods. Eddie's abridgment of speech is a concern to them. But of greater concern are his increased truancy and frequent expulsions. They fear he is headed for dropping out of school. When they suggest he's becoming a "slacker," he retorts, "Word!" (as in, you're right). When they ask why he thought missing school to go to a movie was acceptable, he replied, "Man, it was the bomb!" (translated for his parents as, "you know, really cool").

Circumstances Affecting Underserved Youth

Any of the following circumstances may contribute to the plight of these and other underserved youngsters. More often than not, a youngster will be the casualty of some combination of these conditions. Their frequency, intensity, and duration will affect different youngsters in different ways. Thus, although their individual stories may vary, their collective dilemmas usually can be credited to some assortment of the following circumstances, which can easily interact and overlap.

Poverty

Many underserved youth are from schools that are impoverished themselves and serve a student body that is even more impoverished. The Reverend Jesse Jackson has suggested that many youngsters today "are embittered and hurt. They live amidst violence and rejection, in broken streets, broken sidewalks, broken families, broken hearts. Their music, their rap, their video, their art reflects their broken world" (Payson, 1995). Though most of us identify two worlds (the flawed one we live in, and the better one we dream of), these youngsters frequently become resigned to the former. And by adjusting to it and becoming resigned to it, they reduce their life options.

Most people agree that education is the key to opportunity, to equality, to facing the marvels and perils of a future world, which we can only try to imagine. It is difficult to deny, however, that some of our institutions and practices are not in tune with our best values. Some youngsters live in surroundings with almost unlimited resources, while their poorer neighbors struggle among condemned buildings, inadequate play spaces, gang warfare, and woefully understaffed and underfunded youth activity programs. Both groups are told that all doors are open and opportunities are unlimited. None shall be excluded from the American dream. But the youngsters in the impoverished areas learn quickly to expect more of the same. Worse, their expectation represents a disparity (*discrimination* is a less forgiving term) to which we've become accustomed. But sometimes we get used to things we shouldn't get used to. As John Dewey (1900) put it, "What the best and wisest parent wants for his [or her] own child, that must the community want for all of its children" (p. 3).

What happens in schools is greatly affected by social conditions outside the schools. Some suggest that in the long run, the causation can work in the opposite direction; that is, better schools might produce better social conditions. Although schools could be a fulcrum for social change, the primary aim should be to get kids out of poverty in the first place. In other words, improve the social and economic conditions of the kids, their families, and their neighborhoods. Sadly, a disproportionate number of underserved young people live in impoverished areas where they can make an enviable income through the unreported and illegal "street economy." In these areas, school is often a hostile environment where they feel alienated and bored and where they perceive themselves as chronic failures and headed for low-status, dead-end employment or worse (welfare, jail, homelessness). Staying in school is not worth the effort, and they reject the widely held societal belief that greater education leads to employment and a guaranteed income.

Interestingly, those who drop out say nothing about the lack of quality of the school program. The program simply does not meet the needs of those already struggling with other home and personal problems that arise from poverty.

Unsafe Environment

A safe environment is devoid of physical harm as well as emotional and psychological harm. Ill-treatment can arise from varied sources ranging from gang warfare and family clashes to sexual abuse and verbal insults. Unhappily, the issue of a safe environment has become a story one has read a hundred times: What was absorbing and novel has become routine, with the plot tiresomely repeated and rehashed. Unless one experiences the daily threat of physical violence, it has become glamorized and romanticized to a point where it scarcely commands our attention. And yet today there is unprecedented violence.

For many youngsters, physical and emotional harm are real, constant threats. The most recent annual survey conducted by the Horatio Alger Association revealed that 56 percent of high school students are concerned about their personal safety at school, and 30 percent think violence and crime are the biggest challenges facing society today (decline of family, moral, and social values was the second greatest challenge the nation faces today, according to the 1,200 14- to 18-year-olds interviewed). One bit of evidence supporting their fears is that across the nation, juvenile jails are jammed, and before new ones are built, they are already overcrowded. Moreover, the 40 percent recidivism rate does little to calm youngsters' fears.

Many young people take for granted a sense of well-being, but that pleasure is not shared by many other less advantaged youngsters. With a constant threat of violence in school and on the streets, these youngsters' physical and emotional well-being is at risk. Their families and communities have neither the wherewithal nor the ability to erect a safety net. Their lives are quite unpredictable except for the unsettling nature of their day-to-day existence. Despite such impediments, these young people are supposed to involve themselves in learning, demonstrate socially appropriate behaviors and attitudes, and overcome the adversities that undermine their capacity to do good deeds and to nurture themselves.

Insufficient Support and Empowerment

In many communities, young people are not nurtured and have no sense of themselves as contributors to their families, their communities, or society. Few people ask, "What kind of person are we building?" and partnerships that support young people are not being created among university professors, public school teachers, parents, prevention workers, counselors, business leaders, and other community members. Indeed, many citizens view young people not as resources to be nourished and sustained but as liabilities. The result is a youngster whose weaknesses are exploited, whose apparent shortcomings are heavily weighted, whose individuality (e.g., cultural differences, developmental needs) is not respected, and whose strengths remain undiscovered, unacknowledged, and untested. In short, they are perceived as burdens, not resources.

The institution most frequently assigned the duty of "building" youngsters is the public school. But schools acting alone can provide only marginal support. Furthermore, when asked what our children need from education and what our society needs, the typical response from school officials is more emphasis on academic training and the traditional disciplines. The expectation is that our youngsters will be better prepared to enter the work force, to succeed in today's changing world, and to live a fuller and more prosperous life while also avoiding crime, poverty, and other social ills.

These expectations hold little promise for the many young people who reside in communities burdened by crime, drugs, violence, and poverty. It is shortsighted for schools to focus on advancing students' cognitive capacity and their respect for learning without fostering students' self-esteem, motivation, character, civic responsibility, and respect for individual, cultural, religious, and racial differences. The disconnectedness between academic basics and nonacademic basics results in a school experience that offers little vitality or significance for youngsters. Thus, it is not surprising why some students do not appreciate education as an opportunity. They do not have a receptive and cooperative attitude, do not understand the impact of their behavior on themselves and others, do not possess conflict resolution and peer mediation skills, do not decide on better ways to act, do not choose to be responsible for their behavior, and do not achieve academically. In sum, academic achievement cannot and does not occur in a vacuum. Youngsters do not learn only in school: They learn at home, on the playground, and on the streets. They are learning all the time, and some of what they learn is destructive.

We might ask, then, how we can support young people in learning things that are beneficial. Alfie Kohn (1991) suggested that we should "try to produce not merely good learners but good people" (p. 497). He and others (Noddings, 1992) contend that both academics and prosocial behaviors are important, and that respect, responsibility, and caring need not occur at the expense of academics. That is, we don't have to choose between teaching youngsters to think and teaching them to become more responsible. We can develop support systems that emphasize qualities such as respect, responsibility, and relationship, and there is no reason to assume that "generous and responsible behavior must be forced down the throats of children who would otherwise be inclined to care about only themselves" (Kohn, 1991, p. 498). Of course, no matter how much we might do with a youngster, other forces (parents, peers) have the power to undo it all, by intent or by sheer lack of support and reinforcement. But we can build support systems that include a larger community (no easy task in a time when Americans are experiencing a dwindling sense of community). And we can act out of an understanding that all young people are valuable and that they should be empowered to discover and develop their individual potentials.

Lack of Enduring and Meaningful Participation

A recent story about one of California's toughest youth correctional facilities described how a group of inmates (drug dealers, burglars, carjackers, and kidnappers) were learning new skills for a good cause—sewing gowns for premature babies. The story highlighted how youngsters in even the bleakest environment (they walk single file everywhere, are routinely checked for weapons, and live where gangs still rule) can benefit from doing something sustained and meaningful.

When asked why they endure teasing from other inmates in order to make warm clothes and blankets for premature babies, one inmate answered, "Because I've always been a taker from society. It's time to start giving back." They are less comfortable talking about the preemies who don't make it. For those babies, the inmates make satin burial gowns. Though no one expects the experience will magically lead these young people out of anger, violence, and crime, most agree that helping infants to keep warm in their struggle to survive is a powerful antidote to the events and circumstances in these youngsters' lives. The story also illustrates the importance of providing young people with long-term participation in meaningful activities.

In programs developed by Dr. Gene Taylor in southwestern Colorado, young people participate in programs in which they learn new skills and experience repeated challenges designed to give them a sense of doing something important and right. For example, some learn carpentry skills from adult volunteers and then build birdhouses that they present to seniors in nursing homes. Others help younger children to rebuild bicycles (donated and assisted by a local 90-year-old "bike collector"); the younger children keep the restored bicycles and ride them in a police-sponsored parade. Later chapters describe other programs that join young people with long-term, meaningful physical activities and that support them faithfully in the face of obstacles ranging from teasing and discrimination to gangs and poverty.

Lack of a Caring Adult

Rachel Carson (1956/1984) said, "If a child is to keep alive his inborn sense of wonder . . . he needs the companionship of at least one adult who can share it, rediscovering with him the joy, excitement and mystery of the world we live in" (p. 45). Young people, particularly adolescents, need the support and guidance of a caring adult not only to maintain a sense of wonder but to discover their sense of self. Searching for and finding a sense of self are earmarks of adolescence, which is often an emotionally intense time, a time of inspection and experimentation and puzzling choices.

The adolescent must face the conflict of accepting or discovering an identity and must deal with doubt concerning possible choices. In our culture, one of the paradoxes in negotiating the path of adolescent identity is the lack of carefully prepared, socially approved, or highly appreciated societal roles. Today's youngster must maneuver among many influences that result in a bewildering number of choices, often with little guidance and support. Influences include electronic media, which plays a major role in dispersing cultural information (often suggesting that fashion and style are the highest values to which a young person can aspire); social changes that occur too quickly to be assimilated; a dearth of suitable role models; a natural period of distancing from one's parents; confusion among many parents about their parenting roles and responsibilities; and young people's increased allegiance to peers. In addition, an increase in family breakups and increased mobility of family members as well as erosion of the nuclear family (providing parents with fewer sources of advice and support) have resulted in turbulence at home and a breakdown of the traditional safeguard, the family.

Compounding the problem of reduced guidance at home is the shrinking guidance provided at school. These days teachers share fewer mentoring responsibilities with parents than before. As noted earlier, teachers are being held increasingly accountable for nurturing the intellect, not the individual. They are neglecting the whole child—mind, body, and spirit. Imagination, intuition, and the inner life are viewed as suspect, and self-examination and reflection receive short shrift. Young people become another "cipher in the snow" (Palmer, 1998). This phrase is from the tale of a youngster who died, yet no one in the school, including his favorite teacher, knew much about him. Teachers who try to attend to the whole child risk being criticized for being anti-intellectual and acting in ways that smack of spirituality.

Inappropriate Values and Role Models

The primary function of school continues to be the acquisition of knowledge, which deals with students' intellectual capacity. Furthermore, the emergence of the school psychologist as a major figure in educational life suggests an additional concern for kids' emotional development, that is, how well they are dealing with life. The question posed by Robert Coles (1997) in his book *The Moral Intelligence of Children*, however, is this: How do we encourage lived moral experience in our students? Coles noted that too little attention is paid in our schools, never mind in our public discourse, to this aspect of life: namely, moral living as children learn it.

Coles further suggested that youngsters acquire a sense of morality in several important ways. One is by observing significant others, chiefly parents and teachers. So we must live out what we presumably want taught, because youngsters measure us not so much by our words as by our deeds. Another way is through stories, particularly those that encourage moral imagination, are concrete, and are connected to everyday experience. Unfortunately, many youngsters are unaware of important moral deeds, are presented with too few models who exhibit positive morality, and receive little moral guidance from adults. Yet these youngsters very much need a sense of purpose and a set of values grounded in moral introspection. In the absence of such direction, many feel morally abandoned.

All young people have a moral hunger and a need to have their humanity affirmed. But without role models and heroes, and without caring adults who share stories about our moral aspects and who attend to youngsters' fundamental concerns (Why am I here? Where, if anyplace, am I going? What makes life worth living?), many will grow up with no sense of purpose and no vision of a possible future, rendering their own presence not very compelling.

Aftermath—Circumstances Affecting Underserved Youth

The upshot of the aforementioned circumstances is simply that many kids live painful lives facing a host of negative influences and confronted with a confusing array of choices. Some are successfully navigating these sometimes treacherous waters, but for the many who are not, the results are upsetting.

Powerlessness

In *A Christmas Carol,* Charles Dickens (1868/1952) created Ebenezer Scrooge, a man with an icy-cold heart whose indifference to others eventually was transformed into compassion and good deeds. Two particular episodes in this story are instructive. The first occurred when Scrooge was visited by the spirit of Jacob Marley, Scrooge's deceased business partner. They spoke together, and as Marley departed, Scrooge heard sorrowful noises outside. As he looked out his window, Scrooge noticed the air was filled with phantoms, wandering in restless haste and moaning. As Marley's ghost floated out into the night, he told Scrooge that the phantoms moaned because they were doomed to wander through the world and witness what they could no longer share but might have shared on earth. In the second episode, Scrooge revisited his own childhood. On several occasions he attempted to speak with former friends and family but was informed that they could not hear or see him because they were "shadows of things that have been." In the two instances, Marley's ghost and Scrooge had lost the ability to intervene in human affairs. They felt helpless, powerless.

Powerlessness reflects a person's perceived lack of control over his or her life. People who feel powerless frequently attribute their successes and failures to inappropriate sources. For instance, they may attribute success to luck or chance rather than to their own abilities or talents. On the other hand, they typically attribute their failures either to others (the "blame game") or to their own suspected shortcomings (the "guilt game"). None of these attributions serves the individual in a positive way. In general, youngsters who feel powerless think that they have few choices available to them and that others have more power in controlling their lives than they themselves have. Their limited sense of control dominates their decisions, behaviors, and emotions (their general consciousness) in a self-defeating manner.

Alienation

A sense of belonging or connectedness is part of the support system that most of us need to succeed. Its opposite, experienced by many young people, is isolation or alienation. The absence of a viable and positive support system, and of the norms and values that underpin it, places many youngsters at risk. Recently, Pope John Paul II contemplated with sadness his warnings about the perils of "human alienation" and its attendant images of desperation and hopelessness. But his is only a recent reminder of a topic that has been discussed through the ages. Alienation, or lack of a sense of belonging, has been a recurring theme throughout history; in ancient Athens the highest punishment was banishment, not execution. Alienation robs the person of human affiliation, of a sense of purpose, of dignity, of a reason for behaving as a human being, of a reason for living.

Mary Shelley's (1831/1984) classic story of Dr. Frankenstein and the monster he created is perhaps the most poignant and compelling work about a person whose alienation from others caused him to become a monster. Unlike Hollywood's twists of the original, Shelley tried to teach a primary lesson concerning the effects of alienation. Today old people are banished to convalescent homes, and worse. Mentally disabled people are banished to institutions. People are sometimes forced to retire before they want to, often perceiving retirement as an immediate and usually irrevocable step into second-class citizenship. All of us are vulnerable and can suffer exclusion from our psychological and social home, from our physical home, from our work and friends, from life as we knew it.

Therefore, when we speak of disconnectedness, we speak on behalf of underserved youth, but we also speak on our own behalf. That's why this condition may be the most serious and most personal in this chapter. As we exclude certain young people, we increase the expectation that we too may be excluded some day. And the consequences are the same—despair, or worse.

The many young people who experience alienation frequently know neither what they are missing nor where to turn to get it. Their hearts and minds are not filled with the hopes and dreams from which to fashion success, nor do they acquire the skills and motivation necessary to wend their way through the system and advance themselves. They do not regard themselves as part of an academic enterprise, especially not one that is bonded with home, neighborhood, and community. In the process of becoming disconnected from schoolmates, neighbors, and the larger community, youngsters are at increasing risk for diminished skills and knowledge, lack of self-discipline, lowered self-esteem, frustration, depression, violence, and a focus on rudimentary survival skills, many of which clash with the values of the greater society.

Resignation and Despair

Shel Silverstein's (1976) book *The Missing Piece* features an unusual hero: a circle. Or, more accurately, an almost-circle, because it is missing a piece the size and shape of a pie slice. Driven by a sense of incompleteness, the almost-circle rolls bumpily through life looking for its missing piece. Before finally finding what it needs to become whole, it tries and discards many stray fragments in the hope of locating one that fits. The happy ending in Silverstein's tale is not shared by many underserved kids. An alarming number of youngsters limp through life with a similar sense of incompleteness. Unfortunately, due to the factors already mentioned (numerous external conditions accompanying frustration, alienation, and self-doubt), many of these young people never find their missing piece. As a consequence they become resigned and even desperate. A growing number try to fill the gap with drugs and alcohol, turning to substance abuse at younger ages than ever before. Others finally despair of finding what they need and end their searches in suicide. By all accounts, suicide attempts among teenagers are rising at an alarming rate (more than 1,500 attempts daily).

For an even greater number of youngsters, dissatisfaction takes a subtler form. First, many choose to drop out of school. In some major cities, the dropout rate exceeds 50 percent. Others simply tune out, perhaps acquiring a diploma but failing to master important content. Such actions carry serious economic consequences for these individuals as well as ominous consequences for society. Dropping out of school or graduating without mastering the knowledge and skills necessary to be effective citizens and to contribute to the economy place the individuals and our society at risk. The problems among minority students are particularly acute, and this bodes ill for our nation's future because minority groups account for a growing percentage of our population.

Inevitability or Possibility?

Cynical, bitter, alienated, without purpose, powerless, and having no faith in the future—these terms describe many young people. Are these feelings inescapable? Is it inevitable that a large number of kids will fall prey to a negative environment and will never obtain the skills and values to become responsible members of society? Must they be so strongly influenced by a despairing environment that they will develop serious behavior problems, will exhibit socially deviant behaviors, and will likely be incarcerated for or victims of violent crimes? Is it unavoidable that certain youngsters, notably those from less prosperous communities, will become troubled and troubling?

All of these questions can be answered from a position of inevitability, that is, that challenges facing many of today's youth are too difficult to overcome, so little will change. Change can be difficult. It requires the courage to try something new, to learn from mistakes, and to try again. People are afraid of change, and changing a system may mean you will have to change something about yourself. Another perspective, however, is what philosopher Maxine Greene called "consciousness of possibility," an ability to imagine a better state of things and to act on that imagined condition, not a seemingly inevitable one. In the next chapter we begin to suggest possibilities.

For Further Study

Gatto, J. (1992). *Dumbing us down: The hidden curriculum of compulsory schooling.* Philadelphia: New Society.

Although critical of compulsory schooling, Gatto provides glimpses of how youngsters can be "occupied in real work, real charity, real adventures, and the realistic search for mentors. . . " (p.28).

Herndon, J. (1965). *The way it spozed to be: A report on the classroom war behind the crisis in our schools.* New York: Bantam Books.

An accurate description of "deprived" (i.e., underserved) children and the forces lined up against them. A record of one ill-fated year in an inner-city school where the educational bureaucracy, the schools, and life itself are all rigged against the underserved kids.

Howe, Q. (1991). *Under running laughter: Notes from a renegade classroom.* New York: Free Press.

From the prologue, "This is a book about children whom no one heard when they cried." This is a book about children struggling against seemingly insurmountable odds, and those who have joined in the task of trying to assist them. A classic on youth development.

Rose, M. (1989). *Lives on the boundary.* New York: Penguin Books.

Rose challenges our assumptions and describes methods of awakening untapped potential in kids defined as "educationally underprepared." He provides guidance on how to determine and honor their voice (their beliefs, stories, enthusiasms, apprehensions) in an ever-changing, frequently uprooted community.

Rose, M. (1995). *Possible lives: The promise of public education in America.* New York: Penguin Books.

Rose provides a renewed hope for public education by taking us into the classroom and introducing us to what is possible and what really goes on in good classrooms. He provides an opportunity to imagine what might be, as an antidote to what will be.

Chapter 2

The Way It Could Be

Melissa Parker

> If I were to wish for anything, I should not wish for wealth and power, but for the passionate sense of potential, for the eye, which, ever young and ardent, sees the possible. Pleasure disappoints, possibility never. And what wine is so sparkling, what so fragrant, what so intoxicating as possibility! (Soren Kierkegaard, 1843/1987)

Todd Koering started his master's project this way:

> Working with young people is difficult. There are moments in coaching or teaching when something so special happens that you want to cry with happiness. Then there are moments something so hard and difficult to explain happens that you want to cry in sadness. It seems that all too often today we are crying in sadness due to some horrible situation that occurs in a young person's life. We ask ourselves why? What were they thinking? Don't they understand what they did? They should know better.
>
> I don't know if we can answer all these questions. Therefore, the common response is to give up hope. Many give up and try to hide from our future generation. I believe that today's young people can be taught morals, responsibility, character, self-esteem, and making positive choices through the lessons they learn in educational settings. I believe some of the best ways to teach such personal and social responsibility are through sport and physical activity. (Koering, 1999)

Why did it move me? It was just the prologue to a master's project, written by a student I had known for four years. So what was so unusual about it? I pondered that for awhile and actually read it aloud to several colleagues. Then I realized—the writer had shared responsibility for what happened to today's youth. They were his concern. He took responsibility for kids he didn't even know. He didn't say "someone else's kids" and he didn't say "kids" in the nonpersonal sense. He said "our kids." All too often we think of them as someone else's kids, and the pain and chaos in their lives are not our problem. The pain and chaos belong to someone—families, neighborhoods, law enforcement, churches, social workers, and hospitals—but not to us. Sadly, all too often, we alienate ourselves from their world.

Beyond our disenfranchisement from the lives of kids in the world, there is another sadness. There is a sadness in our lack of imagination, our inability to dream dreams that we can change the world or even a small portion of it. It seems that the exodus of our ability to conceive extraordinary possibilities accompanied the exodus of our childhood. This loss has been replaced by a propensity to complain about the way things are and to place blame. We have developed the talent of blaming others, and we have become blind to the possibilities. We have convinced ourselves that we can't make a difference in the world and that those kids in chapter 1 are beyond our help.

There are programs for underserved youth, yet we are so blinded by our myopia that many programs are nothing short of disreputable. Kids are put on drugs to control their behavior. They are sent to residential programs that attempt to change their behavior, to make them conform. They go to short-term treatment until they can demonstrate acceptable behavior. Girls are put on birth control procedures that few of us would elect. Children are sent to foster families that often mean well but aren't equipped to deliver what kids need. Some are enrolled in two-week programs to remove them from a problematic environment. Others are sent to jail or juvenile homes, are put in remedial classes, or attend daily programs that deliver an activity to keep them off the streets. As well-intended as all of these programs are, the kids return to their environments having had a good experience but not having learned the skills and attitudes necessary to survive in that environment (or most others). Problems ensue, and, once again, the kids are blamed—someone tried and it didn't work. Those kids are no longer our problem.

The harsh reality is that those kids are our kids. Their problems are our problems, and their voices are crying for us to hear. We are obligated to help solve those problems for them and for our society. For if not us, who will hear them when they cry? If not us, who will give them what they need to survive in our society? People can work together for the good of kids. This working together for youth development, called service learning, is what we are all about.

Programs

Despite the complacent and blaming attitude of society and the horrific problems mentioned in the first chapter, some programs provide glimpses of light for kids who are underserved. There are places where someone is doing something right. There are programs that imagine a different way. There are programs that give kids the necessary skills and attitudes accompanied by the ability to use those skills and attitudes to find a different way.

There is no franchise on these programs for kids, no mold, no blueprint. These programs are all over the country. They are largely in urban areas, but you can find them in rural areas as well. Some are run by adults who were underserved as youth and want to give something back. Others are directed by outsiders—university professors, professional athletes—who simply want to give something. Some are sponsored by agencies with big funding, whereas others are run on shoestring budgets. Many are run by men and some by women. Some meet in reclaimed buildings, others in city facilities. The media they use to reach kids vary: scouting, art, music, sport, academics, and church. These programs are trying to help kids combat their problems. These programs look very different from one another, but in some ways they are alike.

These different programs appear to share several forceful convictions that guide their work with youth, convictions that separate these programs from the rest. These beliefs and how they are achieved give kids the skills and attitudes to break the mold. Just for a minute, dream with me and try to envision what these programs would look like:

Try to imagine programs for youth that focus on youth.

Try to imagine programs for youth that focus on learning before teaching.

Try to imagine programs for youth that focus on empowerment, not control.

Try to imagine programs for youth that focus on circumstances of greater magnitude than the content of the program.

Try to imagine programs for youth that focus on development.

A Focus on Youth

All we have to do is read the newspaper headlines to find out how "bad" kids are. Our society is very quick to blame youth. Their actions are blamed on them as if no one else had anything to do with the average 14-year-old. These are the kids in chapter 1; they are the victims of a life that none of us would choose. They come from homes that have been ravaged by chaos, drug addiction, poverty, crime, violence, and abuse (Howe, 1991). Their plight in life is not one that we would want. The circumstances of their childhood are certainly different from most of ours—they have been dealt a bad hand—but they are not to blame.

The programs that have been the most successful with kids don't blame the kids. Instead of seeing their pathology, they see their potential (McLaughlin, Irby, & Langman, 1994). These programs respect kids' struggles. They understand that these youth have to combat adversity and strife that many of us can never imagine. They listen. In these programs, kids are treated as individuals with their own unique voices and an untouched capacity as decision makers.

Try to imagine what putting youth first would look like. In East Grand Forks, Minnesota, the Coaching Club was a before-school program for underserved middle and high school youth. When a staff member asked the club's most notorious member (by the school principal's standards) why he was so "good" in the program and so "bad" in school, his simple response was, "You listen to us." When Quincy Howe (1991) wrote about teaching at Leake and Watts, a private residential school for underserved children in New York City, he spoke of creating effective bonds with children to minimize the fragmentation in their lives. In the Youth on an Upward Roll Program (1997), the members were asked what they wanted to do with some excess money they had earned. Although the program leaders initially had some ideas, the kids wanted to go to Six Flags, 900 miles away (not what the leaders had in mind!). But the group went to Six Flags, and the experience was nothing short of remarkable. It was also one that these kids would never have had otherwise.

One of the strongest statements about the power of focusing on youth came from a girl in the Arroyo Girl Scout Program in a large southwestern city. When asked what would make a difference for underserved youth, she responded, "I would change people's attitudes, 'cuz some adults, when they look at you, they think, 'She's never gonna do anything because she's already gotten pregnant or she got in trouble.' Instead of helpin' [kids], they're jus' puttin' them down. Why. I don't understand. You can change a person" (McLaughlin et al., 1994, p. 214).

These programs meet kids where kids are, and the people take time to know the kids. If you observe one of these programs, the activities initially may not seem to match the purpose. Howe (1991) indicated that the movie *Lethal Weapon* has been seen so many times in his classes (for the sole purpose of building bonds and meeting kids where they are) that kids know the lines. In the Coaching Club, Hispanic students are allowed to speak Spanish (something they are not allowed in school) if they will teach Spanish to the non-Spanish-speaking kids and coaches.

In all of these programs, the needs of the youth come first. It is not that kids get to do anything they want, but rather their needs, as assessed by the program leaders, are at the forefront of the program.

A Focus on Learning

In 1969, Carl Rogers said that teaching was a vastly overrated function. Yet 30 years later, there seems to be an inordinate focus in education on teaching: effective teaching, best practices in teaching, reflective teaching, etc. We train teachers and, for that matter, recreation specialists and youth workers to give feedback, write grants, maintain facilities, fill out reports, and ensure on-task behavior. Somehow, learning appears to have been left out of the picture. What happens to the students; where do they fit into the equation?

We teach. We do activities. But what do kids learn? Learning is an ongoing process. It isn't complete at the end of a session or a lesson or a year. It is never-ending. As program leaders we must continually revisit the constructs that we want kids to acquire. We have to develop ways to help them experience the concepts we are teaching. Teaching, on one hand, can be very neat, compartmentalized, and pretty. Learning, on the other hand, is very messy, scattered, and unpredictable. Often teachers and program leaders focus on the act of teaching while neglecting the process of learning.

The successful programs focus on what youth need to learn, not what the program leader thinks is important to teach and not the act of teaching. Postman and Weingartner (1969) contended that the critical content of any learning experience is the method or process through which the learning occurs. The difference in focus on teaching or learning may be subtle, but it is quite powerful. The importance is shifted from the program leader or teacher to the child. What happens to the kids is more important than what we do as teachers.

Howe's (1991) example of teaching his students how to write a business letter (as required by New York state curriculum guidelines) may be one of the best examples of focusing on learning (as well as teaching). Most students (underserved or not) see little purpose in learning to write a "proper" business letter. Yet, these same students have a lot to complain about. So Howe teaches them to write a business letter that deals with returning a defective piece of stereo equipment, for example. The results are that his students learn to write business letters that are useful to them (and often ones that many of us secretly wish we had the nerve to write).

A fifth-grade physical education class in south-central Los Angeles provides another glimpse at learning. In the program, the students work on basketball skills, and many want to play games. The skill level is like most physical education classes—diverse. The students choose among playing highly competitive basketball, playing recreational basketball, playing basketball-shooting games, or practicing skills. The result is that four completely different activities occur in class at the same time, and students participate in activities where they can learn best.

Yet focusing on learning is not enough, and learning cannot be separated from teaching. We need to consider the environment in which learning occurs. Learning accomplishes little if it does not empower students to take responsibility for their own lives and decisions.

A Focus on Empowerment

Recently I was invited to teach a session on classroom management. The question that my university students most wanted answered was how to "control" their elementary and secondary students. The same conversation regularly occurs in every teacher's lounge in the country. And, amazingly enough, some have figured out how to solve the problem—build more jails, develop more and stricter rules at school, or even put gates on schools, not to keep intruders out but to keep students in. There are also programs for underserved youth that are designed to "keep kids off the street." All of these focus on control, not on empowering kids to make their own decisions. Some have said that the educational system actually disempowers students (Reyhner, 1992).

If you advance the teaching and learning issue beyond just placing learning before teaching, you must focus on the environment in which the learning occurs and ultimately on the act of teaching. (I use teaching here in a very broad sense, one that includes leading, directing, facilitating. It is interesting that this kind of teaching rarely occurs in the classroom.) The programs that have been most successful with youth, over the long term, are ones that have created empowering environments. These environments help youth actively gain control over their own lives while collaborating with each other to achieve their goals.

Gatto (1992) wrote that we have developed an intellectual dependency in students: We train them to wait to be told what is important and worth knowing. Reyhner (1992) commented that many of the learning difficulties of minority students are caused by the way we teach children who are designated "at risk." He wrote that most instruction confines students to a passive role and induces a form of learned helplessness. Instead, instruction should liberate kids from dependence on instruction and should encourage them to generate their own knowledge.

Instruction that creates conditions for empowerment is experiential and interactive. In such environments, program leaders give kids decisions to make and guidance in making them. The decisions kids make resemble real-life decisions on a smaller scale, but mistakes won't land them in jail or even the principal's office. These programs believe that kids can be trusted, can learn, and can assume responsibility. They are environments in which the leader progressively relinquishes control.

The idea of relinquishing control is frightening for many of us. In classroom management classes, we are taught to control kids. What would empowering environments look like—total chaos? To some, yes. At Cooper House, a YMCA program in the Northeast, youth participants, initially as a joke and then seriously, took turns sitting in the director's chair for an hour or so daily. They practiced being the director—answering phone calls, problem solving, and helping others learn to make decisions (McLaughlin et al., 1994). In a wilderness-based adventure program in the mountains of Adirondack Park in New York State, a participant became angry with his group and decided to leave. One of the program leaders, instead of arguing with him or trying to force him to stay (which he probably couldn't have), let him walk through the mountains for more than two hours, always trailing him at a discernible distance. When the participant finally stopped—without water and food and one shoe—the leader asked him if he knew where he was and how to get out. Together they made the journey back to the group. A Coaching Club in Chicago (discussed in chapter 7) allows members (sixth and seventh graders) to decide what they need to practice before the morning sessions begin. These club members individually or in pairs work to improve their basketball skills based on what they think they need to practice. If the program leaders see them doing nothing or something that they really don't need to practice, a one-on-one discussion takes place—not a boot out of the program. Members of the Harlem Boys Choir are expected to be at rehearsal, but instead of being kicked off the choir for skipping, as some programs would do, the situation is used as a learning experience (Turnbull, 1995).

Each of these programs has designed experiences and situations that allow participants to make choices with guidance. The choices are not about compliance to arbitrary standards—responsibility and empowerment go far beyond simply obeying the rules—but rather are about allowing participants to gain control over their lives

A Focus on Circumstances of a Greater Magnitude Than Content

In the movie *Mr. Holland's Opus,* as Glen Holland struggles with teaching music to unenthused high school students, the principal tells him, "A teacher has two jobs—to fill minds with knowledge and to give those minds a compass so the knowledge doesn't go to waste." She continues, "I don't know what you're doing with the knowledge, but the compass is stuck" (Field, Nolin, Cort, & Herek, 1995). The same is true for many programs designed to serve underserved youth. We give them knowledge about how to change their lives but never help them learn how to use it. Empowerment is admirable, but we need a medium through which to transmit knowledge and we have to teach children what knowledge means and how to use it, all the while avoiding the trap of focusing solely on the content used as the medium. In other words, we have to look at the whole child.

Many programs exist for underserved youth. Midnight Basketball may be the best known, but there are others that have a clear academic or sport focus. They are designed to enable students to develop academic, sport, or vocational skills that will help them succeed. The intent is admirable and does meet a need, but it also falls short, because the program doesn't address the whole child. Underserved youth are often lagging academically, but more importantly they are lacking and are unfulfilled in other ways that affect all else they do. They are missing responsibility skills—both personal and social—and the environment in which to develop those skills. They are missing things that come from the gut and from the heart. And while helping them academically or athletically even in an empowering way solves a portion of the dilemma, it only treats a symptom of the problem. Programs that have been successful focus on the whole child—body, mind, and soul.

In programs that focus on the whole child, what will you see? First, you have to look closely, because what you initially see is the medium that is used. In other words, you will see basketball or music or dance or computer skills. Keep looking. You will see instructional methods that allow kids to make decisions. You will see interaction. You will see program leaders biting their tongues while watching failures, not saying, "I told you so," but asking, "How can we work on it?" You will see teachers offering guidance rather than directives. You will see small victories and personal commitment by both program leaders and kids. You will get a feeling about something happening. But what does this look like? I'm not sure I can tell you. It is hard to see the soul. It is a feeling. As St. Exupery (1943) wrote in *The Little Prince*, "It is only with the heart that one can see rightly; what is essential is invisible to the eye" (p. 87).

One example may help, but I fear the emotion may be lost in the words. In a morning Coaching Club (see chapter 7), Joe was known as the pouter. He wanted everything his way. He threw elbows after rebounds, even when no one was around. He sulked and walked up court when he missed a shot. At times he would even sit down in the middle of games. One day, he was throwing elbows and punching and just being a jerk. He lay down on the court and beat his elbows on the floor after one particular play where someone beat him on the baseline. A coach took him aside and talked to him about teamwork, making mistakes, politeness, and helping others. One of the issues was telling others they had done a good job. During the next session, another player grabbed a rebound that Joe thought he should have. Joe turned to him and stammered, "Goo—oo—oo—d job!" It happened so quickly and at such an inaudible level that we all wondered if we had heard it. It sounded like a kid practicing a foreign language. The teams actually stopped and the rebounding player thanked Joe. A small victory after two years, but one that came from the heart.

A Focus on Development

Some programs that work with kids are one-shot deals (and one size fits all). They provide activities for kids that last for a set period of time, maybe just the summer, and then are gone. The kids come back the next summer and do the same thing. Again, these programs provide kids a safe place to go and teach them some skills, but the deal never changes—the program is always the same. It is like a program where I once worked that brought inner-city kids to summer camp for two weeks. We did great things in the outdoors for those two weeks; the kids went on backpacking trips on an island in Lake Michigan and bike tours up the western Michigan coast, but then the kids went home. They went home to the south side of Chicago where all the backpacking skills in the world weren't going to help them when confronted with gang violence, drugs, and dysfunctional homes. If they were lucky, they came back a second summer to camp, did the same thing all over again, had a great vacation, and returned home to the same problems and without any new skills to help them. A colleague (McBride, 1984) conducted his doctoral research on putting adjudicated youth through ropes course adventure activities—about a three-shot deal. The kids' behavior changed while on the ropes course, but there was no change in their group home.

Programs that have an influence stick with kids and focus on the development of leadership skills. Programs that have a profound influence grow with kids and develop their content over time. Where are these programs? What do they look like? One such program in Chicago started out as one of Hellison's Coaching Club programs and grew into the Nike Scholar Program (see chapter 10). In the program, kids typically started in sixth grade in a morning basketball program. As they grew and gained more responsibility skills (as well as basketball and coaching skills), they began to assist with other Coaching Clubs, and then they taught in a summer program for other kids. These kids are now high school students, and if they graduate from high school there are funds available for them to attend college.

The things that are bigger than content—empowerment, responsibility, leadership—happen over time. Development happens over time.

A Big Picture

The five convictions that underlie successful programs have been presented to you as five separate pieces. The examples have been extracted to illustrate points. In reality, it is not that neat (much like learning). The convictions are all interdependent and interwoven much like a Navajo rug. If you watched the weaver work you would see piles of different colored yarn, all integral to the finished product. To describe each yarn and the berries from which it was dyed and where they were collected tells part of the story of the rug. But in no way can it describe the finished product, the most intricate creation that tells a legend of the Navajo life. The whole is truly greater than the sum of its parts. And so it is with successful programs for underserved youth.

You may say at this point that we are dreamers, that we can't change the world. But as the little boy who was throwing starfish back into the ocean when they had washed ashore at low tide said, "I can help this one." We are dreamers.

John Gatto (1998) wrote: "The primary goal of real education is not to deliver facts but to guide students to the truths that will allow them to take responsibility for their lives" (p. 13). If true, who will (not "should") provide this necessary guidance? If not solely parents or teachers, who? Religious training, or the Boy Scouts and Girl Scouts, or Little League? These can be admirable teachers, but many youth are not connected to such organizations. Who will ensure that young people will acquire a drive for public service and be willing to blow the whistle when something is wrong? Who will ensure that young people will develop compassion, a willingness to work, loyalty to family and friends and organizations, fairness and honesty, and the courage to face temporary defeat without losing forward motion? Who will pledge that yet one more young person will not become a cipher in the snow? Perhaps anyone sensitive and committed enough to accept the responsibility of becoming a youngster's caring adult. One who will say, "You won't be alone as you go out to meet the future. Together we can develop programs that make a difference in the lives of kids."

> Some men see things as they are and say why. I dream things that never were and say why not.
>
> Robert Kennedy

For Further Study

McLaughlin, M.W., Irby, M.A, & Langman, J. (1994). *Urban sanctuaries: Neighborhood organizations in the lives and futures of inner-city youth.* San Francisco: Jossey-Bass.

Urban Sanctuaries *is probably the best book available to explore the range of possible and successful programs for underserved youth. The book describes six programs for underserved youth. The strategies that leaders and their organizations use to create and sustain successful programs for youth despite the challenges they face are explored in a lively, personal manner.*

Reyhner, J. (1992). *Teaching American Indian students.* Norman: University of Oklahoma Press.

Teaching American Indian Students *is one of the few books that explores the education of Native Americans as a process to empower Native American children while not forcing them to choose between their culture and the culture of the school. The book begins with the empowerment of students and then develops those ideas through the various content areas.*

Rose, M. (1995). *Possible lives: The promise of public education in America.* New York: Penguin.

Possible Lives *is an account of teachers who have created promise in public education. Mike Rose describes classrooms around the United States (in such places as Los Angeles, New York, and Hattiesburg) that he visited and the people in those classrooms. In these classrooms he found teachers who not only were surviving despite all odds but were enthusiastic and creative—in short, heroes. His book shows us what is possible and offers hope for what might happen in educational settings.*

PART II

Serving Underserved Youth Through University-Community Collaboration

Part II describes the conceptual basis for moving from the way it is to the way it could be. Chapter 3 describes a different way of working with kids and shows how this approach can be used in a variety of underserved community physical activity and support programs designed to promote youth development. Chapter 4 develops the concept of university-community collaboration in the service of underserved youth, for example, by developing service learning experiences for university students. The specific physical activity youth development programs shown in figure 3.1 are described in detail in part III.

Chapter 3

Serving Underserved Youth Through Physical Activity

Don Hellison

Kids in underserved communities don't have access to the programs and resources they need for their full development. Sometimes programs are available, but often they are underfunded or in need of reform. Sometimes there aren't any programs. Moreover, studies of the attendance patterns of children and youth in underserved areas show that as kids get older, they drop out, not only of school but of the available extended day programs as well. Yet these same studies (e.g., McLaughlin et al., 1994) point out that a few programs are oversubscribed, and that even gang members stand in line to join.

Guidelines for Youth Development Programs

Why do kids join some voluntary programs and not others? You might think that sport programs would pull kids in like a magnet; however, most "gym and swim" programs designed for underserved youth can attract younger but not older kids and cannot keep those who do show up. Certainly the influx of physical activity programs aimed at addressing the many social issues facing underserved youth, such as Reviving Baseball in Inner Cities, Midnight Basketball, and the National Youth Sport Program, have captured the attention of the media and funding agencies and have provided some heated debates among politicians. However, the success of these programs varies. Table 3.1, drawn from several recent studies and scholarly analyses of current youth programs and policies, shows why (Hellison & Cutforth, 1997). These key criteria for state-of-the-art youth development programs describe a program that is, among other things, holistic in nature, suggesting that focusing on a single activity, even if it is basketball, is not enough to keep kids involved.

Although most or even all of these criteria may make sense to you, just the opposite takes place in most programs, perhaps even the ones you experienced as a preteen or teenager. Programs in underserved areas in particular tend to "blame the victim" by treating kids as if they are the causes of the problem, rather than placing the blame where it belongs, on community and societal economic, social, and political factors (Benson,

Table 3.1

Key Criteria for State-of-the-Art Youth Development Programs

1. Treat youth as resources to be developed. Build on the strengths they already possess, and emphasize their competence and mastery.
2. Focus on the whole person—the emotional, social, and cognitive as well as physical dimensions of the self.
3. Respect the individuality of youth, including cultural differences and developmental needs.
4. Empower youth.
5. Give youth clear, demanding (but not unreasonable) expectations based on a strong, explicit set of values.
6. Help youth envision possible futures for themselves.
7. Provide both a physically and psychologically safe environment.
8. Keep program numbers small and encourage participation over a long period of time; emphasize belonging and membership.
9. Maintain a local connection.
10. Provide courageous and persistent leadership in the face of systemic obstacles.
11. Provide significant contact with a caring adult.

Note: From Hellison, D., & Cutworth, N. (1997). Extended day programs for urban children and youth: From theory to practice. In Walberg, H., Reyes, O., & Weissberg, R. (Eds.), *Children and youth: Interdisciplinary perspectives* (pp. 223-249). Thousand Oaks, CA: Sage. Copyright 1997 by Sage Publications, Inc.

1997; McLaughlin & Heath, 1993). Once program leaders and policymakers decide that kids are the problem, it is a short step to planning a program designed to control and "remediate" them. A common example of attempting to control youth is any program that has as its primary goal keeping kids off the streets. Remediation has many forms, basic academic skills instruction being one very familiar example. Of course, there is nothing wrong with programs that value safe, structured, enjoyable activities, and lots of underserved youth do need basic academic skills (just as all of us can make lists, sometimes long ones, of our own deficiencies). The point is that kids are most attracted to, and most supported by, programs that

- focus on their strengths;
- attempt to meet their emotional, social, and cognitive needs, not just their physical skill needs and sport interests;
- give them important decisions to make individually and collectively within a framework of clear expectations and values, instead of making all the decisions for them;
- respect not just their culture and gender but their individuality; and
- help them expand their possible futures and ways to get there.

Of course, the environment has to be a safe place, but that means not only physically safe but emotionally safe as well. Program participants must know they can show up without fear of being laughed at, criticized, or bullied. As table 3.1 shows, the most successful programs make participants feel as if they belong; a commitment to the program and to other members is part of the deal. Belonging and commitment, as well as the opportunity for the program leader and the kids to develop meaningful relationships, are greatly facilitated by the size of the group and the duration of participation. Not surprisingly, youth in smaller groups that stay together over several years tend to experience more benefits.

The program leader, who might be you, is crucial to making all of these things happen. Program leaders need to really care about kids and to support them continuously. They also need to confront and overcome the numerous obstacles involved in developing and sustaining a good program. Finally, they need to maintain a connection to the community. For example, I have run a before-school program in one of Chicago's most violent neighborhoods for several years. While exposing my students to the university environment and to various educational and career opportunities, I also help the principal with discipline problems, speak at graduation every year, and invite the principal and vice-principal to university meetings they might be able to contribute to and enjoy. Your other authors have had similar experiences in Denver; Greensboro, North Carolina; Los Angeles; Greeley, Colorado; and rural North Dakota.

The Responsibility Model

Although these state-of-the-art criteria can open our eyes to what is missing in most youth development programs, they fall short of providing enough guidance to start a program. First of all, their advice is fairly general; they don't really give specific strategies. Second, the role of physical activity is nowhere to be found. And third, if the goal is to offer a variety of community programs, for example in school as well as after school, we cannot rely exclusively on small clubs to do so. Fortunately, these gaps can be filled by an approach to teaching physical activities that has been in existence for over 25 years. This approach is most commonly referred to as the responsibility model (and more formally as Teaching Personal and Social Responsibility).

The origin and early development of the responsibility model were primarily experiential and autobiographical, and this tradition continues today (Georgiadis, 1992). My teaching career began in physical education programs in inner-city high schools and a detention center in the early 1970s, followed by 10 years of teaching in alternative schools for court-referred and dropout-bound kids and 10 years teaching in a variety of extended day programs for inner-city children and youth. I spent my first few years trying to survive these experiences, while at the same time struggling to remain true to the holistic values and beliefs I brought with me from earlier experiences and reflections. This holistic perspective coupled with my students' needs, which just about screamed at me every day, led to the discovery of most of the program criteria in table 3.1 well before they were published.

But how could I convert physical activity into a vehicle to promote these holistic, student-centered state-of-the-art criteria? It seemed to me that the kids faced more choices—including some very problematic ones such as drugs and guns—and less adult guidance in all aspects of their lives than in the past (for a variety of reasons), and that a lot of the kids' interactions with each other and sometimes with me were defensive, aggressive, and sometimes overtly abusive. I experimented with this and that and over time focused more on shifting responsibility to my students for making choices that would enhance their own well-being as well as contribute to, or at least not harm, the well-being of others. This meant letting go of some of my authority and spending some time each day with them discussing and helping them reflect on their decisions, including their attitudes and behaviors toward themselves and others. What gradually emerged was an approach that

- treats kids as whole people, with emotional and social as well as physical needs and interests, and as individuals, not just members of a gender or race or other group;
- empowers them to make decisions within an explicit set of life values;
- prioritizes both emotional safety and the need for a relationship with a caring adult; and
- accomplishes all of this through the medium of fitness, motor skill instruction, sport, games, and other human movement activities.

This model has been the focus of numerous teacher and youth worker workshops and publications, and, although it is not sweeping the country or world by any stretch of the imagination, it does have a presence in many states and Canadian provinces as well as in New Zealand (Creighton & Lee, n.d.), England (Smith, 1990), and other countries. These teachers and youth workers, joined by some faculty in higher education, have added their own spins to the model, creating new strategies and modifying the responsibility guidelines to better fit their situations. The model also has spread to public schools in relatively affluent communities, suggesting that many kids today are underserved and in need of help even if they aren't poor.

With the expansion to more affluent communities, people began to ask whether this is really a model for inner-city youth. The answer lies in the history of the model, which was developed by one person who wanted to contribute to the lives of kids he was working with. Whether the model could work elsewhere was, at least in the beginning, an open question. As practitioners working in suburban and rural areas began to adopt and adapt the model (e.g., Compagnone, 1995; Hellison, 1995), their work became examples of applications to other populations. That teachers and youth workers decide for themselves the relevance of these ideas for their settings and students is consistent not only with the origin of the model but with its empowerment emphasis.

Responsibility Model Goals and Strategies

In the movie *Creator*, Peter O'Toole tells his colleagues to keep an eye on "the big picture." Without some sense of the big picture, readers can easily get lost in the details and nuances of any program model. So here is a glimpse of the big picture, which, together with the preceding description of the model's evolution, should help as you wend your way through the responsibility model's details and nuances. At its core, the model's premises are simple:

- It's relational. If the program leader cannot establish and maintain a relationship with students that honors their ability to take responsibility, nothing else will matter.
- It starts with a focus on physical activity and gradually shifts to an emphasis on life. The major message is not necessarily to maintain an active lifestyle throughout life but to live a personally and socially responsible life that prioritizes human decency and self-development.
- The responsibility for planning and carrying out the program gradually shifts from the program leader to the kids.
- Everything else, as they say, "is details." That includes how to develop relationships, how to teach about life through physical activity, and how to empower students.

Three steps are involved in developing and putting these premises into practice:

1. Kids have to be put first.
2. Guidelines that spell out what students need to take responsibility for have to be developed and then integrated into physical activity lessons.
3. Specific instructional strategies have to be implemented.

Putting Kids First

"Tennis is a way to reach kids and teach them things that are much more important than tennis." (commonly attributed to Arthur Ashe)

Putting kids first means just that. Although fitness and sport may be important, life skills and values matter more, especially given current social trends. Because physical activity is active, interactive, highly emotional, and attractive to many kids, it can become a vehicle for teaching life skills and values. Why role-play conflict resolution in the classroom when real conflicts begging for a resolution erupt all the time in the gym? Why teach self-esteem in the classroom and allow trash talk/in-your-face basketball in physical education? Of course, the subject matter cannot take a back seat in this relationship. Fitness, sport, and other movement activities must be taught effectively and enthusiastically even if goals other than improved physical performance are sought. Although some tradeoffs do occur when the responsibility model is integrated with physical activity instructional strategies, a comment by an inner-city high school boy reflects this integration: "We learned basketball, but he also taught us the main points about life."

The integration of kids and content is an attractive idea to many physical education professionals. That's why we brag that "sport builds character." But if we are serious about putting kids first, such claims won't help much. We need to set a student-centered tone in our programs by adopting what Nel Noddings (1992) called a care ethic. This means subjectively caring about kids as people and being sensitive to their emotional, social, and cognitive as well as physical needs. In the words of a fifth grader, "This program is great because in here we're treated like people." The focus is on truly caring, not just teaching kids about caring. One way to do this is to prioritize the relationship with students. Although the phrase "programs don't change kids; relationships do" (Millikan, 1994, p. 60) may overstate the case, it correctly challenges the notion that any model can be successful just because it is based on good ideas. If the relationship with students is weak, the model will suffer. To develop that relationship, teachers need to genuinely and sensitively care about each student's emotional, social, and physical health and to develop a positive relationship with as many kids as possible.

Respecting one's students is at the heart of developing such a relationship. However, respect is a much used and perhaps much abused concept (in our everyday language and especially on the street). As program leaders using the responsibility model, we have learned, sometimes the hard way, that it is necessary to genuinely respect

- students' strengths (especially those that aren't very visible), rather than focusing on their deficits;
- not only their culture and gender but their individuality (treat them "unequal but fair," as Portland State professor Walton Manning used to say);
- their voices (they have a "side"); and
- their capacity for decision making (even though they may need practice to become more effective).

These last two, students' voices and their capacity for decision making, are particularly important in implementing the responsibility model.

We have found that if we do genuinely respect students in these ways, they tend to give it back to us, to "respect us back." They often don't, however, give it to their peers. To address that issue, we need to build a set of guidelines to help them focus on taking on specific responsibilities.

Guidelines for Taking Responsibility

Setting the tone by putting kids first is an essential first step, but, as I painfully learned in my early teaching experiences, it is just that: a first step. Caring about kids, respecting them, and developing relationships with them do not automatically translate into their taking responsibility for their relations with others or for their own development. To help this process along, the teacher probably needs to provide at least some minimal guidelines. It may be enough to focus their attention on taking more responsibility for their own well-being and for their sensitivity and responsiveness to the well-being of others (stated in language kids can relate to). If so, there is no need to be more specific. Sometimes, however, students don't get the point, or they interpret this as doing whatever they want, rather than, as deCharms (1976) argued, doing as they must. In my experience, more focused responsibilities—what students are specifically responsible for in this program—help them to understand how to practice taking responsibility.

Over the years, five student responsibilities, often referred to as "levels" (explained subsequently), have held up fairly well in assisting students to take responsibility for their personal and social development. The names, descriptions, order, and even number of these responsibilities vary to some extent from gym to gym, as program leaders adapt and modify them to fit their students and setting. They are stated here as if the teacher is talking directly to kids:

1. *Respect the rights and feelings of others:* As a student in this program, your first responsibility is to practice self-control of your mouth and temper (including not blaming others), to include everyone in the activities, and to solve conflicts peacefully. These actions will help to protect the rights and feelings of everyone in here, and all of us will be able to have a more positive experience.

There are two modifications to this responsibility. First, you have a voice in how we should fulfill this responsibility (as well as the other four responsibilities) and in negotiating issues that arise. Second, this does not mean being peaceful at all costs. There are times when all of us have to stand up for what we believe in and care about. However, with a world full of war, murder, assault, intimidation, bullying, and other forms of violence, we need to learn when confrontation is necessary and how to conduct ourselves so as not to unnecessarily inflame the situation.

2. *Effort:* Your next responsibility is to work on your self-motivation by giving a good effort to the task at hand and having the courage to persist when the going gets tough (thanks to Tom Martinek). The goal of this responsibility is self-improvement—being the best person you can be—rather than trying to outdo others.

3. *Self-direction:* An advanced responsibility is to be able to work independently, to set and work on personal goals, and to have the courage to make personal choices and set personal goals that may not meet the approval of your peers. Our program can't function if we don't respect each other's rights and feelings and you don't participate in the activities; however, self-direction, although an important factor in personal growth and reaching your personal goals, is a choice you must decide whether to make.

4. *Helping others:* Another advanced responsibility is to help others by genuinely caring about and being sensitive and responsive to them and by assuming leadership roles that will contribute to the group's welfare. Like self-direction, helping others is a choice you must decide whether to make. However, our group won't function very well unless at least a few of you decide to assume helping and leadership responsibilities.

5. *Outside the gym:* Your most difficult responsibility is to try out the first four responsibilities in other settings such as school, playground, home, and street to see if they work better than what you are now doing. If they do, you have a responsibility to yourself to practice them and a responsibility to others to become a role model.

Program leaders need to do the following to support their students' efforts to put these responsibilities into practice:

1. Be under control themselves, give students power to take *self-control*, and practice equity so that everyone is fully included in program activities, thereby modeling and supporting respect for others in the program.
2. Provide instructional and game experiences that honor student differences in ability, learning pace, and competitive drive, thereby giving students the opportunity to become involved and put some effort into the activity.
3. Believe that, even though students will make mistakes, empowerment opportunities will give them practice at decision making and help them to become more self-directed.
4. Help students learn how to help, coach, teach, or lead others in ways that contribute to both the individual's and the group's welfare; teach students how to do these things with sensitivity to

others' feelings and needs; and believe in the importance of student leaders' insights into the ways problems can be solved and the program improved.

5. Believe that exploring the transfer of these four responsibilities to other settings is an ultimate program goal.

Taking on five responsibilities all at once is asking a lot of students. One way to address this issue is to present the responsibilities as a loose progression of levels. As a teaching-learning progression, respecting others is introduced first as Level One, because, to even begin to function effectively, the rights and feelings of all students in the program must be protected. Because effort is fundamental to improvement in physical activity (and everything else), it is introduced second, as Level Two, although in practice the respect issue must be revisited often. Giving students time for self-direction is Level Three, because it assumes that control and motivation issues have been sufficiently resolved to permit independent work. Helping is Level Four, because for many kids it is the most difficult level to reach unless students are socialized to do so at an early age, for three reasons: It requires taking one's own time away from personal interests and goals, it is not usually perceived as being the "in" thing to do (especially with people who aren't friends), and it is to be done without rewards (virtue is its own reward!). However, leadership is often valued and can be defined so that it is synonymous with helping. Outside the gym cannot be explored until the first four responsibilities are being practiced in the gym (Level Five).

Such a teaching-learning progression can help the teacher plan each lesson as well as individualize the program. Kids don't progress in lockstep fashion; some will struggle with the respect issue for a long time, whereas others can almost immediately assume some leadership responsibilities. Therefore, the progression can help the program leader individualize instructional tasks, so that, for example, some kids work independently while others receive (nonpunitive) direct instruction from the program leader or a student leader.

This progression also represents a hierarchy of values: Respecting others is the least one can do for another, helping (responsively) perhaps the most. Putting effort into a personal task or challenge is the least one can do for oneself, whereas being self-directed is a more advanced skill and attitude.

For simplification, many leaders with large classes or in an "open gym" setting choose to use the term *level*, as in Level One or Level Two, to refer to students' responsibilities. This creates an accessible vocabulary for talking about responsibility, for example, when the teacher holds up one finger as a reminder of the need for self-control

(Compagnone, 1995) or when she says "Are you ready for some Level Three time?"

To further simplify, the levels also can be converted into "shorthand" so that students can more easily visualize goals toward which to work and can more easily evaluate their own progress. This is accomplished by presenting them as *cumulative levels* that build on each other. To make this work, a Level Zero: Irresponsible, is added. Level One becomes self-control (or respect) without much motivation to participate. Level Two becomes a combination of self-control and effort and is usually conceptualized as being under the leader's supervision. Level Three adds self-direction, which means more independence and less direct supervision, and Level Four adds helping. Someone at Level Two, for example, is a participant in the class; whereas someone at Level Four is a participant, has shown self-direction, and has contributed something positive to others. This way, one number can be used to set a goal or self-evaluate (but not for program leaders to evaluate or categorize kids). This process is not without problems, because kids bounce back and forth from level to level, often in the same session, but many physical education teachers report that these problems are minor.

Developing and Implementing Specific Instructional Strategies

Putting kids first creates the necessary climate or tone for a responsibility-based program to work. Responsibility guidelines provide students with the awareness and direction to begin assuming some responsibility. However, to really put responsibility into practice, specific strategies need to be identified and implemented. Students cannot take responsibility if they are not given some, so instructional strategies must emphasize sharing power with students and negotiating issues with them. Taken to their logical conclusion, these strategies encourage students to eventually evaluate and, if necessary, to modify the responsibility guidelines.

Five general instructional strategies are used to implement the five student responsibilities:

- *Awareness* of their responsibilities, which involves brief talks and perhaps posting the responsibilities on the wall or bulletin board.
- *Direct instruction*, in which the teacher leads students through experiences designed to teach the responsibilities, for example, requiring all students on a team to pass the ball or puck to teammates (the right to be included) or requiring all students to participate in reciprocal teaching (Mosston & Ashworth, 1986), in

which they pair up and give each other motor skill feedback based on a few specific cues (helping others).

- *Individual decision-making*, so that students can individually learn to make choices and reflect on the benefits and liabilities of their choices, for example, by making an improvement plan if they are disruptive or abusive, by choosing their own optimal number of repetitions, by setting motor skill improvement goals for themselves, by volunteering for coaching or teaching leadership roles, or by evaluating the extent to which they have practiced self-control, given a good effort, and so on.
- *Group decision-making* to problem-solve issues or conflicts that arise or to evaluate various aspects of the program.
- *Counseling time*, which is a fancy name for building in some time, perhaps when students come in or leave the program, so that program leaders can have brief one-to-one conversations with students just to check in or get their opinion about something or to negotiate something. As students become more independent, more counseling time will become available automatically.

A progression accompanies these general instructional strategies and the more specific "substrategies," which are described in all of the chapters in part III (and in detail in Hellison, 1995). At the beginning of a responsibility-based program, most of the time is devoted to awareness and direct instruction, but as the program progresses more time is given to individual and group decision making. Once students are experienced in the model, perhaps no more (and maybe less) than 10 to 20 percent of the time will be devoted to awareness and/or direct instruction. The rest will involve individual and group decision making.

We are often asked about strategies for discipline problems. In the responsibility model, discipline is not addressed by a separate management system; it is a less adversarial way of teaching. Getting started is difficult, because the ideas are new to kids, administrators, colleagues, and parents. But as more students are able to function at Levels Three and Four, the program begins to run itself, and the program leader can focus on those who still struggle with basic responsibilities.

A daily class or session format helps to organize the four instructional strategies:

1. *Awareness talk:* Each class opens with a brief awareness talk to remind students of the program's guidelines—what the program is really about and what they need to focus on. Eventually, students can lead the awareness talks. The awareness talk keeps the idea of taking responsibility for oneself and others in the students' consciousness.

2. *Lesson:* This is the physical education subject matter—for example, a fitness routine, a basketball practice and scrimmage, some kind of motor skill instruction, or even open gym—integrated with strategies such as direct instruction, individual and group decision making, and, if necessary, brief awareness talks. One familiar example is to use Mosston's (Mosston & Ashworth, 1986) more individualized teaching styles, all of which shift some decision making to students. Negotiation is often used with students who struggle with their responsibilities, and some students may choose or need a more structured teacher-directed group because of their level of motivation or unwillingness to take sufficient responsibility for themselves.

3. *Group meeting:* Near the end of the day's program, a group meeting is held so that students can evaluate the lesson and suggest some solutions to any problems that have arisen. In large classes or with limited time, this can be done while standing and by requesting two or three students to volunteer their comments. In smaller groups, kids can sit in a circle and share their opinions and ideas. The group meeting helps students to reflect on the group's welfare and to have a voice in the proceedings.

4. *Reflection time:* Reflection time is set aside for students to reflect on the extent to which they have taken responsibility that day. The lesson closes with the teacher asking students to indicate to what extent they respected others, were self-motivated, were self-directed (if opportunities were given), and were helpful to others in class that day, and whether they tried any of these things outside of physical education since the last time the class met. They can carry out this self-evaluation by using their thumbs (up, sideways, or down; thanks to Nick Cutforth), by raising their hands, by saying one number to indicate what cumulative level they achieved, or by making a journal entry (Cutforth & Parker, 1996). There are many variations of reflection time. For example, Pete Hockett has painted the cumulative levels zero to four on the wall just inside the door, and students simply touch whichever cumulative level they think they reached that day on the way out of class. If Pete disagrees, he takes the student aside and they negotiate. (Pete calls his system tapping in and out. It also includes students touching the level they want to achieve on their way into class.)

Implementing this format and these strategies may appear to be straightforward (or not), but it takes a sensitive, reflective, artistic leader to match the appropriate strategies with individual and group needs (see chapter 4 in Hellison, 1995). The first step, letting go of full control, is enough of a struggle by itself. As I said recently to a university student of mine who could not seem to let go of control, "When you're doing nothing and they're doing everything, you're doing everything!"

How Do I Know If I Am Doing the Model?

All of these things—putting kids first, the students' responsibilities, the instructional strategies, the daily format, the necessary teacher values—are shown in table 3.2. However, this table does not answer the question, "How much of this stuff do I have to do to use the responsibility model?" Although the notion of using a model sometimes conjures up some rigid recipe to which one must adhere, we use the term *model* as Joyce and Weil (1986) do, as having a theoretical-philosophical focus and a body of supporting evidence, as well as actually being in practice, not just some college professor's brainstorm.

Table 3.2

Responsibility Model

PUTTING KIDS FIRST

1. Care about the emotional and social as well as physical well-being of each student.
2. Prioritize the instructor-student relationship.
3. Respect students' strengths, their individuality, their voices, and their capacity for decision making.

RESPONSIBILITIES

1. Respect for the rights and feelings of others
   - Control temper and mouth.
   - Include everyone.
   - Solve conflicts peacefully and democratically.
2. Effort
   - Explore effort and new tasks.
   - Have the courage to persist when the going gets tough.
   - Focus on self-improvement, rather than comparison to others.
3. Self-direction
   - Be responsibly independent.
   - Set and work on personal goals.
   - Have the courage to resist peer pressure.
4. Helping others
   - Be sensitive and responsive to others' needs.
   - Provide leadership to promote group welfare.

5. Outside the gym
   - Try these responsibilities in school, at home, and elsewhere.
   - Be a role model for others.

STRATEGIES

1. Awareness
2. Direct instruction
3. Individual decision making
4. Group decision making
5. Counseling time

FORMAT

1. Awareness talk
2. Lesson
3. Group meeting
4. Reflection time

That theoretical-philosophical focus is, in a sense, a spirit, a "way of being" (thanks to Nick Forsberg), rather than a rigid formula, and leaders need to own and adapt it to fit their setting, students, and style. Posting the responsibility levels on a gym wall does not necessarily mean the spirit of the model is being practiced in this gym. A much better indicator is this quote from an inner-city third grader: "This program is about trying to make the world a better place." Although a bit expansive, this little boy captured the spirit of our work.

Here are some questions that might help you determine to what extent you are doing, or are interested in doing, the model. If most of your answers are "yes" or "I'm working on it" or "I want to do that," you probably support the core principles of the model. Please remember that this model is only one way to serve underserved youth; you don't need to feel guilty if you don't score well. Rather, a lot of "no" answers simply suggest that this is not the approach for you, at least not at this point in your professional life.

1. Do you like kids and can you relate to them?
2. Do you try to treat all kids "unequally but fairly" (that is to say, individually)?
3. Do you spend some time consciously focusing on students' strengths?

4. Do you listen to students, believe that they "know things"?
5. Do you share power with students?
6. Are the students learning to solve their own conflicts?
7. Are the students learning to control their negative statements and temper, rather than relying on you to exert control?
8. Are the students learning to include everyone in the activities on their own?
9. Do the students have opportunities to work on their own goals?
10. Do the students have a voice in evaluating the program and in solving problems that arise?
11. Do the students have opportunities to assume meaningful teaching, coaching, and/or leadership roles?
12. Is some emphasis placed on value transfer from the program to life?
13. Do students leave your program understanding what taking responsibility means and how it applies to them?

State-of-the-Art Criteria and the Responsibility Model

The responsibility model is one way, not the only way, to put the state-of-the-art criteria into practice. To test the match between the criteria and the responsibility model, here are the criteria in the order they appear in table 3.1, accompanied by specific aspects of the model that meet each criterion. Other models can be compared to the criteria in the same way.

1. "Treat youth as resources . . .": Putting kids first specifically includes respecting their strengths and individuality.

2. "Focus on the whole person . . .": Putting kids first honors the holistic perspective rather than prioritizing sport or fitness, and the model's focus on personal and social development as a set of guidelines for physical activity content balances and integrates a whole-person focus with the physical activity content.

3. "Respect the individuality of youth . . .": The self-motivation dimension of effort requires individualized instruction opportunities, and self-direction emphasizes individual goal-setting.

4. "Empower youth": Two of the four instructional strategies, individual and group decision making, are empowerment-oriented, and as the program progresses, these two strategies dominate pro-

gram time. Moreover, some of the language in the five responsibilities—self-control, self-motivation, and self-direction—is empowerment-based.

5. "Give youth clear, demanding . . . expectations based on a strong, explicit set of values": The five responsibilities provide an explicit set of values.

6. "Help youth envision possible futures for themselves": The Neighborhood Scholar Program (see chapter 10) specifically addresses life after high school. In addition, the emphasis on becoming a role model in the community is an early step to possible futures sometimes not envisioned by the kids.

7. "Provide a physically and psychologically safe environment": The responsibility model framework leads off with self-control as a primary responsibility of students.

8. "Keep program numbers small and encourage participation over time; emphasize belonging and membership": Early experiences with the responsibility model in alternative school physical education classes, which are small in size and typically involve students for two or more years to provide special help for kids in trouble (see chapter 8), and similar experiences in small extended day clubs (see chapter 7), have validated the state-of-the art criterion for small class size and participation over time. Extended day programs provided the additional benefit of a club atmosphere.

In-school physical education classes typically have 30 or more students on the roster, often many more if conducted outdoors, and, with the exception of elementary school, are not likely to keep the same groups together for more than one year. With large numbers and a brief time frame, it is difficult to treat participants as individuals, to help them build on their strengths, or to control emotional abuse. The mandatory nature of most in-school programs and kids' attitudes toward "gym class" further hinder the achievement of desirable outcomes. Despite these barriers and the strategy modifications that need to be made in these settings, the model's goals and underlying values—(e.g., respect for students and the whole person, teaching a set of explicit values, some form of empowerment) can be implemented, according to evidence gathered over the years (Hellison, 1996; see also chapter 6). Because public schools are not likely to reduce class size (despite the success of schools that have found a way to create small classes, such as Central Park East in Harlem), physical education teachers are welcome to adapt the model for large classes as long as they don't stray from its underlying beliefs and values. After all, it was first piloted with large classes in two inner-city high schools (Hellison, 1978).

9. "Maintain a local connection": One example of a local connection is the preceding description of one of your authors helping the principal with discipline problems. All of your authors have had similar experiences.

10. "Provide courageous and persistent leadership in the face of systemic obstacles": We try! One thing you (and we) can always do is show up and hang in there, no matter how many barriers face us.

11. "Provide significant contact with a caring adult": This is emphasized in "putting kids first" and in the counseling time instructional strategy.

A Map of Community Responsibility-Based Programs

Based on the preceding principles, what kinds of programs are possible and desirable? How do they relate to each other? How does service learning fit in? The following overview of program possibilities is your six authors' blueprint for doing community work.

Figure 3.1 depicts 12 different kinds of community programs, almost all of which are in operation in one or more of your authors' communities. Ianni (1989) complained that community youth development programs never point in the same direction, and he called for a community "youth charter" to remedy this all-too-common state of affairs. We use the responsibility model in table 3.2 as the youth charter for all of our programs, supported as we have seen by most of the state-of-the-art criteria in table 3.1.

The programs on the left side of figure 3.1 are youth development programs. Note that students who successfully participate in any one of the four youth development programs near the top (chapters 5-8) can then join a cross-age teaching program (chapter 10) to teach what they have learned with younger students and eventually, if they graduate from high school, can become a neighborhood scholar (chapter 10). This progression ties the programs together and requires that they teach the same values. It also provides an opportunity for kids to experience our version of a youth charter from childhood to late adolescence and beyond.

The programs running down the middle of figure 3.1 support the youth development programs as the arrows indicate. For example, mentor programs (chapter 9) help students with their academic work and behavior in the classroom, and family programs introduce parents to the goals of the programs so that they can help at home. The right side

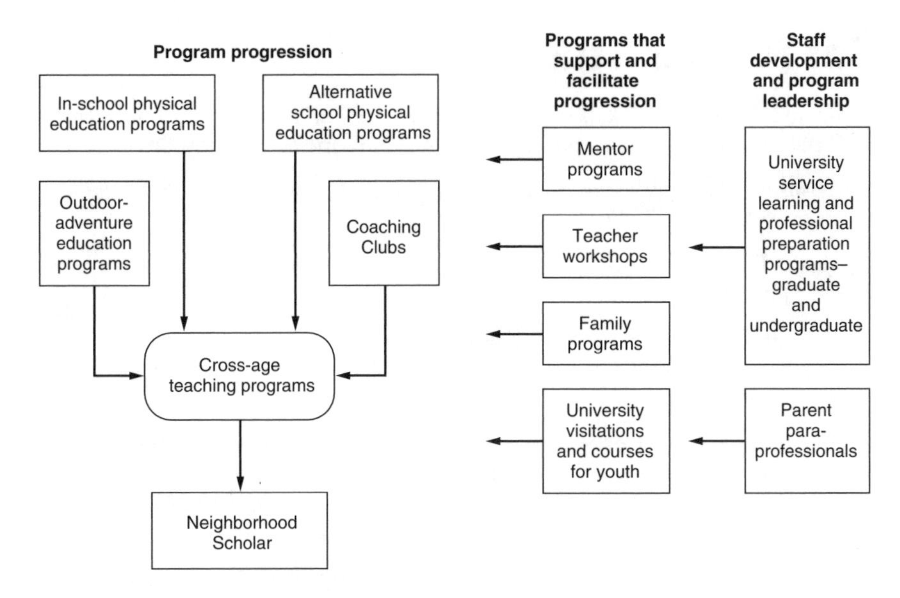

Figure 3.1 Past through present achievements of the responsibility model.

of figure 3.1 is devoted to staff development and leadership programs (chapter 4). Students and parents in these programs learn how to do service learning in the programs on the left side and in the middle of the diagram.

To learn what these specific youth development programs look like—for example, an outdoor adventure program or an extended day basketball club—we will take you to visit each of these programs in part III.

Youth Development in Underserved Communities

This chapter has described a set of generic youth development program principles (table 3.1), a specific physical activity program model based on these principles (table 3.2), and a map of community programs using this model (figure 3.1). Chapter 4 develops a concept and describes some examples of the kind of university staff development and program leadership courses, experiences, and programs necessary to form a university-community collaboration for youth development. These principles, model, map, and university programs provide the building blocks for the specific youth programs described in part III.

For Further Study

Benson, P.L. (1997). *All kids are our kids: What communities must do to raise caring and responsible children and adolescents.* San Francisco: Jossey-Bass.

Benson's "40 developmental assets" support and expand the youth development perspective described in this chapter.

Hellison, D. (1995). *Teaching responsibility through physical activity.* Champaign, IL: Human Kinetics.

Use this reference for a more thorough explanation of the responsibility model including specific instructional strategies and the teacher qualities necessary to put this model into practice.

Hellison, D., & Cutforth, N. (1997). Extended day programs for urban children and youth: From theory to practice. In H. Walberg, O. Reyes, & R. Weissberg (Eds.), *Children and youth: Interdisciplinary perspectives* (pp. 223-249). Thousand Oaks, CA: Sage.

This reference provides a more detailed description of the 11 state-of-the-art criteria for youth development and their origin.

McLaughlin, M.W., Irby, M.A., & Langman, J. (1994). *Urban sanctuaries: Neighborhood organizations in the lives and futures of inner-city youth.* San Francisco: Jossey-Bass.

This is perhaps the single best reference for studying successful extended day programs for underserved youth.

Chapter 4

Toward University-Community Collaboration

Nick Cutforth

So you are a student in physical education or kinesiology and you want to work with underserved kids? Or maybe you are a professor who wants to direct your teaching, research, and service work toward improving the quality of education and life of underserved kids. The good news is that in several universities around the United States, much important collaborative work is being done with social agencies and educational institutions in the surrounding communities to impact the social, emotional, and educational growth of underserved children and youth. In these universities, professors and students are working together to provide a rich array of physical activity programs for underserved youth.

This work takes place at different times (weekdays, evenings, weekends, during the school year, during summer vacations) and in different venues (including elementary, middle, and high schools, alternative schools, detention centers, universities, and Boys and Girls Clubs), and it involves different ages (from third graders to high school seniors). Much of this work has been going on for several years at the same site, whereas other program sites are new and their future may be in question. However, these programs have several things in common: They capitalize on the popularity of physical activity among kids; their framework and focus are based on the responsibility model; and they are taught or directed by your authors—people who are concerned about the plight of underserved youth and who are committed to developing programs that work.

The community programs run by university students and professors began in Chicago, but it is no secret that many of our youth around the nation—perhaps the majority—need more help than our institutions give them. Underserved neighborhoods and communities are everywhere. That's why the authors of this book are working in Greeley, Colorado and Greensboro, North Carolina, as well as Los Angeles, Chicago, and Denver. Thus, the ideas shared in this chapter have relevance for professors and students in all colleges and universities, not just those in major urban areas.

In this chapter you will read about the variety of experiences, courses, and programs that physical educators in higher education can use to develop a community focus within the college, school, department, or division. I will draw on the experiences of your authors and their students who have integrated serving underserved youth into their professional lives. First, I identify the constraints, barriers, and limitations that professors and students may encounter as they establish a university commitment to working in underserved communities. Second, I present several options for professors who are considering how best to integrate experience in community programs into university coursework and degree programs. Third, I conclude with a set of recommendations to guide professors and students as they strive to develop a community focus within larger physical education/kinesiology contexts.

Establishing a University Commitment to Underserved Communities

Despite periodic calls for reform and change, kinesiology and physical education programs have remained largely isolated from their surrounding communities (Lawson, 1997). Granted, teacher education programs place preservice teachers in local schools to fulfill student teaching requirements, but in most cases, the attention of student teachers, university supervisors, and cooperating teachers is focused on children and youth within the "normal" range of ability and attitude. This is hardly surprising, considering that university coursework is usually geared to this population as well as to coaching elite performers or students with clearly defined "special needs." With few exceptions, little regard is given to understanding the lives of young children and youth whom you read about in chapter 1, and even less attention is devoted to considering how their needs can be met through physical activity programs.

A Brief History: How a "Lone Ranger" Community-Oriented Professor Was Joined by Kindred Souls

Don Hellison shared a little about his physical education career in chapter 3. Until the late 1980s, he was perhaps the only university professor in the United States who regularly taught physical activity programs to kids in underserved communities. After having been a "lone ranger" at Portland State University for almost 20 years, in 1987 he joined the University of Illinois at Chicago (UIC), attracted by the promise of then–Kinesiology Dean Chuck Kristufek to support his efforts in teaching urban kids. It wasn't long before a small group of faculty members and graduate students joined him and taught their own programs. Under Don's direction, this group was instrumental in creating a School of Kinesiology commitment to providing physical activity programs for underserved youth in the urban communities that surround the UIC campus. Although students have graduated and faculty have moved on in their professional lives, the group is still in place, and in 1999 nine programs were being run in Chicago schools and social agencies.

As this book shows, Don's efforts have branched out to other locations around the United States. Two of the authors of this book—James Kallusky and myself—are Don's former students who used the knowledge and experience gained from a close working relationship with him to develop a community focus in our universities and implement our own physical activity programs. Two others—Tom Martinek and Missy Parker—used their sabbatical leave to observe and assist in the UIC programs run by Don and his students; on returning to their universities, Tom and Missy applied this new knowledge to develop community programs of their own. The other author—Jim Stiehl—has known Don for many years and has maintained close contact with him by sharing ideas and writing. At the same time Jim has taught kids in outdoor programs, taking along university students with him.

Thus, each author's journey toward a focus on university-community collaboration differs in several ways. In addition, our present commitment to youth programming takes many forms. For example, our kids' programs differ in content focus and populations served (although all participants are underserved); the way we connect these programs to our universities varies; and our organizational styles reflect our different personalities and values. However, we are all connecting community programs in underserved communities to university structures, coursework, and degree opportunities.

Multiple Stakeholders

In university collaborations with local community organizations, there are many participants. Faculty members (including teaching assistants), students (both undergraduate and graduate), other administrators in the college or department, community partners (including community members, community-based organizations, K-12 school personnel), and funders all have a stake in the program.

Naturally, these stakeholders vary in regard to their involvement. For example, college or department administrators don't usually venture out into the schools and may be distanced from the efforts of the other stakeholders. However, their moral and fiscal support and concern are crucial to the establishment and development of the programs. At the other extreme, professors are the primary facilitator of the programs and are always deeply involved. Somewhere in the middle of the commitment scale are the other stakeholders who, although they are dedicated to serving underserved children and youth and play a crucial role either teaching or organizing programs at individual sites, do not usually take home all the headaches associated with sponsoring an entire program.

Personal Abilities and Dispositions

Directing the talents of individuals within a kinesiology/physical education program to the needs of surrounding communities is hard work, and the quality of the final product, as in other realms of human endeavor, depends on the personal abilities and dispositions of those who do the work. Faculty colleagues and students at our institutions differ greatly in regard to several abilities and dispositions. These include their commitment (specifically, their willingness and ability to invest time and energy in the needs of underserved kids, attend meetings with community partners, and seek out funding sources); their receptivity to change (their intellectual curiosity and open-mindedness about addressing the social problems facing schools or community organizations); their attitude toward risk taking (e.g., their degree of confidence about stepping outside the university to serve in neighboring schools and community); their values (particularly about directing their intellectual efforts toward serving the community—a task often conceived as marginal by the professorate); and their orientation to task (e.g., their ability to communicate across the different cultures of higher education, K-12 education, and community-based organizations).

Intellectual Dispositions

Professors and students also vary in regard to their intellectual posture toward working with underserved kids. Their life and teaching experiences contribute to a view of teaching and learning that determines the way they view such matters as, for example, content, discipline, and the degree to which the program leaders and instructors share decision-making powers with their students. Of course, such views can always be challenged as previous experience is meshed with the present and with views of the future. However, such transitions don't come easily and often require serious inquiry into educational issues. On the one hand, some professors and students have a broad, deep understanding of the role that physical activity programming might play in underserved kids' lives. On the other hand, the "underdeveloped" intellectual posture of other professors and students can be reflected in a number of ways. For example, some may see themselves as sport-specific experts (e.g., basketball, soccer, or martial arts) or as experts in a particular field (e.g., sport psychology or pedagogy) and not as teachers of young children and youth who are growing up in adverse circumstances and who possess complex and profound needs.

Political Dimensions

When professors and students commit to putting their energies into a collaborative relationship with community partners, their actions do not exist in isolation. For example, a professor's new course offering in Youth Development or At-Risk Youth Leadership has to be approved by colleagues and may affect class schedules and colleagues' course assignments. External worries (e.g., about accreditation) and internal concerns (e.g., about credit-hour generation and teaching load) may also surface.

External Influences

Any attempt to infuse a community focus into institutional structures is also influenced by national dialogues calling for reform on urban, racial, and education issues (to name just a few) and by a complex, often conflicting array of external trends—for example, changing demographics in an increasingly pluralistic society, the restructuring of teacher education programs, the need for interdisciplinary programs, and calls for programs to address the needs of students at risk (Lawson, 1997). Understandably, professors and students vary in regard to their familiarity with these trends. Rather than making up our minds on such issues, we need to listen carefully to all sides so that we can address the realities affecting underserved children and youth.

Other potentially strong external influences on university-community youth development programs are the organizations that provide support. These include the university, local schools and social agencies, philanthropic foundations, and other funding agencies. All of the authors' universities provide varying degrees of financial support for students. These include scholarships, work-study positions, and teaching and research assistants. Similarly, local schools and social agencies such as Boys and Girls Clubs, local parks and recreation districts, and the YMCA may be able to pay university students to teach kids in their programs. Such assistance goes a long way toward helping people who might not otherwise be able to participate in youth development programs. However, inevitably there are strings attached to such support, and these should be clarified so that all parties enter into the relationship with as thorough an understanding as possible.

It is quite possible to collaborate with community partners without financial support—indeed, the early community efforts of several of your authors were undertaken with no resources and in addition to university duties. However, philanthropic foundations and funding agencies provide important financial support to maintain existing programs and develop new ones. Although some organizations allow complete autonomy in how their funds are spent, others have requirements that must be satisfied. These include pragmatic issues such as the number of children to be served, guidelines for program organization, and methods of evaluation, and also administrative issues such as how funds can be used, methods of reporting progress and impact, and providing matching funds. Such requirements need to be fully understood; otherwise, program directors may find themselves pursuing directions that not only take up their time but also may clash with their values and program philosophy.

Integrating Experience in Community Programs Into University Coursework and Degree Programs

The university-community programs in the authors' university settings take several different forms. They are distinguishable by the kinds of experiences available to students and the accompanying degree of intellectual depth. They also reflect professors' and students' motives for participating in such programs and their desired levels of involvement.

Your authors range from tenured full professors to untenured assistant professors. Their motivations vary from always having done this kind of work (Don and Jim), to an expanding interest in applying many years of success in their disciplinary field to the needs of underserved kids (Tom and Missy), to a desire to pursue the challenges of university-community collaboration for the rest of their careers (James and Nick).

The students range from first-year undergraduates trying to find something worthwhile to do to doctoral students writing their dissertations. Their motivations range from the simple desire to have such an experience to an interest in pursuing a career in youth development work (including public school teaching). Their reasons for participation illustrate the variety of commitments one can make, ranging from a one-semester experience to an entire career change.

In this section we will look at several options, including

- visitations to existing programs,
- independent study,
- optional (or mandatory) service learning experiences in current courses,
- graduate concentrations,
- special programs, and
- faculty and student collaboration on research and scholarship.

Visitations to Existing Programs

These are opportunities to visit and observe existing programs taught by professors, university students, community youth workers, or public school teachers. They could be voluntary or could provide credit for students who show interest and promise. The student's role could be an observer or, if sufficiently motivated or confident, he or she could assist the teacher by working with individual kids or small groups. Although these visits need not be connected with coursework, they could be one option for a course assignment (for example, Curriculum Issues in Physical Education or Psychosocial Aspects of Physical Education and Sport), in which case they could be followed by a written paper or class presentation.

Independent Study

An independent study involves a student and a professor having regular one-to-one exchanges on a project tailor-made for the student—for example, Effective Programming for Underserved Youth (Cutforth). The pair meets weekly, biweekly, or monthly to discuss readings or an issue or idea about underserved youth and effective programming. Often, the resulting personal relationship enables the professor to add meaning to course readings, discussions, and perhaps visits to existing youth development programs. Sometimes, as a result of the course, the student may be motivated to become further involved with the professor's work by visiting existing programs or developing and teaching a program in the community. The drawback is that the professor has to budget time to meet with the student, read and respond to the student's journals or papers, and prepare for the next meeting, and often this work is "off-load" and therefore in addition to usual professorial duties. Although new assistant professors, in particular, may be concerned about this drawback, independent study arrangements provide them with a valuable opportunity to discuss readings and issues related to their academic interests.

Optional (or Mandatory) Service Learning Experiences in Current Courses

Service learning experiences involve community placements in which students assume helping roles with youth. Such experiences can be mandatory or optional. When mandatory, *service learning* may even be included in the course title or course description to reflect the focus of the class. However, a service learning assignment can also be one of several options within a course. As a pedagogical process, service learning involves four elements:

1. Planning
2. Implementation and project monitoring
3. Reflection and celebration
4. Evaluation and reporting (Witmer & Anderson, 1994)

University students are placed in community settings to "serve and learn" through various roles. These might include mentoring a child or a small group of children through physical activities; assisting teachers with a physical education class, athletic team, or after-school program; or directing their own physical activity program.

The first step of the service learning experience involves planning. Here, the students work cooperatively with the professor and the community partner to describe and agree on the major components of the service experience including tasks, schedule, outcomes, supervision, and assessment. This step also involves preparing the university students and the host site as to how to act and what to expect, identifying the needs of the placement population, and planning a series of activities to meet these needs.

The next major component to be considered in effective service learning experience is project implementation and monitoring. During implementation, a good monitoring process is needed to ensure that the project is meeting the expectations of the professor, the student, and the community partner. It also allows modifications to be made during the implementation process.

Reflection and celebration distinguish service learning from other community service activities. Through reflection, students analyze, synthesize, and evaluate their service experiences while also learning youth development concepts. Reflection is an ongoing process and can include writing diaries, logs, or journals and oral reflections such as presentations and discussions with peers, site supervisors, or the professor. The written materials enable students to compile a record of their experiences, thus creating a system for reflection and growth; written materials also enable students to reflect on the meaning of these experiences, thus increasing the power of students' application of theory and research to their work with children. The oral medium offers contexts for sharing experiences, questioning particular activities or events students observed, probing new possibilities, discussing successful activities, and exploring new solutions to problems. Students should be encouraged to develop their own culminating experiences that integrate reflection with the celebration component of service learning. Tom and I provide some examples in chapter 10: Cross-Age Teaching Programs.

The final stage, evaluation and reporting, should be based on the objectives of the service learning activity and should be designed during the planning process. The students should learn how to use both qualitative and quantitative techniques to collect, analyze, and report data. The evaluation should show the extent to which objectives were met, the degree to which the activities were carried out as planned, and the impact of the experience on the children's academic, social, and personal development. The reporting could be done through traditional class papers or oral presentations or through more nontraditional approaches such as poster presentations, video documentaries, or Web pages.

Thus, service learning is a complex process that involves careful planning, implementation, reflection, and evaluation (Erickson & Anderson, 1997). The time spent on these elements will be reflected in the quality and impact of the experience on the community partners, the professor, and the students. The community partners benefit when the service experience is tailored to young people's needs (Cutforth, 2000) and from the enhanced relationship with the university. Potential benefits for the professor include increased student motivation, an increased knowledge of the community and the extent of services available, better relations between the university and the community, and the experience of using a nontraditional pedagogical approach.

The students benefit from learning by doing and from reflecting on their learning with the professor and fellow students. Service learning experiences offer opportunities for students and professors to link theory and practice in ways that stimulate discussion, refine pedagogical strategies, and develop new teaching approaches. For example, challenges such as diversity and youth alienation can take on real faces and specific locations for students. Such shared, collaborative learning experiences enable students to learn actively rather than passively, and their discourse is wide-ranging and interdisciplinary. Students in these small learning communities often say that these are some of the most beneficial learning experiences of their degree program. Furthermore, the students' involvement in planning, practicing different skills, and reflecting on these experiences reinforces basic pedagogical behaviors common to teaching. Many students continue to work with kids long after completing the class.

Special Programs

Several of the professors have built an administrative home for their work by establishing special programs. These programs differ in regard to the academic experiences offered and their form of university-community collaboration. At UIC, Don offers an undergraduate elective course in At-Risk Youth Leadership, a master's program in Urban Physical Education, and a doctoral program in curriculum design with the College of Education with a concentration in Urban Youth Leadership. Students work in youth programs in Chicago's inner-city communities. At the University of Northern Colorado, Jim's students can pursue master's and doctoral degrees in Outdoor Education while teaching outdoor and experiential education in alternative schools in the Greeley area. At the University of North Carolina at Greensboro, Tom directs a master's degree in Community Youth Leadership and teaches courses in underserved youth and program evaluation. Students work in Project Effort, a mentoring and cross-aged teaching program held at the local Boys and Girls Club. At the University of Denver, Nick offers a two-course specialization in Urban Education at the master's level. In addition, graduate students in the College of Education and undergraduate students in the Department of Service Learning provide numerous educational, curriculum, and mental health services to three Denver public schools as part of the University of Denver/Northwestside Schools Partnership.

Although different in structure, these programs share several similarities. The students enroll in master's or doctoral programs; take several classroom courses and one or more service learning or field-based courses; develop, teach in, and evaluate programs for underserved kids; and write theses and dissertations to expand their knowledge and their connections to real-world problems. The purpose of these programs is to prepare students to take leadership roles in a variety of institutions and levels. Several graduates are teachers in private or public schools and community recreation programs, whereas others are pursuing careers in higher education as faculty members in physical education teacher education, kinesiology, recreation, or urban education.

Also, these special programs adopt modes of organization in curriculum, pedagogy, academic work, and assessment that promote educational community among students and faculty. Student learning spans the disciplines and is shared and collaborative both in the university and in the community, so that students learn together rather than apart. These classes often follow an inquiry approach into the dilemmas and challenges of teaching and learning in underserved communities. The professors ask questions of students, direct them to a variety of resources, share perceptions, suggest some possible alternatives, and encourage them to persist in their own learning until they resolve the dilemmas of their teaching practices to their own satisfaction.

When students study the same topic, they will naturally form their own associations to give each other academic and social support. The professors have found that students spend more time together out of class than do students in traditional, unrelated, stand-alone classes. The common study of a subject within the context of kids' programs brings students together quickly as small communities of learners.

These learning communities have several benefits. First, students become more actively involved in classroom as well as after-class learning, and by spending more time learning, obviously they learn more. Second, the students spend more time learning together, and learning together enriches everyone's understanding and knowledge. Third, these students form social bonds outside the classroom. They tend to learn and make close friends at the same time. This last outcome is especially important in an era of what Robert Bellah (1996) called rampant "expressive individualism" and of growing racial, gender, sexual, and ideological divisions on university campuses. Collaborative experiences teach students that their learning and the learning of their peers are inexorably intertwined, and that regardless of race, class, gender, or background, their academic interests, namely working with underserved youth, are the same.

These special programs require faculty to work and think in a different way. Often the traditional professor–student relationship is replaced by a team approach in which team members spend many hours discussing what specific topics should receive focus and how best to study them. Each person should feel able to express his or her opinion, and decisions are often made by consensus rather than as directives from the professor.

Faculty and Student Collaboration on Research and Scholarship

Each of the preceding options may include varying amounts of teaching in community programs; presenting papers and conducting workshops at local, national, and international conferences; and undertaking research. Numerous applied research opportunities are available for students and faculty interested in contributing to the academic community and to the advancement of the youth development model. Such opportunities illustrate how the university tripartite mission of research, teaching, and service can be combined rather than being seen as separate entities (Cutforth, 1997).

Recommendations for Developing a University-Community Focus

In closing, I offer suggestions to help you think about forging university-community collaboration. The authors' experiences have led to the following recommendations.

Problems Can Consume a Great Deal of Time and Energy

Collaborating with social agencies and educational institutions in local communities takes a considerable amount of time, support, and intellectual energy and is often messier than working on research projects and teaching. Problems are inevitable, but you won't learn or be successful without them. Expect to experience both struggles and victories in gaining support at the departmental, college, university, and community levels. Also, be selective in where you put your resources, because many gatekeepers, rules, regulations, and structures can make collaboration difficult. Furthermore, without careful planning and negotiation, school and agency staff can be threatened by the appearance of other professionals.

Stay True to Your Program Philosophy

Underserved communities are everywhere and most are desperate for additional help and services. Although such neediness can be an asset (there is no shortage of settings in which to focus your energies!), there is also the danger that you will be asked to take on more than you can handle. For example, on several occasions I have been asked to take 30 kids in my after-school programs. I make it clear that large numbers will take my focus away from the responsibility goals of the program to classroom management and behavioral strategies (for additional thoughts on this issue, see Hellison & Cutforth, 1997).

Start, and Start Small: Vision and Strategic Planning Will Come Later

"Start small" is appropriate because the options for university-community collaboration discussed earlier take time to develop and require professors and students to be receptive, ready, and willing to teach and learn in new ways. All your authors started by teaching in their own community programs. Sometimes interested students visit these programs, several get their feet wet as assistant teachers, and a few go on to direct their own programs. Others may approach their professor about doing an independent study.

Over many months, the professors and students begin to foster university-community collaboration, often without much experience in doing so. As the years progress, they gain access to additional public schools and community social agencies, and they gain the trust of school and agency officials. Often the practical questions that arise from such efforts merit thoughtful consideration back at the university and generate a demand for service learning experiences and the infusion of youth development concepts into university coursework. Several years later a graduate concentration or a special program may develop, with faculty and students collaborating on research and scholarship.

Although this scenario may sound like a blueprint, it certainly is not. Rather it is nonlinear and loaded with uncertainty. Because of individual, group, and institutional values, priorities, and needs, the extent to which these developments occur may vary. The important point is that one has to start somewhere, and without the professor's initial efforts to venture beyond the university setting, there would be no opportunities for the seeds of university-community collaboration to take root. Vision, although necessary for success, emerges from action more often than it precedes action. Remember, also, that productive educational change is really a journey that doesn't end until we do.

Professor-Student Roles Tend to Be Informal

In the authors' university-community programs, students are more like colleagues than subordinates, colleagues to be supported in any possible way. Social functions play a large part in all the authors' programs, and these occasions reflect the view that most of us possess minds capable of cultivation beyond classes. Also, they reduce the isolation that innovators typically experience. These professors are almost always available to students in their offices and homes and they have a solicitous concern for their students' well-being—a concern that is usually reciprocated. Such practices embody the view of looking beyond labels such as "inexperienced," "beginning teacher," "graduate student," or "member of a research team" and replacing them with appropriate recognition for contributions to various projects, whether these contributions be teaching in community programs, writing research reports, making presentations, or submitting manuscripts for publication.

It has been the authors' experience that neither centralization nor decentralization works in efforts to reach out to the community. These efforts require a two-way relationship of pressure, support, and continuous negotiation, amounting to simultaneous top-down and bottom-up influence. Each of us—whether as individuals or in groups—has learned to manage this paradox.

A Final Word

The most important ingredients for successful university-community collaboration are the commitment, preparation, and persistence of the faculty and students involved. Every person can be a change agent but must forego the hope of discovering a set of easy-to-follow steps. Likewise, a commitment to university-community collaboration by itself is not good enough. A commitment needs an engine, and that engine is individual, skilled change agents pushing for changes around them, intersecting with other like-minded individuals and groups to form the critical mass necessary to bring about continuous improvements. Indeed, this is the spirit in which the partnership involving your authors was formed.

Physical education/kinesiology programs in higher education are well-positioned to direct more of their energies to their local communities and to develop leaders in the youth development field—people willing to accept challenges and take risks. This chapter has provided several examples and guidelines for doing this kind of work and for developing and implementing programs. It is up to you to decide the level at which you want to get involved.

For Further Study

Erickson, J., & Anderson, J. (Eds.) (1997). *Learning with the community: Concepts and models for service learning in teacher education.* Washington, DC: American Association of Higher Education.

A comprehensive review of approaches to service learning in teacher education, including the perspectives of university professors and students and school administrators, teachers, and students.

Lawson, H.A. (1997). Children in crisis, the helping professions, and the social responsibilities of universities. *Quest, 49,* 8-33.

The author argues that the physical education profession should forge new directions for research and practice toward the needs of poor and vulnerable children, youth, families, and their local neighborhood communities.

Siedentop, D. (1998). Regaining the public trust: Complex social problems meet specialized academic disciplines. *Quest, 50,* 170-178.

Using the College of Education at Ohio State University as the context, the author argues that problems of urban communities and their potential solutions should become part of the teaching, research, and service mission of university faculty and programs.

PART III

Physical Activity Programs for Underserved Youth

The map of specific physical activity youth development programs for underserved youth in figure 3.1 is based on the responsibility model and the state-of-the-art criteria for program development described in chapter 3. Part III describes in some detail these specific youth programs in a variety of settings, including the wilderness, public schools, alternative schools, and social agencies, and in a variety of program structures, including outdoor and adventure education, physical education, extended day clubs, mentoring, cross-age teaching, and postsecondary education.

Chapter 5

Outdoor and Adventure Programs

Jim Stiehl

Lifetime or "carryover" activities such as golf, tennis, bowling, and badminton are now included in most school and community physical activity programs. However, many youngsters desire alternative activities that provide excitement, challenge, and a degree of risk. They also prefer activities in which the emphasis is not on winning or losing but rather on cooperating and facing the challenges of a natural environment. The use of outdoor and adventure activities (e.g., backpacking, rock climbing, map and compass reading, cross-country skiing, winter camping, white-water paddling, and challenge ropes course events, all of which include important choices with sometimes weighty consequences) in association with a program of responsibility can provide a powerful alternative to conditions that lead to feelings of alienation and powerlessness, which often result in withdrawal and rebellion.

In the following pages, you will read about similarities and differences between adventure and outdoor activities and how the responsibility model can be tailored to both. I also provide glimpses of three distinct programs: an adventure program in an after-school setting, an outdoor program infused into a school's curriculum, and an outdoor summer program. Next are suggestions for applying responsibility concepts in adventure and outdoor settings. And finally I include a few closing thoughts for university faculty who wish to be involved in these sorts of programs.

Adventure Programs Compared to Outdoor Programs

For purposes of this chapter, outdoor activities are considered as distinct from adventure activities in several respects, although one may incorporate elements from the other. Adventure programs typically offer individuals the opportunity to increase communication, cooperation, and trust while becoming effective members of a team capable of group problem solving. Although activities and problems are presented in a playful, nonthreatening manner, the attempt is to simulate obstacles and situations that occur in everyday life and then deal with them in ways that are enjoyable, creative, and productive. Some adventure programs include a challenge ropes course, which involves elements (constructed of wood, rope, and steel cable) near the ground and off the ground that simulate challenges found in a more natural setting (ascending trees, crossing streams using logs or ropes, and climbing over walls). The responsibility of the instructor or program leader is to facilitate individual and group achievements and to ensure that the entire process occurs in a physically and emotionally safe environment.

A similarity between adventure and outdoor activities is their focus on personal and group development. One important difference, however, is that outdoor activities occur in open environments, with little to no control imposed on the environment and where hazards may sometimes be beyond the participants' control. Dangers in the natural environment must be understood, and participants and program leaders must exercise appropriate judgment in attempting to minimize potential hazards. Also, outdoor educators and leaders of backcountry excursions have the opportunity to inspire participants to alter their outlooks on the environment. Participants in outdoor activities must be especially mindful of minimizing their impact on fragile habitats. Finally, flawed judgment, poor planning, inadequate technical and medical skills, or misuse of equipment can quickly and easily jeopardize an outdoor venture.

For these reasons alone, outdoor educators require extensive training and experience beyond that expected of instructors in adventure programs. For example, the instructor in an adventure program places considerable attention on being a "facilitator;" that is, encouraging individuals to plan, describe, analyze, and communicate experiences; helping them make sense of the experiences; and helping them carry this learning into subsequent activities and into their everyday lives. The leader's role is to present scenarios and problems, and then to back off and allow the group to experience the joys of success and agonies of failure. Successes and failures are then discussed with the group. In contrast, although the outdoor instructor may assist in processing experiences, a more prominent role is that of "teacher," someone who ensures that participants acquire specific technical skills (e.g., canoeing or rock climbing) and essential knowledges (e.g., backcountry medicine, land navigation, weather) and who provides participants with an opportunity to explore and shape their attitudes toward the environment.

Thus, although activity offerings will vary among programs, skills often expected of an adventure facilitator and, to a greater extent, an effective outdoor leader include

- technical skills or competencies (e.g., knot tying, paddling, orienteering, climbing);
- safety skills (e.g., inspecting equipment, weather interpretation, wilderness first aid, avalanche hazard evaluation);
- environmental skills (including minimum-impact travel and leave-no-trace camping);
- organizational skills (e.g., managing risks, planning routes, securing permits, arranging transportation and equipment);
- instructional skills (e.g., teaching progressions, analyzing tasks, matching teaching strategies to learner characteristics);
- facilitation skills (e.g., fostering productive group dynamics, resolving conflicts, cultivating personal trust and group cooperation);
- flexible leadership style (e.g., employing a democratic, delegating, or autocratic style as appropriate to a situation); and
- professional ethics (moral standards that include a positive outdoor ethic as well as a vision for a clean, sustainable environment; it is truly disturbing that our society has come to rely more on its citizens' ability to spend and consume than on their ability to do and save).

Few college and university programs prepare individuals with all of these skills in mind. However, each is important if a program is to advance and expand safely and effectively. Noted at the end of this chapter are a few of the many resources available for developing outdoor and adventure programs.

Despite the aforementioned differences between outdoor and adventure programs, two outcomes often promoted through both types of programs are a healthier sense of oneself and a stronger sense of community (connectedness). Outdoor programs often go beyond these two outcomes, also emphasizing a heightened sense of place (in part, an appreciation and respect for one's surroundings).

Many young people are seeking activities that promote better self-understanding, provide for more satisfying relationships with others, and permit active participation in outdoor environments. Thus, more and more teachers, program leaders, and teacher educators are beginning to incorporate adventure and outdoor activities into their programs. When the responsibility model is incorporated into these programs, the result is a powerful means for offering young people a sense of identity and an ability to act independently, the experience of making responsible commitments to themselves and others, a chance to learn problem-solving skills, and valuable social competencies that include empathy, caring, and communication skills. The desired outcome is an individual who embraces an ethic of valuing people and his or her surroundings.

Outdoor and Adventure Programs and the Responsibility Model

The responsibility model is flexible enough to embrace goals typically espoused in adventure and outdoor programs. Although the specific adaptations of the responsibility model may vary among programs and populations, I have found the following general version to be a valuable one.

Level One: Expedition behavior. Many an expedition has failed because of conflict among its members. As a member of this group, you are expected to keep your language and actions under control. The single rule here is "be appropriate." Working together and respecting each other and our surroundings are the keys to a successful team.

Level Two: Determination. Another responsibility is to accept challenges and to keep trying, even in the face of adversity. This includes accepting encouragement and support, particularly when you might least want to. Determination is also a form of courage.

Level Three: Independence. A more advanced responsibility is to set your own goals and work independently on your skills and attitudes in an attempt to reach those goals.

Level Four: Leadership. The greatest responsibility when we are together is to honor our group by looking out for the entire group's welfare. This involves sharing your knowledge and skills, being sensitive to others' needs, and trying to serve them, even if it may be uncomfortable for you. This is sometimes the most difficult responsibility because it requires going beyond yourself ("me first") and sometimes even beyond your friends ("us first") to advocate for what is best for the whole group or the environment.

Level Five: Beyond the fence. Responsibility for yourself, others, and your surroundings does not only occur when we are together. You will be asked to try to act responsibly at school, in your neighborhood, and in town, as well as in more remote outdoor settings.

Each level of responsibility is presented within a framework of making choices. Because every choice has consequences, we emphasize the concept of choice as the most essential ingredient to successful participation in the program. For activities and settings that involve some degree of risk, it is imperative that we make choices which minimize the possibility of negative outcomes. In an outdoor setting, natural obstacles such as weather, rockfall, swift water, and snow bridges can present hazards with negative consequences ranging in severity from minor to enormous. Consequently, each participant must develop respect (not fear) for hazards and the ability to maximize a group's margin of safety through good judgment (i.e., anticipating and recognizing hazards and knowing how to avoid them). In other words, making appropriate choices is essential. Although in most adventure activities, perceived risk typically surpasses actual risk, the consequences of making inappropriate choices in these activities can also result in serious injury, both emotional and physical.

Thus, when promoting responsibility, the concept of choice is central in our adventure and outdoor programs. The following examples illustrate a few of the many possibilities available through outdoor and adventure activities that have been coupled with an emphasis on developing responsibility for ourselves, others, and our surroundings. Teaching strategies for these programs differ somewhat from those described in chapter 3 (awareness, direct instruction, individual decision making, group decision making). Depending on specific goals, group characteristics, available resources, and the nature of a specific activity, strategies may vary from session to session. Nonetheless, we usually include the following in our instruction: awareness, direct instruction or self-instruction (including practice time), and debriefing and reflection.

After-School Adventure Program

This program was developed for middle school youngsters in our community who demonstrate leadership potential yet exhibit or are in jeopardy of demonstrating violent behaviors. It is an ongoing multiagency program involving a partnership among the university, public schools, the city parks and recreation program, and alternative homes for youth. Hence, this is a collaborative effort to combine community resources in a way that makes them accessible and useful to these youngsters. The specific purpose is to develop personal and social responsibility through adventure activities. The following is a glimpse of the program across several sessions. Each session involves a loose sequence of activities: icebreakers, awareness talk, direct instruction (may include trust and spotting activities, problem-solving activities, knot tying, and belaying), and debriefing and reflection. Sessions occur on Friday afternoons for three hours, initially at the community recreation center and later at the university's challenge ropes course. We will observe day one and then skip ahead to day six.

Day One

The 18 youngsters (10 boys and 8 girls) arrive, some rowdy but most appearing to be listless. After getting acquainted using a name game, we seat the group and discuss goals, standards, and logistics. Each participant is provided an opportunity to share what he or she is hoping to accomplish today, and we remind them of our roles as leaders. Minimum goals are to be safe, have fun, respect others (Level One), and challenge yourself (Level Two). Minimum standards include having required signed forms (necessary for participation), not using alcohol or nonprescription drugs, and staying with the group and away from areas not supervised. Logistics include location of restrooms, determining tobacco policy, asking about medical issues, and confirming the group's commitment to the goals, standards, and any other agreements.

After briefly discussing this afternoon's schedule, we begin with some tag games to get the youngsters active, and then play several silly games (deinhibitors) that give participants an opportunity to be playful and to appear inept in front of their peers. One such game is an animal game (Speed Rabbit) in which players stand in a circle with one player in the center of the circle. The center player points to anyone in the circle and designates her or him as either "elephant," "moose," or "rabbit." The designee and both adjacent players must quickly form the identified animal in a manner suitable to the center player who, if dissatisfied with the performance of any one of them, may then designate that person as the new center player. The activity proceeds with a great deal of laughing, which can prove useful in involving those young people who spend much of their time trying to be right and look good.

Next we demonstrate and practice a few spotting and lifting procedures. These are necessary to ensure safety in later group problem-solving activities, most of which involve physical contact and often require safeguarding one another's movements. Also, spotting enhances team building because each participant must assume responsibility for the well-being of others during each event. This in turn develops trust among group members and enhances individual confidence due to the supportive atmosphere.

An example of a group problem-solving activity, or initiative, is Full House. Players balance themselves on a four-by-four-inch beam and are asked to rearrange themselves, nonverbally, according to birth date and without touching the ground. Talking or touching the ground by any group member results in a restart. Another such activity is Nuclear Fence, in which the group must cross from one side of a horizontal, waist-high bungee cord to the other. The crossing must occur with all participants connected at all times. If anyone touches the cord, or if the connection breaks (akin to one defective Christmas tree bulb causing the others not to light), the group must restart.

After the final group initiative of the afternoon, we conduct a closing session in which all participants gather in a circle to reflect on what the day has meant to them. At first, I try to elicit some comments about what they learned or experienced. We then discuss items that pertain to the responsibility model and that might improve teamwork in subsequent meetings. For example, I explain that today I noticed how everyone appeared to be challenging themselves and taking some risks (Level Two: determination). I ask why this might be so, and one player mentions that she did not feel "stupid" when acting silly or making a mistake. We proceed to discuss a supportive environment (Level One: expedition behavior) and examples of how support might appear in others' actions and comments.

One youngster reports that some of the activities are boring for him. A discussion arises about playing the "blame game" and what he might do next time to create more value (i.e., less boredom) for himself. He and the others agree that this is a worthwhile challenge for him (Level Two: determination). One player even offers to help him think of ways to reduce his boredom (Level Four: leadership). Someone else says that she heard a few disrespectful comments during one of the activities. We review the group's agreement to speak and act with respect and explore briefly the impact that such comments might have on a group member. All are then asked to write a journal entry describing an example of a Level One and a Level Two behavior that they noticed during today's session.

Day Six

This is our final session indoors. The group has been working on Level One and Level Two behaviors in a context of increasingly difficult group initiatives and trust activities. In one of the sessions, we dealt with specific alternatives to violent behaviors and ways of thinking. Discussions and journal entries included topics of keeping cool (being cool-headed versus hot-headed), sizing up the situation (defining a situation as hostile will influence the solutions you pick, and you'll likely treat others automatically as adversaries), thinking it through (think about alternatives and their consequences), and doing the right thing (pick a response that is most likely to be effective in solving the problem and preventing violence). All of this was presented in a context of Level One expectations.

We have noticed considerable progress to the point where the group successfully completed a trust fall last week. The trust fall involved a controlled fall from the four-foot level of the bleachers into the arms of arranged spotters. This activity involves emotional and physical trust, clear and assertive communication, sensitivity to gender and body issues, and focus on the task. If we are to proceed next week to the challenge ropes course, success in activities such as the trust fall is imperative. Also necessary is each youngster's competence in knot tying and belaying. Though we will teach belaying (a technique that protects the climber) next week, we have already established the importance of proper positioning (for spotting), being focused, and mastering commands. Today's emphasis is on tying several important knots.

As they arrive, each youngster practices two knots that were presented last week: an overhand and a figure eight (Level Three: independence). Once everyone is in the gym, we first play a quick warm-up game to break mental sets ("I didn't finish my soft drink!" "Who took my keys?" "It's cold in here!"). We then form a circle for a brief awareness talk to remind everyone of their responsibilities. Next, the lesson begins with tying a studebaker wrap, which is a self-tied harness to be worn next week for climbing and belaying. Though commercial harnesses are available, I explain that by tying their own harnesses they must accept more responsibility for safeguarding themselves and their teammates. Those who learn quickly are asked to support others (Level Four) who are still learning (Levels Two and Three). In similar fashion, they learn and practice a few other critical knots.

Time remaining for the closing session, or debrief, is only about 10 minutes. I begin by evaluating their efforts thus far. Then team members evaluate their performance. One youngster is anxious about next week, because he is afraid of heights. I reassure him that our philosophy is "challenge by choice" and that he has the right to say "I choose not to . . . yet" instead of "I can't." I further mention that it might be useful in frightening situations to ask ourselves, "Do I have fear, or does fear have me?" He chuckles, suggesting that he might change his T-shirt's catch phrase from "No fear" to "Manage fear."

Because we are out of time, yet have agreed to complete a journal entry after each session, one youngster volunteers to collect the completed journals and return them to me by tomorrow. Everyone consents to deliver their journals to this person (a confirming example of trust on their part, because journals are confidential, and a welcome act of initiative on his part, substantiating the leadership that he has displayed for the past several weeks).

In-School Outdoor Program

The second program we will visit is an outdoor program that has been operating for almost two years in an alternative high school. The program started with a small and select group of students described by the principal as "troubled and troubling." Although the principal viewed with some skepticism our proposed program of outdoor activities and responsibility, she was willing to give us a chance (largely, we think, because we were convincing in our commitment to the welfare of these kids). To receive support from teachers, parents, and other school administrators, the principal defined our program as promoting youth development and leadership, a part of the school's charge.

Surprisingly, outdoor activities have proven so popular at this school that they are being woven into much of the school's curricular fabric. For example, orienteering is linked with reading and geography, and rock climbing is linked with math and earth science. This is not without its problems, however, because expanding the outdoor program has required resources beyond those now available at the school. Nevertheless, the faculty and staff are committed to including outdoor activities and responsibility in the school's programs and mission. In fact, we were taken by surprise a year ago when the custodian made an unsolicited monetary contribution to the program. Recently he asked if we will accept another donation because it was his "favorite and most personal gift" last year.

It is midsemester in the spring, and the class we are visiting consists of 23 youngsters, 13 boys and 10 girls. Although all of them will participate in some outdoor activity during the course of the year (e.g., orienteering, white-water rafting, winter camping, rock climbing), and several are preparing for an upcoming backpacking trip in the canyonlands, this particular 90-minute session is a daily science class. Students are studying the night sky. Much of their learning is experiential and involves group projects.

After a brief reminder of today's goals, groups of varying sizes proceed to their projects. In one corner of the room, three students are constructing a telescope while several others work on a presentation they are calling "The Polestar: Our Puzzling Partner." One member from each group departs for the school library, an unsupervised move that was unthinkable just a few months ago. Meanwhile, a group of four students are working on a model of the moon that they will include in their PowerPoint presentation on the moon's history. They are busily building while also chatting about harvest moons, blue moons, the moon illusion (why does it seem so enormous at the horizon?), and even origins of the term *honeymoon*. Another group of four argue that the night sky is simply a version of the day sky, thereby "convincing" the teacher to permit their construction of a giant sundial outside in a corner of the playground. Finally, the largest group of 10 students are already in the gymnasium building a planetarium of sorts. Using pieces of heavy black plastic taped together in the shape of a dome, they have inflated it using a box fan. Some are inside marking constellations with glow-in-the-dark stars and paint. Others are adjusting the entrance, because air has been escaping thereby preventing the bubble from remaining fully inflated. Each project will be shared with other students in the school.

Toward the end of the period, all students gather again to discuss the progress of their projects. One member of the planetarium project scolds another for not listening to her ideas about how to improve the entrance. He apologizes, claiming that the entrance problem had frustrated him beyond his ability to hear her suggestions. After accepting his apology, she again admonishes him, saying, "I can't imagine how the entrance had enough power to control your hearing!" Anticipating an escalation in this conversation, the teacher interrupts and asks the group for their point of view. One mentions that the apology would have been more genuine had he not also played the "blame game." Another remarks that it was the sort of miscommunication that distracts people from their goal. The teacher observes that although this incident was not a major breakdown, the accumulation of seemingly minor miscommunications can spell disaster in the backcountry. He further suggests that in English class (where their journal writing occurs) some topics worth considering are how to manage miscommunication among team members and some negative consequences that can result from inappropriate communication.

Summer Outdoor Program

Our final program takes us 19 miles into a remote wilderness area in the Rocky Mountains. The entire group is relieved to find an appropriate campsite after being delayed by several of the area's brief, violent summer cloudbursts. Up to this point, our group of 11 teenagers (7 boys, 4 girls) and 3 instructors have experienced high winds, temperature extremes, and difficult terrain mostly above 10,000 feet. Though not yet savvy veterans, the youngsters are no longer the bunch of map-illiterate tenderfeet who began with us nine days ago. Our early emphasis was on living and traveling skills with mostly off-trail travel. There have been no safety incidents, a primary aim. Apart from a few early blisters, one upset stomach, and general travel aches and pains, we have had no other problems. As we continue to refine camping and moving skills, our next goal is to scout and climb several peaks. This evening, however, we will practice fly fishing.

Unlike our experiences on some other expeditions, these young people seem to like each other. They understand the importance of taking care of themselves and one another. Although few courses are unmarred by typical expedition behavior blemishes, this group thus far has been amazing. No one has been ostracized; no one person has been singled out for critique or ridicule. They are taking care of one another in funny but effective ways and really enjoy being together as a group. Their progress will allow us to concentrate on other aspects of being in the mountains, which is great. It also permits more emphasis on independent work, small-group achievements, and leadership.

How did our expedition get to this point? Luck played a part, no doubt. Accounts of groups that cannot form as a team are countless. The mountains play their part as well. They are unforgiving of improper choices and actions. But an equally important factor was our instruction, which was deliberate and sometimes unconventional. For example, rather than begin trekking right away, we agreed to spend the first two days at a nearby climbing site. We speculated that by emphasizing knots, belaying, top roping, and basic movement on rock at the beginning of our expedition, we might be afforded an excellent and early opportunity to instill concepts of responsibility. Thus far we have spent six days above 10,000 feet, often in winterlike conditions. Our initial plan was to relax and fish for two days before embarking on a route that will involve some harder traveling and navigating. But now with the apparent change toward milder weather, we may explore the group's interest in fishing for only one day and undertaking either a tyrolean traverse or some snow travel and ice axe use. Our most immediate responsibility, however, is to interact with tomorrow's three leaders of the day who have just arrived at our tent.

Leader of the day is but one of many opportunities for team members to develop Level Four (leadership) skills. Other leadership tasks (thanks to John Gookin at the National Outdoor Leadership School) have included bus loadmeister (take charge of loading the bus), ration supervisor (execute quick rationing), chief chef (organize a cooking class or group dinner), tent group coordinator (agree on method for assigning tent groups, then execute the plan), journal editor (ensure group journal is being completed as agreed), among others. The discussion we will now have with these three leaders of the day involves some very real responsibilities. Their choices and actions can help the expedition progress more smoothly and also can help them acquire better leadership skills and habits.

Earlier we talked with today's leaders of the day. We used both reinforcement and constructive criticism to alert them to our perceptions of the day's events, especially as the events related to their performance as leaders. One leader felt that she had too much difficulty mustering support from her team. Upon further reflection she thought that her attempts to be aggressive and charismatic were not natural for her. This led to a discussion of leadership styles, that each of us must develop our own style, and how we may discover that a repertoire of styles can be useful. The instructors then shared how, when our styles have clashed, we have endeavored to resolve those differences for the good of the entire group. By personalizing the discussion, noting our responsibilities and our own imperfections, we hoped to increase the value of our debrief.

We further made it clear that the purpose of our debrief comments is to coach participants for success and that lessons learned from personal experiences are how we develop our own best judgment. We also discussed how simple human errors and imperfect decisions should be tolerated in ourselves and in each other. Before participants returned to their respective tent groups, one leader announced that he would be the next recipient of the group journal. They agreed to collaborate on a group journal entry that might benefit subsequent leaders of the day. First, however, they planned to acknowledge their respective teams for individual and group accomplishments and to ask what they might have done differently as today's leaders.

Now, back to the three who just arrived. Thanking them for being on time, we note their slightly glazed look of tiredness and immediately decide to keep our meeting brief. The sole purpose of this meeting will be to develop more ownership in this expedition. To do so, we plan to involve the entire group in deciding what to do next. Although we believe they are ready to tackle the added challenge of only fishing for one day and then moving to a location that would favor more advanced mountaineering skills, we want them to help shape their own expedition. Avoiding the temptation to subtly steer things toward our leaning, we outline different options and considerations. Their task is to develop a consensus about how to proceed and then report back to us. As they explain their task back to us, we remind them of a few safety issues that must enter into their forthcoming deliberations. Their decision will become part of tomorrow's large-group morning meeting (our "daily forecast"). We offer to lend a hand in their deliberations but only if invited. One asks to borrow my copy of *Gold Nuggets* (see "For Further Study" at the end of this chapter) to locate an "inspirational" reading for their meeting. We then sit back, relax, sip hot chocolate, and look at the map, wondering how the other two expeditions are doing. One group is somewhere on a segment of the Colorado Trail, and the other is at a climbing area in Wyoming.

Techniques for Promoting Responsibility

I am sometimes asked, "What is the most effective way to promote responsibility in an adventure or outdoor setting?" A flippant response is akin to a comment frequently attributed to W. Somerset Maugham (W. Zinsser, personal communication, 1989) about effective writing: There are three tricks, only no one knows what they are. In truth, there is no single best way. But in all of the previously described programs, several colleagues and I have found these ingredients to be helpful: Be explicit, advocate, model, and practice responsibility.

Be Explicit

We are explicit about the levels of responsibility, explaining that they are not meant to categorize or label anyone. Rather they are meant to communicate important values and behaviors. Furthermore, they are arranged in a progression that is meant to help all of us prioritize our efforts. In general, Level One (expedition behavior) needs to be established first, Level Four (leadership) is most difficult for most participants, and so on. Our intent is to help young people become aware of the levels, and to make decisions about and reflect on what they think and believe as well as how they act.

Level One: Expedition Behavior This goal is aimed at protecting the rights and feelings of everyone in the group. In part this means creating a safe learning environment. It also means being able to work together and respect each other in a unique setting. Certainly, working together in possibly harsh conditions and sometimes in close quarters 24 hours a day is different from most people's experience. By explicitly addressing the goal of expedition behavior, we lay a foundation for youngsters to discuss, develop, and demonstrate appropriate behaviors. This level does not necessarily include participation in program activities, but it does require taking another's perspective and not intruding on others' right to learn and participate. In Project Adventure (Rohnke, 1989), this level of responsibility is addressed through use of a "full value contract," which asks each youngster to participate in a group that is physically and emotionally safe, to make a conscious effort to avoid devaluing or discounting oneself or others, and to give and receive honest feedback. It is anticipated that by using the full value contract, the group will find positive value in the efforts of its members.

Level Two: Determination Also referred to as perseverance, tenacity, persistence, participation, and effort, this goal means stepping out, taking reasonable risks, and challenging oneself, as opposed to "cruisin' in neutral." At first this goal seems to some individuals more like a predicament or a requirement than an opportunity. But as they become involved in choosing realistic, personal challenges, they soon move beyond going through the motions. Part of Project Adventure's philosophy toward learning involves "challenge by choice," whereby the youngster is permitted to try potentially difficult and frightening challenges in an atmosphere of support and caring (a Level One atmosphere). In discussing Level Two with young people, we sometimes mention that determination is a form of courage: not the kind where we act well at the risk of deadly danger, but rather the kind where we persevere in tough circumstances. Once young people realize that the attempt is more significant than performance results and that opportunities for future attempts will be available, they become more motivated to try again. Hence, the next level.

Level Three: Independence Emphasis is on self-improvement, frequently in areas of personal preference as identified by the youngster. Personal preferences might include aspirations (to be a competent rock climber) as well as problems (to manage fear of heights). This choice is seen as the ability to work on specific tasks independently, without supervision; to develop some kind of personal vision, goal, or intention (gradually being confronted with such questions as "Who do I want to be?" and "Who can I be?"); to seek and develop a knowledge base to achieve goals or intentions; and then to make plans and persevere especially in the face of boredom, performance plateaus, or other obstacles. The intent is not necessarily to "go it alone." In fact, youngsters frequently are encouraged to invite support from others, but the source of the request is the youngster herself or himself.

Level Four: Leadership This is sometimes the most difficult because it requires going beyond oneself ("me first") and beyond one's friends ("us first") and sometimes beyond long-held prejudices and stereotypes (such as sexism, racism, and physical elitism). Leadership involves genuinely helping others, sharing one's knowledge or skill with another person, and working toward the entire group's welfare. In our outdoor programs especially, leadership also means being responsible for our surroundings. The national Leave No Trace education program, for example, emphasizes certain principles designed to promote informed and responsible use of wilderness and other outdoor localities.

Advocate

Essentially, advocacy means taking a stand and letting others know that certain principles have personal meaning to you and that they fit into your program's mission of serving people and the environment. For instance, regarding responsibility for our surroundings, I try to make young people aware of Western culture's estrangement or separation from nature. I try to elicit vivid childhood memories of contact with wild places and wild things. That goes beyond informing someone about the principle of minimizing impact at a pristine campsite. It includes telling how I listened to one south-central L.A. adolescent as he listed a half-dozen different automatic weapons used on the streets and was able to identify each by its sound. He did not see this as an unusual piece of discriminatory knowledge for someone his age. These were the sounds he heard, learned, and sensed to be vital to his own existence. In another place and time, he would have spoken as matter-of-factly about the calls of six common species of hawks and owls.

And I try not only to be an advocate for Leave No Trace principles or for protecting wild places but also to be an advocate of advocacy itself. I may tell them of the Native American elder whose grandmother used to say that if you treat every step on our earth as a prayer, then you are showing a responsibility toward yourself, toward your fellow people, and toward our earth. I may tell them how members of one Native American tribe, when they impose on the land, always imagine how that action might affect seven generations hence. I may tell them how Albert Camus, when he won the Nobel Prize, said that part of one's duty is to speak for those who cannot speak for themselves—and that this extends to all living things and all places.

Of course, in the wilderness these messages seem to hold more sway than in town or in the city, perhaps because our advanced technology seduces us into believing that we are in complete control, that we can make or break or fix anything. And then we go to the outdoors, where nature reminds us that we are not in complete control, that we're not really on top; rather, we find ourselves within nature, not separate from it.

Model

It is becoming quite clear to me that, at least with young people, you must *demonstrate* responsibility. Not only when you know they are watching, but in whatever you do, because they are always watching. "Jim, you aren't wearing a helmet." "Jim, you aren't drinking enough water." They're always watching, and they seem to remember whatever they watch. "Do as I say, not as I do" is a most ineffective way of teaching responsibility.

I also am obliged to be conscious of my own speaking, especially with regard to the messages I send to others. I still find myself using language whereby I can dodge responsibility. I'm not so much concerned with minor examples such as using "kinda," "sorta," and "like," or even, "I wish to thank you for . . ." (why not just go ahead and thank them?). Rather, I try to remain more alert to language that attributes my thoughts and deeds to others and not to myself. As an example, when helping youngsters to select language that puts more choice and more possibility into their lives, one type of language that I explore with them is "makes me" language. "Makes me" language sounds like this:

- "My group leader makes me happy."
- "Billy makes me nervous."
- "I hurt her feelings."
- "The snow made me lose my white spoon."
- "The river caused my sleeping bag to get wet."

All of these say that someone or something else is in control of us, or that we control others. And if that's true, then I'm not responsible for my thoughts or actions regarding other people and events. But if I replace "That's boring" with "I'm allowing myself to be bored"—or "You really make me angry" with ""I'm angry about..."—or "He annoys me" with "I let myself be annoyed by him," then I become the origin of the thoughts and actions, and I don't give others the power to tie me up in knots, or wear me down, and generally control me. This was illustrated to me one summer when a fellow instructor exclaimed, "Nobody lives rent-free in my head!" She was quite clear about the degree to which others would control her own thoughts and feelings.

Practice

Although seemingly obvious, critical to becoming more responsible is having opportunities to practice responsible behaviors, which includes accepting the consequences for one's choices of action and language. In outdoor and adventure situations, this typically means discussing with a youngster what he or she might be willing to be responsible for (managing equipment, being a team leader, arriving to class on time, arriving to class at all, choosing one of the responsibility levels, or creating value for oneself), and then exploring possible costs and payoffs (getting into trouble, being laughed at, failing, doing it wrong, being scared, feeling bad versus feeling good, being praised, looking good, managing a fear, feeling a sense of importance or belonging). This eventually can lead to making commitments (I will learn to fish, or to speak up more, or to be more patient, or to rock climb) and associated promises (in rock climbing, for instance, to learn such skills as tying specific knots, rope management techniques, belaying and signals, hazard evaluation, and placing protection).

Finally, it means confronting the outcomes, such as dealing responsibly with a broken promise, or acknowledging what isn't working and then making a plan (e.g., beginning again, or trying something different, or requesting support). These are in contrast to typical irresponsible responses such as complaining, blaming, unfairly criticizing, and being silent or withdrawn. Basically, it requires acknowledging the situation, addressing it in an honest and gainful manner, and then proceeding without fanfare, drama, and other unnecessary and unproductive baggage.

The essence of what we're trying to do is to make kids aware of alternatives, and then encourage them to make choices, accept the consequences, and learn in the process. Most of us long to be a good person, a pretty good person at least (Smedes, 1990), and being responsible is a large part of that. Responsibility implies making choices, and "we define ourselves by the choices we have made. We are, in fact, the sum total of our choices" (Allen, 1989). Thus, practicing responsibility and being role models for making appropriate choices are at the core of who we are and what we do as outdoor and adventure educators.

In summary, combining adventure and outdoor activities with responsibility presents grand opportunities to young people. They become aware of responsible behavior and language, they practice those things, and they then can choose whether to engage in them in other circumstances. If we emphasize responsibility as an important value and behavior, and if we don't impose it but give kids opportunities for making authentic, meaningful choices, they will rise to the occasion. By being explicit about responsibility, advocating responsibility, modeling responsible behaviors and language, and letting young people practice being responsible, we as program leaders and instructors can provide an immeasurable service to these youngsters and to our communities.

Closing Thoughts

I believe that young people possess an inordinate amount of unrealized potential and possibility. The consequences of this state of affairs are tragic, both for our youngsters and for our society. The answer to this problem does not lie in education per se. Education is no guarantee of decency, prudence, or wisdom. In fact, more of the same kind of education will only compound problems. We need not education, but education of a certain kind—a kind where knowledge does not supersede feelings and experiences but becomes compatible with them; where young people's feelings, dreams, and imaginations will be encouraged, supported, and legitimized; and where their struggles will be respected by caring and knowledgeable leaders and teachers.

To create the specific programs mentioned in this chapter, we have had to undertake a considerable amount of "navigating and creating." Each program is the result of collaborations between university faculty and various community agencies, including public schools. Navigating the bureaucratic seaways of large institutions, and creating more opportunities than one finds, are part and parcel to program development. Because our success has depended on establishing university-community partnerships, potential deterrents to these efforts are worth considering.

Conversations with university colleagues reveal that two conditions often prevail in obstructing program development. The first condition is a university's self-justifying denial of real-world problems; that is, real-world problems hold little relevance to the university. Many universities have become institutions with lives of their own, rarely impinging on or having much relationship with the world outside. A second disaffirming condition is lack of incentive for faculty to be involved in ameliorating these problems. Faculty may feel obliged to pursue an institutionally defined career versus the more personal callings represented in this book. In some universities, research takes precedence over teaching, which takes precedence over service, with the three seldom integrated. In such places (criticized by Michael Lewis as "an academy grown unacceptably self-indulgent," 1997, p. xiv), the faculty member must avoid being dispirited by adopting the courage demanded in Level Two (determination), by stepping out of the dominant university paradigm as part of Level Three (independence), and by encouraging the university to reach out and make a larger connection to the communities that surround it (Level Four: leadership). As reiterated throughout this chapter, it all boils down to choices.

For Further Study

Dougherty, N.J. (Ed.) (1998). *Outdoor recreation safety.* Champaign, IL: Human Kinetics.

Practical guidelines for presenting a broad range of outdoor activities in ways that will lead to better experiences for participants and less likelihood of injuries and litigation.

Graydon, D. (Ed.) (1992). *Mountaineering: The freedom of the hills* (5th ed.). Seattle: The Mountaineers.

An excellent comprehensive and contemporary tool and resource for novice to advanced mountaineers.

Project WILD elementary (and secondary) activity guide. (1986). Boulder, CO: Project WILD.

"The goal of Project WILD is to assist learners of any age in developing . . . informed decisions, responsible behavior, and constructive actions concerning wildlife and the environment upon which all life depends."

Rohnke, K. (1989). *Cowstails and cobras II.* Dubuque, IA: Kendall/Hunt.

The classic guide to games, initiative problems, and sample curriculum that promote self-confidence and group cooperation in the face of contrived obstacles.

Rohnke, K., & Butler, S. (1995). *Quicksilver: Adventure games, initiative problems, trust activities and a guide to effective leadership.* Dubuque, IA: Kendall/Hunt.

A recent compilation of adventure activities that challenge people to go beyond their perceived boundaries and to work with others to solve problems.

Schoel, J., & Stratton, M. (1990). *Gold nuggets: Readings for experiential education.* Hamilton, MA: Project Adventure.

These readings—over 350 poems, essays, and songs—help identify concepts that relate directly to what a group might be experiencing, prompting the group to view itself in a larger perspective.

Chapter 6

In-School Programs

James Kallusky

Imagine a university professor, two graduate students, and four undergraduate students promenading through the grounds of a public school, with three bags of equipment slung over their shoulders, to teach a physical education class to 30 high school students. Something special is happening, indeed, as can be seen on the questioning faces of teachers, students, and maintenance personnel as the group meanders through the hallways. This parade does not occur without meaningful purpose and agreement from school administrators; but, unfortunately, it's not a part of many school physical education programs.

The peculiar stares that this event receives are common only because schools are oftentimes perceived as fortresses, with no contact or relationship with the outside world (Perrone, 1991). Although schools are typically located in the center of communities or near universities, one rarely sees professors or others from the neighborhood freely walking around in schools. This is curious, because if schools are to teach students about functioning in the world that surrounds them, it should not be unusual to include people from this world in the culture of schools. Furthermore, if universities are to inform schools about effective practice, university students and faculty should spend a substantial amount of time at public schools. However, this is typically not the case.

This chapter furthers the notion of university and public school collaboration by describing a physical education program where university students and their professor (me) actually teach in the public school system. Subsequently, I will discuss the reasons why many students in the U.S. public educational system learn to discount their schooling (leading to being institutionally underserved), much to the consternation of adults and universities. In essence, the focus is on why some students' attitudes and behaviors directly reflect the ways in which they are treated and, to some extent, the discontinuity between the school environment and their lives outside of school. The chapter includes a description of one secondary in-school physical education program located in an underserved neighborhood. Based on the responsibility model, this program creates a learning environment unlike most schools, partly by treating students differently and partly by shifting responsibility to the students.

The Context of Schools

A growing number of students are becoming unhealthy, both physically and mentally. Many suffer from the direct and indirect effects of child abuse, poverty, substance abuse, inadequate child care, family breakdown, and a multitude of societal problems that plague them daily. All of them want a break, but the opportunities are limited. For many, the idea of obtaining a high school education seems hopeless, and attending college is a mere fantasy.

Schools do not appear to be helping many of these students. Therefore, I write this chapter with a premise regarding school practices: that processes of public schools (especially large ones) tend to overshadow the needs of underserved students, leaving them, at times, to wonder whether they should attend at all. Some of these students typically do not feel wanted or needed, and most of them have difficulty in relating what they are learning (or not learning) to their daily lives. Some school issues like bus schedules, supervisory lunch placements, and enforcing hall passes often take precedence over the student; moreover, details of obedience, silence, and control appear to be omnipotent in schools. Students who do not adhere to these components for "successful" teachers and schools have difficulty finding the purpose of their schooling regimen. In addition, these students notice that other things in school, including other students, tend to be more important than them; it is a vicious cycle.

I base this premise on my own experiences (as a student and a teacher), supported by comments from the kids with whom I have worked. Student declarations such as "every bad thing you do they like to count and count it, and once they get enough on you it's like 'get outta here' and they kick you out" are all too frequent in schools. Make no mistakes about it: Public schools can be unfriendly places to some kids.

Too many students today say "schools don't care," and they say it with indignation and with a glimpse of genuineness that they rarely otherwise convey. They say it with such passion because although "not caring" is anticipated in other places (even home on occasion), they are told that school is good and is there to help them. They have difficulty, then, understanding why school is often not helpful. Although schools typically claim that the underserved population (which, by the way, can be an entire school in some communities) consumes a great deal of their time, as a rule these students are provided less guidance for success than for failure.

Over the past 10 years, the American public has been exposed to a succession of news reports, television series, and motion pictures that attempt to reveal school life in urban settings. Much of the media exposure about urban schools suggests overwhelming dehumanization. That is, typically urban schools are depicted as dirty, lawless, and uncivilized. Many of these accounts set the story line by chronicling unruly environments. Commonly highlighted in these riotous allegories is the notion that particular students are to blame for the unbridled ambiance of the school. And repeatedly, these notorious students are rebuilt by showing their true selves and are "cured" when a teacher who "cares" enters their classroom. Of course, the notion of magically healing kids is fantasy, and too often it takes more than caring to help kids; the antidote remains elusive.

Although the whole idea of fast cures is senseless, the dismal environmental conditions delineated in these stories are real for certain inner-city schools. Both teachers and students face serious challenges inside these schools. Within these "educational" settings, most teachers become policing agents who constantly search for control; administrators become judges who make daily decisions that easily may affect a student's entire life; and the students themselves become pawns in a bureaucratic system gone awry.

Still, year after year, educators choose to work (and care) in these places despite the system, and students still show up every September. Some students are placed in what is commonly referred to as a prevention or intervention program. The following is a story of teaching physical education in an urban setting where school administrators deemed our classroom a dropout prevention program. Compared to what we see on television or the big screen, this story is messy (messy as life itself), and no instant, curative potion is involved. And unlike films, the following is not based on a true story; it is real.

The School Program

Metro High School sits quietly away from the deafening railroad tracks that separate a no-income from a low-income neighborhood in East Los Angeles. Though the high school building itself is designated for learning, it is imposing, plain, and not unlike a prison in appearance. A visitor once commented to me, "Man, this place looks like a detention center, not a school." This "place" has tall buildings, tall walls, and tall fences. There is nothing small to embrace here.

Even the two Los Angeles Police Department officers who roam the campus full-time every school day have large bodies and big attitudes. Their batons and handguns often shelter them from the students. The officers are there to protect, and this is their only service. The graffiti that blankets the outside and inside of the school hints at the talent, frustration, and passion of the protected ones inside the covered walls. Every day, on average, maintenance personnel use 40 gallons of paint to cover the wall scrawl. It is an expensive attempt to deter young perpetrators, usually to no avail.

Most of what the students offer through their restricted writings is gang affiliated. Members from approximately four large street gangs and numerous smaller gangs attend Metro. The smaller gangs (usually called crews) constantly seek the power of the solidified gangs and in so doing automatically place many kids in an unfortunate circumstance; some students join one of the organizations solely to avoid the pressures of others.

It has not always been this way. The area surrounding the school used to be undeveloped land. As the job force moved east of downtown Los Angeles, the school was built to serve the children of the newly formed working-class neighborhood. At that time, Metro was a diverse educational setting that parents wanted their kids to attend, and students were excited about attending. Today, as you walk the fifth floor hallway of structure H and view the multimillion-dollar buildings that line downtown Los Angeles, you can only speculate on the excitement of the panorama when this school opened in 1951. Sadly, however, the student body (98 percent Hispanic, 1 percent Asian, 0.5 percent African-American, and 0.5 percent Caucasian) does not look over there anymore.

Entering the School

In fall 1995, I provided a workshop to the physical education department at Metro. As time passed, I made more informal visits to Metro and, as a component of my university students' capstone course in teacher education, was eventually invited to introduce them to this site. In due time, my undergraduate students not only were introduced to the field of teaching physical education but actually began to teach at Metro. It was not long before some of the university students had keys to the facilities; Metro became a lab school for my physical education teacher education program.

Needless to say, the university students received an eye-opening education regarding teaching physical education in an inner-city school.

It was not easy for some of them. Many struggled with their teaching experience, and others had difficulty adapting to the environment.

In one incident, three university students, while talking in the high school parking lot, decided to intervene when they noticed four boys escaping school by climbing one of the detainment fences. One of the three university students yelled, "Hey, get back to class!" In recounting his experience, one of the university students said, "James, they just turned around, looked at us, and shouted, 'F— you.' They didn't run or anything—we got scared and left." The ruggedness of the physical appearance of the school is reflected in many of its inhabitants.

While working at Metro with my preservice teachers, I had many conferences with site administrators for promoting my Urban Youth Leadership Project (UYLP). This university-based project focused on serving underserved youth by having university students implement the responsibility model in field-based experiences. In one meeting with Metro's administration, I explained that I wanted to teach 32 students every second period for an entire semester in physical education. These 32 students were considered the most disruptive of Metro's 3,200 students. The assistant principal glared at me and said, "You're the craziest professor I've ever met." I grinned, and the assistant principal stated sincerely, "You are smiling now, but wait until you get all of those kids in one class." Immediately after these comments, the gatekeepers approved the idea and, for the first time, I became nervous about my request. The following is my story.

Beginning the Program

After much anticipation, the first day of the spring semester and of the program arrived. Twenty minutes before meeting my high school students I was informed that because I was not a school employee, I would be required to have a "teacher of record" shadow me throughout the semester. They assigned Mr. Frost to me that morning, the morning of his 64th birthday.

My initial encounter with Mr. Frost had taken place the previous semester during the workshop that I had provided at Metro. At that time, he did not take very well to my ideas concerning teaching physical education. I was aware of this because throughout the workshop he continuously shook his head in disagreement and even sarcastically laughed aloud a few times.

Mr. Frost had taught at Metro High School for 40 years and had been head football coach for 33 seasons. Moreover, he attended Metro as a student and was one of its first graduates. He is well known throughout the campus and is considered a natural relic of this institution. Although he appeared tough and set in his ways, I decided that I was not going to allow him to interrupt my teaching process. However, his presence did make me nervous.

Most of the other physical education teachers warned me about the chaos that was bound to take place on the first day of the semester when all of the teachers' students (over 300 of them) met in the gymnasium. Mr. Frost remarked under his breath, "Just take roll and let them sit there." On my way to the gym, I walked the hallway among hundreds of kids and I was the target of both interest and blind stares. As I entered the gym, the teachers were calling students to their "kingdoms" on the bleachers.

The gym bleachers were old, wounded by carvings, and blemished by markers. The gym floor was slippery from the mottled grime that lay upon it, and trash was scattered about. I briefly introduced myself and told students to call me by my first name. After I had finished providing them with a 10-minute overture to the class, Mr. Frost turned to me and said, "I think they'll like you; you don't yell at them."

Before my second meeting with the students, I went to the physical education teachers' lounge prior to first period. My class did not start until second period, but I wanted to get a better feel for the environment of the school. While sitting in the lounge I listened as three male teachers discussed what they were "planning" to teach that morning. One of them remarked, "It's a nice day, let's take 'em to the track." The other two agreed and that was that. I was surprised that no planning had been done whatsoever. First period started and I was stunned as each teacher took roll (students stood on their respective painted numbers on the perforated blacktop) and then indifferently escorted their students to the track. I followed their leisurely pace, anticipating what was to transpire next.

My curiosity was soon satisfied. Any students who dressed out (i.e., who dressed in gym clothes) learned to walk the dilapidated dirt track. Those students who did not dress out learned about sitting at the top-right corner of the aluminum bleachers. The three teachers modeled for the latter group by sitting at the bottom-left corner of the grandstand. The separation of students and teachers that breeds the "us versus them" mentality became apparent.

After some additional observation, I returned to the physical education lounge. On my way back I noticed a janitor who was sweeping around the area in which roll was taken. In the thrill of going to the track one student apparently had forgotten his or her jacket. The janitor swiftly picked it up and hurled it into the garbage can that he was dragging behind him. I wanted to say something but felt inhibited because of my newness. His actions appeared to be common practice, and who was I to challenge that?

Getting to Know My Students

My university student (Christa, who volunteered to help teach in the program) and I had decided to begin the program by offering basketball and weight training as content. We surmised that it would be beneficial to offer our students one team sport and one individual activity. Our reasoning was that since we both would be teaching every day, students eventually could choose whichever activity they most desired.

Only 19 of the scheduled 32 students showed up for the first day of class, and half of those were tardy. I greeted each of them as they entered the musty gym. The boys lined the top of the bleachers while the girls lined the bottom; they had discovered their determined spots. I began the lesson by asking the boys to move down to an acceptable level on the fully opened bleachers. Despite my request, not one of them budged. I then politely beckoned them to move and again waited. Finally, one student descended and the remaining accompanied him. The student who broke the tension by moving down a few rows was Saul, but everybody called him Peanut. He was a small kid with a large reputation. The dean of students at Metro had already informed me that Peanut was a hardcore gangster with notoriety unequaled in the ninth grade.

I proceeded to introduce the course and attempted to provide students with a savor for the class. Of course, they were aware that this was a peculiar physical education class because of the collective reputations of their fellow classmates. I briefly addressed this issue by conceding my awareness that many of them were struggling in school and that we would work on some of their struggles in this class.

Using a mobile chalkboard, I explained the goals of the responsibility model. During this initial exposure, most of the students copied the goals into their journals that had been handed out. After this was accomplished, I distributed individual folders into which students were to secure their daily self-assessments (a grade tally for participation and effort) and journals (they would write every day to evaluate themselves and, at times, the program). As I explained their folders and the folder contents, it became obvious that writing was not to the students' liking. And they did not hesitate in letting me know. For instance, Reynaldo (Rey-Rey) shouted, "This ain't English!" I simply replied, "No, lucky for you it ain't"—accentuating *ain't*. A few students laughed, including Rey-Rey.

After spending 25 minutes on the responsibility model and assessment forms, most still did not seem to understand the essence of this class. After many clarifying statements I finally realized that I was telling them too much, too fast. I was surveying a band of blank faces. By talking too much, I had contributed to this lesson's downfall.

In recognizing my evangelistic start, I informed them that we would postpone discussing this material until later. For the remainder of the class session we would try something different. However, when I called them to the middle of the gym floor, again there was no response or movement. I was standing alone in the middle of an old gym looking at 19 kids who were staring back at me as if I were crazy. My earlier enthusiasm was quickly blurring into pounding anxiety. What do you do when every one of your students boycotts your statements? I didn't know. I decided to give one more encouraging cue. I said, "Come on, give it a shot?" Again, Peanut came to my rescue. When he moved onto the court, 10 others followed.

We then made an intrepid attempt to play add-on tag, which is an all-inclusive, noneliminating, nonthreatening cooperative activity: everything that is politically correct about teaching physical education. The student who volunteered to be "it" was only walking, so she never tagged anyone. In due time, Christa and I ended up doing the chasing, but we could not tag anyone because the gym floor was too slippery to change directions. The participating students eventually sat down (one by one) while laughter directed at the teachers echoed throughout the gym. Christa and I inevitably stood alone once again in the middle of the gymnasium floor.

I concluded the session by communicating to the students that putting effort into this class would make it much more successful and enjoyable (although for most of them, success and enjoyment were probably achieved on this first day of instruction). My last words to them that day were, "Dress out for tomorrow's lesson." As they exited the gym, one student told me, "I have a locker, but I've never dressed out and I never will." One more obstacle to face.

I considered my first day of instruction to be a disaster. I had no idea what Mr. Frost might think after observing this fiasco, and I didn't want to know. After explaining my experience that day to another physical education teacher at Metro, she explained that I received all of the students who despised activity, who never dressed out, and who failed physical education in the fall semester. Apparently, the administration generated an ample list of students who fit my criteria for enrollment in the program and then permitted the physical education teachers to choose my group from the list. Of course, the physical education teachers chose students whom they did not want on their rosters anymore. In other words, I received kids who were identified as the most disruptive to the school environment and who hated physical education.

On the following day, 22 students arrived for class, but only three of them dressed out despite the previous day's request. Again, we briefly discussed the self-assessments and I confirmed that we would disregard the journals for now. I decided to emphasize participation and effort as the sole criteria for the class through their self-assessments. My decision was based on their malevolence for physical education. We also discussed the physical education dressing policy. The department policy reads that a student must dress to participate and refusal to dress out requires that a detention be served. I explained that I was not going to hand out detentions in this class, saying, "Personally, I believe they defeat the purpose of our class." The students liked this idea. I was beginning to capture their attention.

Quickly, it turned into a day of questions. For instance, "Where are you from?" "Do you smoke the bud?" and "Do you have a girlfriend?" They were curious. I answered their questions yet still focused on the day's activity. Today, only two of the three students who dressed out chose to participate. We played two-on-two basketball: Christa and I against Peanut and his partner, Rey-Rey. While the rest of the class (20 students) observed us, we enjoyed a good game that was interwoven with some instruction on skills and strategy.

As the students completed that day's self-assessments, one student (Christina, who sat on the bleachers during the entire class) explained that, for simply attending class, she was going to give herself 30 percent for participation and effort. I asked her if she had a hard time coming to school and she said, "Oh yeah." I slowly replied, "Well, maybe if it's that hard for you to come to school you should give yourself 50 percent for showing up." I don't think she expected that response. At the end of class I explained that dressing out was not required for our next meeting.

Before our next class, one of the other physical education teachers commented that Mr. Frost had spoken to her about the UYLP. Apparently Mr. Frost informed her, "The guy does pretty good with those kids. . . . He's taking his time breaking the ice. . . . I may learn something from him." I was flabbergasted when she mentioned this to me. I had been under the impression that Mr. Frost perceived me as a clown, simply there for the kids' entertainment.

In preparing our next class session, I realized that such goals as self-directed learning and helping others had taken a back seat (limousine style) to participation and effort. I yearned for the students to abandon the bleachers and to become engaged in activity, any activity. Still, I refused to force it onto them; instead, I composed a few strategies.

The first strategy was to arrive early and push in all of the bleachers so that students had no place to sit, except on the dirty floor. I knew that my students were proud of their clothes and would be reluctant to soil them by sitting in dirt. A second strategy was to not attempt basketball again. I sensed that the students would be more likely to participate in individual or dual activities than in a team sport. So, I planned a few combative activities such as mat push (three or four kids on each side of a mat, all pushing to gain territory), playground hand-slap (one student places hands together in front of chest and the other student, starting with hands on hips, attempts to hit the opponent's hands by slapping at them), tug-of-war, and one-legged chicken fights. I knew that these activities would compel the class to experience the need for another goal, self-control.

I achieved my goal! All 23 students who attended that day also participated. I taught them about reflexes, leverage, and stability. Before the close of the session we discussed the importance of participation and effort, along with their ability to control themselves in such activities. We also shared views about the rewards gained from taking risks, such as attempting unfamiliar activities. I infused this talk with excitement and praise for that day's behavior.

On that particular day, there was substantial interaction between myself and the students: both positive (laughs and smiles) and negative (reminding them to listen and to respect my right to teach and others' right to learn). It appeared as though a few of the students, especially Alejandra, were blatantly striving to get under my skin, by constantly disrupting the class. Although to a small degree they achieved their goal, I suspect that they were not aware of their victory.

Because the students had not yet been introduced to weight training, the final session of the first week focused on that component of the class. Of the 22 kids who attended this lesson, six now had consented to dress out. After introducing concepts concerning safety in the weight room and lifting techniques, I instructed them to try different lifts with their partners. The lesson was unfolding smoothly until Rigoberto started cursing (using minor profanity) at George. I decided to stop the class to have a brief discussion regarding profanity. I explained the difference between simply cursing (saying "d—" when you miss a lay-up in basketball) and verbally abusing others. The class agreed that minimal cursing would be tolerated, but verbal abuse would be unacceptable. They agreed that this was fair and applicable for everybody.

Earning Access to the Students—Developing Relationships and Trust

Though the first week of the program was peppered with problems, in the next weeks Christa and I began to develop strong relationships with some of the students. Still, others decided to keep their distance. Most of the relationships were positive, but some were not. For example, Alejandra was still being very disruptive. The negative effects of her disruptions were practically incalculable. One day I directly asked her, "Why are you treating me like crap by being so disrespectful?" She said, "I don't know." Because she did not know or was unwilling to state her reasons, I discussed the idea of establishing a relationship of mutual respect with her. Our conversation was honest and it worked.

With most other students, establishing a relationship came easily early in the program. I had decided to let them search me out instead of chasing their attention. It worked. For instance, Elias was hanging around a lot after class. He was curious about why we were teaching at Metro and much of our conversation could have been classified as "small talk." However, one day he informed me that he was legally blind (which I verified with the nurse the following day). This explained his contempt for basketball and why he always chose to participate in weight training. When I asked him if he had corrective glasses, he said, "Nah, I'm gonna wait till I can buy contacts . . . I ain't runnin' around like a fool with lenses." He then proceeded to explain the classic, "I can't see the front of classrooms, but I still choose to sit in the back." This scenario touched me deeply. Thus, I attempted to locate a service agency or a private optometrist that would provide him with free care: all to no avail.

Another student, Mando, and I began to loan each other music. He would bring me the "current hip-hop" and I loaned him some of my "old school music," as he called it. He considered himself an artist and shared his drawings with me regularly. They were very good. Mando disliked Metro High School and felt he was not learning anything. He explained to me that he would rather attend the University High School of the Arts. I explained that I would assist him in the application process, but he felt it was a waste of time.

One day he brought one of his poems for me to read. The title was "Fly Away or Stay and Fight." The essence was in the title, and he was constantly making plans to leave the Los Angeles area. He was heavily into the drug scene, and violence surrounded him. He wanted to escape from his own life. Eventually (in week 7), he left to live in the desert with his grandparents. He did not return, and I thought of him often throughout the remainder of the program.

Early in the program, many students told stories of violence and drugs. I recognized that not all of them were true, but I was amazed at their glorification of brutality, fury, and altered states of minds. However, Peanut, the student with the most personal stories to tell regarding these subjects, never spoke of them. He was secure in his reputation, and he used a soft-spoken voice to perpetuate it. Many times he would assist in quieting the class during discussions, and no one ever challenged him. In one particular incident he told the class, "Hey, shut the f— up.

He's talking." I turned to him and said, "Peanut, you could ask that nicer, but thank you." Three days later under similar circumstances he told the class, "Hey, be quiet!" Then he whispered to me, "That's better, huh? . . . I'll be your teaching assistant." I told him I would like that.

As the weeks progressed, more students (but not all) chose to dress out and to become engaged in activity. By the sixth week, two thirds of the students had dressed out at least once. Many of them dressed out for the first time all year. More surprising was Carlos, a tenth grader who already exceeded 280 pounds. He dressed for the first time ever in physical education, including his junior high school years. Because of this, I felt as though we must have established a somewhat safer and more desirable environment for these students.

I joked with Carlos on the day that he dressed out by pretending that I couldn't see him even though he was standing right in front of me in his XXL blue sweats (cut off at the knees) and white T-shirt. However, the greatest number of students who dressed on any given day was still only 14. This led me to question the Metro policy of not allowing students to participate if they did not dress out for physical education. Most of my students were sitting out for the majority of our class sessions. Obviously, the policy and its outcome adversely affected the quality of interactions (or lack thereof) between student and teacher, and among the students themselves.

Nonetheless, Mr. Frost was impressed by how many students had been dressing out. He remarked, "You've got kids to dress that have never dressed before." Yet, I was not satisfied. I informed the other physical education faculty that the dress policy was hurting the program and asked them to consider making an exception for my class. Mr. Frost's opinion was clear. He supported me, saying, "I don't care if they're required to dress. It's your program." But the other faculty maintained that the kids needed to learn to dress out because they would be "mainstreamed" next year and that was the department's policy. I argued that if the students were required to follow policy, then because of their noninvolvement, they could not learn anything in class. I further explained that if we allowed them to participate now, they might learn to enjoy activity and want to be involved in physical education next year. My rationale was that if the students desired involvement, they would be more likely to follow policies.

During the struggle over dress policy, I realized that the other physical education teachers did not perceive kids in the same way as I did. The faculty tended to complain frequently about their students, and I concluded that they viewed their students as a burden to their daily routines. Once, I overheard a teacher literally yelling at one student in front of her entire class. She was screaming, "You get over here or I'm turning your name over to the dean and you know I will, especially you." The student just left anyway.

The same teacher had once commented to me that the students in her first-period class were "horrible" and that many of them should be in my class. It was her impression that I should have 60 to 80 students. I wanted to give her a line from *The Simpsons* (Homer to Bart, "If only you could find something more fun than complaining"), but I restrained myself.

By the sixth week of the program we only had 28 students on the roster. Although the administration had deemed us a dropout prevention program, ironically they were expelling our students. Rigoberto was the first victim. I will not soon forget that day. He entered the gym with a mournful look and handed me a yellow card. I asked him what was happening and he explained that it was a dropout card. Of course, I asked why he was dropping out. He replied that it was not his choice and that if he wanted to receive "home-bound" educational services he needed to drop; otherwise, they would expel him with no educational access.

All that was requested on the yellow card was a signature, but it was obvious to me that Rigoberto wanted to stay in school. The yellow card won. I signed his card and as he was walking away, he stopped. He looked over his shoulder and asked in a melancholy voice, "Are you going to have the program here next year?" I told him that I did not know. The other three students who were expelled during this time simply disappeared from the roster. About a week after each was erased, an expulsion notice was circulated to all of their teachers. I often wondered how many teachers smiled when they saw certain names appear on the list.

As I began to understand many of the challenges that my students faced in school and their negative perceptions of it (see table 6.1), I decided that the program had to somehow detach them from their regular experiences at Metro. So, one day we had a social with homemade food, students' choice of music, and plain conversation: nothing related to school. The students were initially shy about eating the muffins and cakes that Christa and I had baked, but the food was eventually devoured. As the music blared through the gymnasium we sat, ate, and talked.

Mr. Frost joined in as well. While eating a muffin he told Christa, "I was your biggest critic, but I'm impressed. You're winning them [the students] over. I learn something every day." At this stage in the program Mr. Frost became a familiar friend, always willing to lend support. He even started to call me "Coach." From him this was more than a compliment; it was a commendation.

Grade reports were due at the end of the sixth week. Mr. Frost handed me a bubble sheet and a comment sheet with numerical codes. The

Table 6.1

Students' Attitudes Toward School

1. School is boring. It makes me bored.
2. It sucks.
3. School, I really don't like it, but I gotta come.
4. I use to do good in junior high, C's and D's, but then high school threw me off.
5. It ain't all that.
6. School sucks.
7. I like to come cause my friends and homeboys are here and I don't like it at home, but school's boring.
8. It's too hard.
9. It sucks, nah, it's cool, nah, it really sucks.
10. I like it cause we're not at home.
11. It sucks. I hate coming to school.
12. I think its dumb, but they think I'm dumb.
13. It's alright, I guess.
14. It's boring.
15. It's alright. Some people think it's boring.

comment sheet only had two numbers on it (13 and 16), which indicated nondressing and attendance problems. I asked him where the rest of the codes were and he replied, "Oh yeah, you'll want some good comments for those kids." He found them, and I used them.

I calculated grades by averaging students' self-assessment sheets. I figured that their own evaluations were what they deserved. The results were eighteen F's, five D's, two C's, two B's, and one A. I reported the grades individually to the students by giving them their percentages. Not one of them complained. In fact, Mando asked, "What's a 64 percent?" I explained that it equaled a D. He replied with sincerity, "Alright, I've never passed PE before!"

I was absent during the seventh week of the program, attending an academic conference. When I returned, some of the students were upset with me. I had notified them earlier that I was not going to be at school during that week. Yet some were still angry at me for missing, to the point that one student even told me that I was "fired." I felt it. They were beginning to care about the dynamics of the class. My absence had not been a motive for celebration. Moreover, I learned that I also needed to better appreciate the program and reflect on my level of commitment.

That week, the students also informed me that the activities (basketball and weight training) were becoming stagnant, even though we had augmented them throughout the initial seven weeks of the program with different activities. Therefore, on the day after my return, we attempted a "trust-building" activity. After I explained "Willow in the Wind" (one student, the willow, is encircled by seven others and must trust the group to support him or her in a fall), none would surface from the bleachers. The scenario was remarkably reminiscent of the first day of the semester.

When the students finally agreed to participate, after much prodding, they suggested that I be the "willow" for demonstration purposes. I acquiesced to their request and they coarsely threw me about in the middle of their circle. I commented that this activity was not called "willow in the tornado," but they neither cared nor cooperated.

I terminated Willow in the Wind prematurely (20 minutes before the end of class) because I wanted to discuss what was happening. Despite my intentions, I did most of the talking that morning. I tried to explain that I did not want the class to lose momentum because it would be hard to regain. I ended by saying that to regain some sense of community, we would attempt large-group, cooperative activities for the remainder of the week.

Though the cooperative activities were, for many of them, tough pills to swallow, the medicine was effective. We implemented a variety of outdoor adventure activities (some of which are described in chapter 5) that focused on outcomes such as communication, trust, and problem solving. In doing so, we accomplished the goal of "getting back together" and rebuilding what we had lost during my absence.

During the eighth week, although we had recaptured our sense of community through implementing cooperative activities, I realized that I was being forced daily to change my curriculum and that it was not a matter of choice for me anymore. Something was missing and they needed that something. Ironically, during this time when the program was struggling six university students (not those involved in my teacher education capstone course at Metro) inquired about teaching in the program. To me, this suggested that the existence of the project had somehow spread to the university student body. I solicited four of the inquiring students and prepared them to teach the responsibility model. By the beginning of the 10th week of the program, we had created an arsenal of teachers who now invaded Metro High School every second period.

I slowly introduced my students to the new teachers. The kids rotated in groups of five or six to each teacher. The teachers were separated in the corners of the gym, and the students spent five minutes with each of them. After completing the rotations, one of the new university students explained that he had asked each group what they were learning in here. Each group replied, "respect." I should not have been surprised, but I was. We were regaining lost territory.

To introduce the activities that would be offered by the new teachers, students rotated in clusters of six and experienced each activity for three full sessions. The choices included Christa teaching racquetball, Stephan teaching contemporary games, Karina teaching basketball, Ramon teaching volleyball, Juan teaching football, and me teaching fitness and weight training.

We split the offerings by days so that on three days per week students could choose among contemporary games, football, and racquetball; twice a week they could choose from volleyball, fitness and weight training, and basketball. This set each learning environment at six to eight participants on any given day. In addition to the small-group instruction, this also allowed teachers to "float" on days when their activity was not offered. A floating teacher could either participate in the activities or spend one-on-one time with a student.

The new structure was successful. The majority of students were now participating, and for the first time we were able to focus on the responsibility model goal of self-direction. In doing so, the students began to set personal goals for their individualized programs. We continued our regimen of choice, and the positive outcomes became increasingly evident. Some of the other Metro physical education faculty took notice of this change and didn't like it. Some even began to undermine the efforts of the university students.

For instance, halfway through Stephan's "flicker ball" lesson, one Metro teacher made him remove his class from an outdoor basketball court. She told him that she had a "large group" and needed the court. In a separate incident, as Karina was gathering her equipment, another faculty member said, "Those are the good basketballs for other classes to use." Karina replied, "Well, these are my good kids and they deserve the good basketballs." Karina quickly turned away from the faculty member and commenced to teach her section of the class.

Furthermore, one of the aforementioned faculty was continuously trying to transfer some of her students into our class. It came to the point where, after I had given many important reasons for not wanting to add students at this time, I said, "Listen, this is not a dumping ground for any students that you do not want in your class." She never asked again.

Sometimes I felt like Jaime Escalante (the teacher portrayed by Edward James Olmos in the film *Stand and Deliver*) because it seemed as though despite their success, my students were supposed to retain their negative stereotypes. Nevertheless, we had a supportive team as well, which was led by Mr. Frost. I asked him how I should go about handling this situation and he replied, "They're only envious of your small groups . . . just ignore them." So I did.

Struggling Students—It's a Wonder They Are Here at All

In the 11th week of the program, I noticed that Peanut had been absent three days in a row. This had not happened before, so I began to worry. When he returned he was dressed in black and wore a hairnet stocking. I sensed that something bad had happened, so I asked to speak to him in private. He confided that over the weekend when walking with his cousin to a mall, they fell victim to a drive-by shooting. One of the bullets hit Peanut's cousin in the leg. Peanut ran and hid in the bushes, while his cousin lay on the sidewalk clutching his wounded leg. The car then was pulled into reverse and its passengers shot the boy twice in the chest. Before the ambulance arrived, the kid on the bloody sidewalk died in Peanut's arms.

Peanut cried as he told me his story. All I could do was listen with my hand on his knee. But when this solemn, earnest, 14-year-old kid finished describing that fatal weekend, he became angered and spoke only of revenge. I explained to him that revenge would not help, but he was beyond my advice. He knew it was a bad path but said, "I gotta do it." He lived by the rules of the street.

Death on the streets was a topic that did not recede easily with this group of youngsters. Only two days had passed since my talk with Peanut when Ernie, the next casualty, emerged. Before entering the UYLP, Ernie had been locked up for three years at California Youth Authority (CYA), a prison for kids. He often expressed how much he enjoyed our class because we trusted him to play football without starting a fight.

Though Ernie was absent for most of the program, we had built a strong rapport. He was a 16-year-old ninth grader who stood about six feet tall. He was more mature than his classmates and was quite eloquent in his dialogue. He had no friends at Metro because of his long detainment at CYA but stood out in the crowd because of the exaggerated dipping-strut in his walk. You could spot Ernie's gait from a considerable distance.

Unlike Peanut, when Ernie experienced the death of someone close to him he showed no signs of a problem. In fact, I was unaware that anything had happened until he asked to talk to me in private. He explained that he had disowned his estranged father before being locked up because his father beat his mother and the rest of the family, Ernie included. The man Ernie now most admired was a neighbor who took care of Ernie's family and often visited him in CYA.

Ernie and I were walking the hallways of Metro as he told me about the senseless shooting of his role model (the neighbor) that had taken place two days earlier. Suddenly, he stopped, looked at me, and said, "I've never walked like this before." Sure enough, his trademark strut was gone. I didn't understand what that meant, but it chilled me to the bone.

In week 12 of the program, the school echoed the story of Samuel, who was gunned down on school grounds. I did not know Samuel, but my students did. In fact, Samuel was one of our student's (Danny) childhood friends. Samuel and Danny were best friends and our class was aware of their relationship.

Upon Danny's return to class following the disturbing incident, the students immediately offered their condolences. They lined up and took turns offering comfort (similar to that of a respected elder). It was fascinating to observe how respectful they were regarding death. Danny and I never spoke of his loss; the students took care of that.

In class, we were still experiencing decreasing enrollment. Michael was expelled for tagging the administration offices after school hours. Carlos was expelled (and arrested) after being tackled in first period and disarmed by the two campus police officers. He was carrying a loaded .38 caliber handgun. Ernie was ousted as well, but I didn't know what for. He simply appeared one day in the middle of a class session and asked me for my telephone number. He explained that he tried to find me at the university but couldn't. I asked what had happened and he confirmed that he did not want to tell me now but that he would call soon. I told him where he could find Christa to say good-bye and he stated, "I gotta go before I start cryin'." So he exited, without strutting.

Grade reports were requested again at the end of the 12th week. They were less time-consuming now because enrollment had decreased to 23 students. Though enrollment was down, grades were up. The students earned two A's, three B's, seven C's, four D's, and seven F's.

Knowing the Students: Living the Responsibility Model

The students were really starting to open up and share their lives with us by the 13th week of class. I attributed this to the idea that the responsibility model, at least at this stage of the program, became less of an everyday ritual for discussion. Before this point, we were diligent in bringing the model to the forefront of every lesson, but it slowly began to fade into the background. This is not to say that the model fell into an abyss. It simply blurred into everyday operations. To some degree, the model allowed us to create an open atmosphere in which students felt comfortable sharing their lives with us.

For instance, Alma began to share some shocking facts about her life with remarks such as, "I have an overactive night life and am sore." This was her reason for not participating one day. Teresa, a typically timid and quiet student, appeared to be depressed one day. I noticed her unusual mannerisms and inquired into her situation. She explained that five other girls on campus were harassing her and had threatened to beat her up on her way home from school. I asked if there was anything I could do and she somberly replied, "Do ya got a gun?"

Ernie, who was no longer in the program, stopped by my office at the university with his mother, unannounced and unsolicited. The three of us discussed his "hard life," as she described it, and designed a contract that he would try to follow to restructure his life. The contract included issues surrounding drugs, gang involvement, and education. Following our lengthy discussion, his mother decided that it was time to leave. He asked if he could stay awhile longer. She and I agreed, and Ernie and I talked for another hour. I then drove him to his church, where he was involved with a youth group. Clearly, he wanted to change his life, and he expressed a strong desire to attend college.

Ernie was not the only student to visit my office at the university. On the day that Elias was suspended for allegedly tagging (with a marker) the cafeteria area, he dropped in to explain what had happened. He adamantly denied the charges, and I thought, "Why shouldn't I believe him?" Here is a kid who tells me about his drug and alcohol consumption, and other negative activities he's engaged in regularly. In my mind, he would surely confess to marking on a wall.

It became clear that I was beginning to empathetically understand these students, and what they viewed as unjust made sense to me too. Therefore, I pursued Elias's issue further, and the next morning I addressed my concerns about his innocence to the principal. Although she fully supported our program, on this morning she just smiled and directed me to take up the issue with the dean of students. I suspected that she was viewing me as a "sucker." She did not believe it was possible that these kids were being honest with me.

On the day that Elias was apprehended, his accusers didn't even find a marker on him. It seemed to me that in these walls, if you are a student, you are guilty until proven innocent. You are simply guilty if a teacher says so. To be considered a problem student, one did not even need to be accused of any wrongdoing. To illustrate, one day Andres was wearing his shirt inside out. He told me that his first-period teacher made him wear it that way because there was an "8-ball" (from the game of billiards) emblem on it. He said that the teacher told him that an 8-ball insignia meant that he was a cocaine dealer and he could be expelled for that. She told Andres that she had learned this during a teacher in-service day. He asked me if he could change his shirt properly. I said, "D— right, that's a stupid rule and wearing your shirt inside out makes you look stupid."

I was not following school protocol, but to me, the whole idea of degrading children for what they wear to school was absurd. I was aware that the school policies were trying to curb gang and drug activity, but they were going about it the wrong way. Since when does ridiculing a student become a means for teaching a lesson?

However, in not following school protocol and policy, I had to deal with sketchy situations at times. Some students took advantage of the open policy in my class. They arrived in the gym under the influence of marijuana. I could tell that they were high just by looking at them. Nevertheless, by this point in the program they trusted me enough to tell me when they were high. On one occasion, a kid even showed me a bag of weed. For some of them, being high was their excuse not to participate in class. For me, this was unacceptable. I used their own words to try to help them understand the problem of coming to class stoned (i.e., you don't participate in learning).

Regardless of what I told them, some students still came to school stoned. However, a few listened to me. This was brought to my attention by Rey-Rey, who, one week after the program ended, came to my office at the university. He brought his girlfriend and asked if I would help her enroll in a nearby alternative school. I made a few calls and secured her an interview with the school. As they prepared to leave, Rey-Rey said, "Well, James, we're gonna go blaze it [smoke pot]." His girlfriend's eyes just about popped out of her head. She looked in astonishment at him and said, "You say that in front of your teacher?" His reply to her was casual but meaningful. He said, "Yeah, he ain't gonna bust me cause he knows that don't help. But I never got high in his class 'cuz I respect 'im."

Like Rey-Rey, Peanut was another student who respected the openness of the program and understood its limits. I truly missed him during the two consecutive weeks that he was gone. Through his absence, Peanut was confined to the largest detention center for juveniles in Los Angeles County. Upon his return, he acted upset and admitted that he was angry. He originally was sentenced to 10 days for theft, but they extended his stay because he was involved in a fight at the detention center. Remarking about the cot on which he slept, he said, "Rehabilitation, my a—!" Once again, one of my students encountered an out-of-order system that clearly does not work.

At the same time as Peanut was released from the detention center, Ricardo was released from Metro. The dean of students informed me, "Ricardo was sent to the Skills Center where he'll study English and learn to drive a forklift." I inquired into why he was expelled and the dean replied, "Well, he'll be better off down there."

In the 17th week of the program, Christa came to class in tears. She had just spoken with Ricardo, who came by for a visit even though he could have lost his educational services at the Skills Center for returning to the grounds of Metro. He only made it to Metro's parking lot. She invited him in, but he avoided seeing me. He said to her, "If I go in I might start cryin'." His comment made Christa realize that our group of students were only kids, kids who yearn for nurturing environments. I am beginning to believe that a very few of us consider this notion.

With this series of misfortunes, I needed to hear something positive, and I did. The principal informed me that we would receive funds for the following year. She confirmed that she had seen campus-wide improvement with our kids and that she was receiving fewer referrals from them. She asked if there was anything that she could do for me, and I jokingly (but very seriously to myself) replied, "Stop kicking our students out of school."

It was during this time that activity reached an all-time high with our students. Elena was active for the first time all semester. We now called her the "terminator" because of her overzealous approach to playing floor hockey. The students were now constantly remarking about the perspiration on their foreheads, as if it were a trophy. Most of them were putting effort into almost everything that they attempted. As their effort increased, problematic behaviors decreased.

Andres, who asked, "Are you going to teach here next year?" exemplified their enjoyment of the class. I asked him why, and he stated, "Because all of the other teachers are a——— to me and you're pretty fair." This notion was obvious to most of the students who were still in the program. This, however, did not mean that the class was without problems. I was constantly reminding the students about taking advantage of the freedom they were given regarding their individualized learning programs. On many occasions, students were not being responsible for their learning and I had to intervene.

In regard to the students' individualized programs, I noticed that many kids were choosing teachers rather than content areas (activities). For example, Sandra once asked, "What is Christa teaching?" She then chose all of the sections that Christa was offering irrespective of the activity being taught. Although the program was imparting some content to the students, the relational aspects of teaching—exemplified in the responsibility model's commitment to putting kids first—were more meaningful to the students.

As the end of the program approached, a sense of indolence had set in with a couple of the university students. Karina and Ramon were absent from time to time and did not put forth much effort in their teaching. Though I was speaking less and less to the students about the responsibility model's goals, some of them reminded me of the goals, saying that the teachers needed to follow them more precisely. Elena typified the feeling of the students by remarking, "I stick to my program, but then you change it when they [teachers] don't show up." She was right. On the next day, I resolved this issue with Ramon and Karina, but it was uplifting to be reminded by our students about the goals within the responsibility model.

Some of the Metro faculty should have been reminded about the goals of the model from time to time as well. Mrs. Avery once disrespected my whole class as they were waiting calmly for me in the hallway as I had requested. She approached them and remarked, "Why is everybody just standing around and how come you're all not dressed?" She paused and then said, "Oh, it's the special kids." Rey-Rey proudly said, "We're not special, we're at-risk." All of the students laughed in harmony. I then realized, in regard to "labeling" kids, that they don't care how you classify them, as long as you treat them with dignity. To confirm this point I overheard one of our students tell her friend who had asked what class she was in, "I'm in the drop-out class. It's pretty cool."

"How do I get in this class?" was a question posed by several unfamiliar faces during the last weeks of school. These were the voices of our "refugee" students. They somehow discovered us and we took them in. One of them even approached me after class and asked, "Hey Mister, can I have one of those folders?" I still do not know the purpose (or meaning) of his request to possess a folder. He may have been searching for a place to belong and wanted to be treated as everyone else. He may have been searching for a responsibility.

Apart from this, during our last weeks together, the students who had attended class regularly were now occasionally absent whereas the newcomers became regulars. Apparently, when students are aware that there is no possible way to pass a certain class (or group of classes), they stay home or they find somewhere else to pass the time or seek learning.

Our Final Meeting

The class was scheduled to meet only once during finals week: a two-hour block. Ironically, the last day mimicked the first, with students sitting on the bleachers. Additionally, on the first day of class, 19 students sat before me—the same number that now sat before me on our last meeting. Except this time, of the 32 students who started the class, I knew the 13 who were missing and whose names were now replaced with "deleted from class" on the roster.

Though we mostly visited, exchanged addresses, and reminisced about the program, I did present them with a final exam. The exam, which they had a choice to complete anonymously, required simply a piece of paper and a pencil. The task was to write briefly about what they had learned in the program.

It seemed an uncomplicated task until I became aware that Elias was not writing. I thought he was sarcastically exercising his right of choice, but when I inquired into the situation he remarked, "What I've learned I can't put on that paper." Although he did not realize it, his statement confirmed why I do this work.

A few days later I submitted the grade sheet to Mr. Frost and said my summer good-byes to the Metro faculty. Of course, we talked about the program a little. In our conversation, Mr. Frost also confirmed the value of this type of work. He said, "Those kids respond a lot better to people now. They used to say 'f—you'; now they say 'hello.'" Their final grades consisted of four A's, four B's, five C's, two D's, and four F's.

Evaluation of the Program

The following student voices were derived from postprogram interviews, in which 15 of the 19 remaining students participated. In all of the interviews, Elena probably provided the most poignant example of the feelings surrounding the students' lives. She answered the question, "What do you want to do when you get older?" With a look of sadness she said, "I always wanted to be a secretary." She voiced the remark in such a way that she had already resigned the dream to her past. Then she looked at me and commented with a tear in her eye, "I don't wanna talk no more."

The students' thoughts regarding the teachers who worked at the school were just as negative as their perceptions of schooling itself, as noted in table 6.1. For example, Rey-Rey said, "They yell at us and give us detention for no reason. Most of 'em are punks." Alma remarked, "Some just hate you. I know this one teacher, he's Mexican, and he don't like Mexicans and that ain't cool either." Alejandra commented, "The teachers are dumb. I don't like them. They don't like me. They say, 'Why do you bother to come, you can't pass anyway?' Forget them. They tell me not to come, then they get me in trouble for ditching. They tell me not to come, then they tell me why don't you come?" Danny said, "They're too strict. They're like strict, strict. They need to loosen up 'cuz the more strict they get, the more we hate it." Angie simply said, "Some are cool, most are not, some are mean. They scream at you." Elias remarked, "They f— with me all the time, nonstop." Teresa complained, "They always yell." Peanut said, "Most of them don't understand you or even talk to you. They just do their job. Like they say something, you do it, that's it. They don't care." Frank remarked, "They just give you the worksheet and that's it. They don't teach us or nothin', don't even explain it." Elena said calmly, "They yell too much. They give me headaches."

These youths' comments send a strong message, one that goes beyond the obvious overtones of their negativity for the school environment and their teachers. The message is that school is not helping them. If it were, they would not disregard it so. According to McLaughlin et al. (1994), "Helping institutions do not help consistently. Schools, too often below par by any measure, are experienced as hostile and demanding environments where neither youth nor their interests are heard or taken seriously" (p. 213). I agree and would add that these institutions are aware that they are not helping youth, yet they choose to remain unhelpful. It is not surprising that the hopelessness in Elena's weeping eyes is overlooked in many schools.

These kids deserve more. At the very least, they deserve to be associated with a place that believes in them and where they can believe in themselves. Too few are afforded these places. I hope that the in-school program provided such a place, a place that enlarged their perceptions of education.

Students' Reflections on the Program's Impact

First, I turn to the students' perceptions of the program. Again, I will let the kids' voices carry the message.

> This is a cool class here. It's better than the others. There's more communication, you know. People get along in here. Other classes, there's no communication so you don't get close to the people in there. . . . In here everybody cooperates, you know. You tell us why we shouldn't be fighting and stuff and other classes don't tell you anything like that. . . . Other classes, they're not really watching 'eh. They might be watching if you're ditching, but not what you're doing in class. Here it's different, you keep more in touch, you know, closer. Hopefully, I have you again next year. (Jose)
>
> I like it. It's fun. And like, you guys aren't always telling us what to do. You guys care what we think too. You care what we say too, like, you listen to what we have to say, other teachers aren't like that. Shh, I like talking

to you guys. I can tell you stuff and you won't tell everybody else. I feel safe in telling you things. (Alejandra)

It's fun. At first I thought it was boring 'cuz I wasn't participating but then I started liking it. . . . You guys are different, I don't know, just, there's something about you guys. . . . I feel respect here. You don't yell at us. You treat us nice. It makes me want to participate. (Elena)

This is the best class I have. How we all get along and play and the games that we do. 'Cuz we help each other in what we're doing. In other classes, if you do something bad they just send you away. They don't care what you do. You guys care, talk to us, tell us what's up, you know, you respect us. (Danny)

Fun. Better than the other classes. . . . You didn't put us down. You guys cared more because you pushed us and made us feel that we should try more. My other teachers don't do that. They give up on you. You guys didn't do that. (Teresa)

I met new friends in here. This is my first time passing. . . . Well, here you ain't that strict. You don't force anything on us. You only encourage us, but it's still up to us. I felt like an adult. (Alma)

This class is cool. . . . This class is like better, you know, 'cuz you get choices in what we want to do, you know, you gotta give yourself an honest grade and what you think you deserve and 'cuz you guys have a lot of respect, they don't be talking s— you know, they talk to you cool so we have respect for you. That's how I see it. . . . This is my favorite class. I come more to this class more than any other class 'cuz this class ain't boring like the others. Other teachers just come to make money, they just do what they have to do. Put on the board some s— or give you a worksheet. Right here it's not like that. You talk to us about stuff and you explain it if we don't know. We ask you and you explain the whole thing, not just parts. You let us understand. (Peanut)

It was alright. Something different that's for sure. I liked getting to know you guys. I'm glad to have all of you here. Oh, you know what's different? We were all treated equal in here. In other classes we're all treated different, like, it's like, do this and that's it and they leave you. They're not there for you. (Angie)

This is a cool class, the best one here. You let us do our own stuff, take our own responsibilities. You didn't treat us like regular teachers, you know, like, 'Hey you, come over here right now.' . . . You talked to me. I felt like an adult, like, more mature. (Frank)

That first week nobody liked this class 'cuz of the stupid games you had, but then after, like, everybody liked it. It's just that there was a lot of defiance at first. But once you get into playing, it's alright. It just changed and everybody helped change it, us and you. Then, everybody just changed. We all get along together and talk to each other and we play together and everything and you don't yell at us. We just help each other. . . . In this class I get to show what I can do. This is the best PE I've had since early in junior high. (Hector)

My Reflections on the Program's Impact

For the most part, the program seemed to be an appealing place for the students. This does not necessarily mean that they gained anything from the experience simply because they enjoyed it. They enjoy being at the mall, but I am wary of what they learn there. Therefore, the following analysis will focus on the students' perceptions of what they learned in the program. I feel compelled to share what Andres said he had learned. When I asked him, "What have you learned in this class, if anything?" he honestly replied, "Nothin.'" He was clear about his statement and I believe it to be true. There is no fault here. There was simply no connection between Andres and anyone else in the program. Fortunately, this was an isolated case.

Many of the students' responses to the same question were much more positive, and I must say, equally honest and frank. It was clear that they were not simply telling me what I wanted to hear. How do I know? By this point in my interactions with them, I was adept at discerning genuine and inauthentic comments and behaviors.

Many of the students stated that they had learned new activities, but in their responses there also is clear evidence of the effect of the responsibility model. Much of this evidence had to do with learnings surrounding issues of self-control. In regard to what he learned, Rey-Rey commented:

> All kinds of sports I never knew before, how to work in a team and control myself. . . . About how we shouldn't be cussin' at our teammates if they do something wrong. At first I was like, no, we can't do that 'cuz if you're doing something wrong on the team you have to be yelled at or somethin'. That's all I knew before, but now I think of it that you shouldn't be talking to teammates like that, well, cussin' them out. You should just tell 'em, 'Next time get it,' you know.

Alejandra's response was very similar to Rey-Rey's. She claimed that she learned "lots of activities and how to respect others." She proceeded to justify her comment stating, "'Cuz I don't cuss as much as I used to. You know . . . I used to cuss a lot, even at you, but now I try not to, especially at other people." Alejandra related her learning to self-control. She said, "Learned some self-control too 'cause I'm not as mean anymore, except to that little girl 'cause I can't stand her [pointing to Alma]. I act better I guess, treat people better everywhere, even at home. I try to be like the best I could." Alejandra then explained that her attitude changed because of the program. She remarked, "My attitude changed all over the place, everywhere, school, everywhere."

Regarding the responsibility model's goal of self-control, a few of the students claimed that they didn't need to learn that. Teresa said, "Well, today I didn't control myself because I told Antonio off, but I'm usually good at that. I just learned about being responsible for myself." Peanut expressed the same notion regarding self-control. He said, "I learned some stuff, but not that self-control. I don't even pay attention about that. I was learning what I gotta do to pass this class. S— though, I learned that all PE classes ain't boring." Along the same line as Peanut's latter remark, Hector replied, "I learned that PE is alright. It's cool."

Some of the students responded in broader terms that related to many aspects of the responsibility model and the environment of the program. Frank commented: "I learned a lot of s—. I get along with others. I never got along with other people before, till this time. . . . About being polite and s—, workin' as a group. Now, I talk to them on the streets, wherever. And with teachers, s—, I used to disrespect all the teachers. I don't do that now. I respect them all now. I learned there ain't no point in disrespecting them."

Respect was a topic throughout the students' remarks. Angie concisely stated, "[I learned] how to throw a football, hmm, I have a lot of respect for the other people in here." Elias was more blunt about what he learned. He commented, "Respect and how to be honest and s—. F—, I respect the teachers for the first time. I don't know, I'm even respecting people that don't respect me." Danny commented, "To get along with others. To help others and respect each other."

Jose and Maria corroborated others' comments through answering the question, "What did you learn, if anything?" Jose said, "A lot 'eh. I show more respect in here than in other classes. In here, we learned to cooperate, you know, in other classes you just sit around. We just respect each other more in here." Maria said, "Getting along with other people. Getting to know other people, respecting them." I questioned Maria's response and immediately asked her, "In what ways?" She said, "What do you mean in what ways? To tell you the truth, I even respect myself now, plus them others. I can't believe it either. It's hard to explain."

Three students supplied vague comments, but I believe their thoughts were very important. Antonio said, "You taught us how to do our own things, I don't know, that's a tough question." Elena replied, "A lot. I really don't know." Alma said, "Different things: I can't explain it. It's weird." It is not my impression that their responses lack meaning; conversely, their responses had a point. Even I am not sure what the point is, but I have been in situations where I have had to respond in the same manner as they did. In my recollection, there was import to what I had learned, with possibly too much significance to answer in mere words. I agree with Maria that sometimes it is hard to explain.

Concerning what they had learned, several students followed their comments with specific notations about our teaching methods (see table 6.2). From the students' comments, I inferred that adolescents make what works for them sound simple. In reality, it just may be that uncomplicated. But somehow, in some way, the problems inherent in public schools complicate in-school programs. A program leader must be persistent in using the responsibility model with public school students. Perseverance is necessary. However, the reward gained through establishing trusting relationships with the students is well worth the effort.

Table 6.2

Teaching Methods That Complemented Model's Goals

You talked to us. (Rey-Rey)

You tell us what respect is. That's it. I take it to other classes and home now 'cuz I didn't know what it was before. (Angie)

You talk to us about things. You put us into groups and you just treat us better. (Danny)

By talking to us. That's all it takes for anyone to listen. (Peanut)

'Cuz you talk to me even if something wasn't wrong. You check to see if I was okay. Actually, because you cared. It helps me to know that if I'm in trouble you're here to talk to me. (Teresa)

The teachers are nice. They wouldn't yell at us or put us down or anything. Other teachers just say, "Why do you act so dumb for?" You never did that to me. (Alma)

Because we get the responsibilities in here, taking care of each other, learning different things. (Maria)

'Cuz you teachers want our respect. Like, you're always telling us things.... 'Cuz you get along with us, you know. You don't act like a d——. And we're closer, you and me. You're friendly. It's like this, you respect us, we respect you. (Jose)

S——, I learned in here 'cuz you guys respect me and then I respect you back. And in this class we have choices, we have options. (Alejandra)

It's just the way you act. The way you talk to us and s——. The first time I ever came late you didn't get on my case. Then it's my responsibility. What kind of teachers don't get on people's case? And you don't talk s—— 'bout us to the dean or anything. You stand up for us when other teachers get on our case. (Elias)

It ain't that you taught us, it's just that we learned it on our own. (Frank)

For Further Study

Perrone, V. (1991). *A letter to teachers: Reflections on schooling and the art of teaching.* San Francisco: Jossey-Bass.

Perrone clearly speaks to teachers about a flawed educational system and about what needs to be part of particular classrooms to make a difference in kids' lives.

Chapter 7

Extended Day Clubs

Don Hellison and Nick Cutforth

Extended day programs are community youth programs offered before or after school, on weekends, or in summer by schools or youth agencies such as the YMCA, Boys and Girls Club, or park district. Chapter 5 described one kind of program that is mostly conducted during out-of-school hours. Extended day programs enjoy several advantages over in-school programs. For one thing, more opportunities exist for developing one's own curriculum. If kids are attracted to martial arts, for example, such a program can be offered. Also, unlike in-school physical education, extended day programs don't have to require specific uniforms, showers, or formal address (e.g., Ms. Smith or Coach Jones). More flexibility exists not only with the curriculum and rules but also with attendance requirements, which can be looser or tighter than in-school programs. Because strict school attendance rules do not apply, teachers usually can ask disruptive or abusive participants to leave without having to deal with a set of rigid procedures. More flexibility is also characteristic of extended day program meeting times, meeting days per week, number of years the same kids can participate, and length of meetings as well as who is eligible to participate. All of these decisions can also be changed more easily, because in many of these settings the program leader is not encumbered by a several layer policy-heavy bureaucracy.

The state-of-the-art criteria for program development described in chapter 3 and shown again in table 7.1 were actually drawn from exemplary extended day programs in underserved communities, although we use them as guidelines for all of our youth development programs. It therefore comes as no surprise that extended day programs can more easily meet these criteria. One criterion in particular—"keep program numbers small and encourage participation over a long period of time; emphasize belonging and membership"—is perhaps the most important advantage that extended day programs enjoy over in-school physical education, although "open gym" and "gym and swim" programs do not take advantage of this criterion. To fully capitalize on small numbers, we organize most of our extended day programs as clubs which by their nature emphasize membership—something to belong to—and commitment over a long period of time.

Of course, organized sport also offers a chance to belong to a team over a long period of time (in multiyear programs), and in some sports such as basketball and volleyball the program numbers are small. However, organized sport programs must overcome problems of elitism, the emphasis on winning, and other influences of professional sport if they are to benefit kids.

Three kinds of extended day clubs are described in this chapter. For each, we visit a specific club so that you can visualize the setting and the kids as they interact with the responsibility-based goals and strategies.

Table 7.1

Key Criteria for State-of-the-Art Youth Development Programs

1. Treat youth as resources to be developed. Build on the strengths they already possess, and emphasize their competence and mastery.
2. Focus on the whole person—the emotional, social, and cognitive as well as physical dimensions of the self.
3. Respect the individuality of youth, including cultural differences and developmental needs.
4. Empower youth.
5. Give youth clear, demanding (but not unreasonable) expectations based on a strong, explicit set of values.
6. Help youth envision possible futures for themselves.
7. Provide both a physically and psychologically safe environment.
8. Keep program numbers small and encourage participation over a long period of time; emphasize belonging and membership.
9. Maintain a local connection.
10. Provide courageous and persistent leadership in the face of systemic obstacles.
11. Provide significant contact with a caring adult.

Note: From Hellison, D., & Cutworth, N. (1997). Extended day programs for urban children and youth: From theory to practice. In Walberg, H., Reyes, O., & Weissberg, R. (Eds.), *Children and youth: Interdisciplinary perspectives* (pp. 223-249). Thousand Oaks, CA: Sage. Copyright 1997 by Sage Publications, Inc.

Our first trip is to an inner-city before-school Coaching Club designed for team sports; our second to a low-income Mexican-American community where an after-school club offers fitness, sport, and cooperative-adventure activities; and our third to an inner-city after-school martial arts club.

You will notice some modifications of the five student responsibilities (or levels) as well as some specific examples of the four instructional strategies and daily format described in chapter 3 and shown in table 3.2. Extended day clubs put kids first in the same way as other responsibility model programs, except that small program numbers and voluntary membership in a club provide more opportunities for the program leader to know the participants' whole selves, to develop more and deeper one-to-one relationships, and to show these youth that they are genuinely respected for who they are and what they bring to the program as well as for their potential to evaluate the program and make decisions.

Coaching Clubs and the Responsibility Model

Coaching Clubs are one version of an extended day program for underserved kids (see Hellison, 1993, 1995, and 1999, and Hellison & Cutforth, 1997, for earlier versions of the coaching club). They use a team sport—or more than one team sport—as a vehicle for teaching club members to take responsibility for coaching themselves and for coaching, helping, and providing leadership for other club members and for the club itself. Club members are also encouraged to become leaders and role models outside the team sport setting. This purpose is reflected in the five responsibilities that club members are expected to carry out. The responsibilities are stated here as if the reader is a club member:

1. *Self-control:* As a club member, you are responsible for controlling your temper and mouth so that others can have a positive experience. You also need to help solve conflicts peacefully.

2. *Teamwork:* Another of your basic responsibilities is to practice teamwork and cooperation in team practices, games, and meetings. This includes being coachable when you are a member of a team and learning to solve conflicts democratically.

3. *Self-coaching:* A more advanced responsibility is to learn how to learn on your own, by working independently on your skills and attitudes and by setting goals and trying to reach them.

4. *Coaching:* Another advanced responsibility is to help others (such as by complimenting them), to take on coaching roles, and to provide leadership so that the club runs better and everyone has a positive experience. This level of responsibility requires sensitivity toward others' feelings and, in some cases, specific leadership skills.

5. *Outside the gym:* After you have some experience in these four responsibilities, you will be asked to try them out in the rest of your life—in school, at home, and with friends. You will also be asked to try to become a positive role model for others. You can then decide whether these responsibilities work better for you than what you are now doing.

Note that both the language used and one of the five responsibilities differ from the program model presented in chapter 3 and table 3.2. The language—teamwork, self-coaching, coaching—attempts to connect the program model to team sports. The substitution of teamwork for effort as the second level of responsibility first evolved in an inner-city basketball Coaching Club where kids were highly motivated to play basketball but did not value teamwork and cooperation. Therefore, teamwork, which is more or less hidden under the first level of responsibility as the right to be included, was made more of a priority. This modification has held up well in other Coaching Clubs such as soccer.

Instructional strategies for Coaching Clubs are the same as those described in chapter 3—awareness, direct instruction, individual decision making, and group decision making. Some "substrategies" in each of these categories have been developed specifically for Coaching Clubs—for example, direct instruction includes required passing, and individual decision making includes calling an NBA 20-second or full time-out depending on the time needed to solve the problem. These and other strategies are described subsequently.

The daily format follows the same sequence:

1. *Awareness talk:* This is used to remind club members of their responsibilities. Club members gradually take responsibility for conducting the awareness talks.

2. *Lesson:* In team sports, the lesson consists of some self-coaching time, team practices eventually led by coaches who are club members, and game play.

3. *Group meeting:* Club members share their evaluations of the program and solve problems that arise. Eventually, club members lead these discussions.

4. *Reflection time:* Club members evaluate themselves in relation to their five responsibilities. A club member can eventually lead reflection time.

A Basketball Coaching Club

For a first-hand look at a team sport Coaching Club, we will visit a before-school basketball Coaching Club in an inner-city Chicago neighborhood. This club meets in a kindergarten to eighth grade school gym on Wednesday mornings an hour before school starts. The school serves low-income African-American students in a community that has one of the highest violence rates in the city, many boarded-up buildings, and no banks or chain grocery stores. The club has 15 or so members, all of whom are referred to the club by the vice-principal because they have been in trouble. Most of those invited, representing a range of basketball skills from the best to the worst in the school, choose to attend this voluntary program (in fact, the vice-principal was recently asked, "How bad do I have to be to get in that club?"!), despite having to get up an hour earlier on club meeting mornings. Most are invited as sixth graders so that they can attend for three years, although in practice "recruits" come in as early as fourth grade and occasionally as late as eighth grade. Because club members often bring brothers, sisters, and cousins who are under their supervision before school starts, the club provides limited "day care" (they sit on the sidelines). Some of these young kids eventually graduate to club membership without the referral process, a privilege of being a "legacy." Although in this neighborhood basketball is viewed as a boys' sport, girls are also invited to participate, and they do. (However, most participants are boys, because fewer girls are referred.)

Self-Coaching and the Awareness Talk

We arrive about 10 minutes early, and a couple of kids are waiting for us in the parking lot. We enter the overheated, dimly lit, cramped gym, where more kids are waiting. Some change shirts and shoes; others grab a basketball as soon as they walk in and begin dribbling and shooting. More kids straggle in, get balls, and participate in the shootaround.

Club members are still coming through the door when everyone assembles in a circle on the floor for an awareness talk. Because most of these kids have been in the club for over a year, the program leader asks for volunteers to "remind us what the club is about." Someone says "don't yell at anyone," someone else says "be responsible" as if that covers it, and someone else chimes in "pass the ball." Although what they said doesn't fully cover the five responsibilities, the program leader looks around for other hands, seems satisfied that the purpose of the club is understood, and asks for two volunteers to coach. (With 15 club members on the roster and one or two absent plus a couple of others straggling in halfway through the session, one full-court game works well. However, the club has also used four coaches with half-court three- or four-a-side games.)

While the coaches meet with the program leader, a university student who is assisting asks the remaining club members to work on the goal they have set for themselves—shooting a lay-up with their weak hand, posting up, shooting off the dribble—and then record what they did on a clipboard. Meanwhile, with the guidance of the program leader, the student coaches make fair teams (teams change every meeting) and are given a few pointers on conducting their team practice. The awareness talk, self-coaching session, and coaches' meeting take about 10 minutes, and then the coaches gather their new teams together.

Team Practices and the Game

Both practices follow the same format: Run two or three drills (e.g., lay-up lines, weave, jump shots), set up the defense (e.g., zone or one-to-one), and work on a couple of plays to use in the game (e.g., post up, pass and cut, pick). In the beginning, the drills, defense, and plays are chosen by the program leader. Gradually, coaches make more of these decisions. To help the participants (some need more help than others), the program leader provides sample drills and plays. At first, zone defenses are required to minimize defensive aggressiveness and permit the other team to pass the ball. Later, coaches can choose the defense and switch during the game if they want to.

At the end of practice, the two coaches are called together and reminded of their duties during the game. Surprisingly, coaches sometimes want to continue their practice for a while before playing the game. (Question: When have kids ever wanted to practice when they could play? Answer: When they are responsible for the team's performance!) When the coaches are ready to play, they are told that if either the program leader or assistant has to take charge during the game, even to help resolve an argument, the coaches aren't doing their job. The program leader also reminds them to call 20-second and full time-outs (as in the NBA) to solve problems and make offensive and defensive adjustments.

Before the game begins, the program leader explains the absence of a referee. Having a referee, he says, takes the responsibility of calling fouls and keeping order out of the players' hands; all they have to do is not get caught! This club is about responsibility, not "traditional" basketball. Other nontraditional features of this game soon become apparent. For one, most of the players on the offense touch the ball at least once before anyone shoots. For another, unskilled players are given some space to pass, catch, and shoot, and the rules for them, for example, dribbling without traveling, are relaxed. This is called playing "soft defense" to help the less skilled learn how to play the game. Surprisingly, some teammates even encourage beginners to shoot, even though the shot has little chance of making it through the hoop.

All of these things were once rules, and the club members with basketball backgrounds were not happy about any of them. The rules are relaxed once they learn what it means to belong to a Coaching Club and to understand why these rules are in place. A reminder here and there, as well as a discussion once in a while in the end-of-class group meeting, is sufficient to sustain these modifications.

Eventually, one team falls behind and the players begin to gripe or lose interest. The coach calls a time-out, and both teams meet to evaluate their team play and, if necessary, make adjustments. The game resumes, but an argument breaks out over a foul. One of the coaches touches her shoulders for a 20-second time-out, and the problem is resolved quickly (no one wants to stop the game). However, the one who started the argument is still angry, so the program leader asks him whether he needs to sit out to cool down. He doesn't want to leave the game, but, because his sullen face leaves little doubt that he is still angry, he is told to "either change your face or sit down until you can." He sits, and a few minutes later, when asked whether he is ready to return, shakes his head no. A little later he gets up on his own and gets back in the game.

The Group Meeting and Reflection Time

With about 10 minutes to go before school starts, everyone circles up again. Coaches for the day talk first, evaluating their practice, the game, the coachability of their team. Then players volunteer evaluations of the practice, game, and their coach. Coaches are expected to name specific players who made a positive contribution in practice or the game (positive comments are uncommon but club members learn quickly) but to discuss individual problems either in general terms or with the player off to the side (or to refer the player to the program leader). Sometimes problems that arose during practice or the game need to be solved by the group. The program leader and university student talk last; both emphasize the club's goal of everyone having a positive experience.

Then it's reflection time, in which all club members are asked to evaluate themselves on their self-control ("did you make a problem for someone else?"), teamwork and coachability, self-coaching, helping others and leadership ("helping everyone have a positive experience"), and whether they tried any of these responsibilities or were a role model for any of them at home, in school, on the playground, or on the "street." For each responsibility, club members point their thumbs up (which means they took on the responsibility), sideways (which means they did it to some extent), or down (which means that it needs work). For each responsibility, the program leader and assistant look around to gain some sense of the group's perceptions as well as whether these individual evaluations match their own. One kid, whose thumb is pointing down for teamwork, is criticized by a couple of club members, but another club member interrupts them: "Thumbs down don't mean he's bad; just means he needs to work on it. It's like a goal for him" (thanks to Jimmy Wilson). The program leader smiles, nods, and says nothing. Then it's "see you next week" and the kids leave for class. The leader stops one of the older kids and says, "Gerald, I love you, but you've got to step up and provide some leadership when things break down." Gerald, who had a bad game, nods, then hesitates, smiles, and gets up to leave.

Student and Teacher Evaluations of the Club

After they straggle out, you leaf through a stack of anonymous evaluations of the club written a few weeks ago by club members:

- "The club helps me to understand people more."
- "I'm learning that girls can play basketball."
- "It is helping me, because before I was in the club I had a very bad attitude."
- "I've learned that I have responsibility, and you all helped me find it."
- "The club helped my self-control in school with the teachers."
- "The club made me put my attitude behind and gave me enough skills to make the school basketball team."
- "When we played the teachers in basketball I thought that we was going to lose, but we didn't. So I think that this club improved my skills in a great way. It also helps me to look at things in a new way."
- "You believe in me, even though I do a lot of wrong things."
- "The club don't have to be improved, because it's improved enough!"
- From the school basketball coach: "I've got five of your kids on the team, and I can tell they are in your club. Thanks for helping me out."
- From the principal: "Your club has changed the culture of this school."

At the end of the eighth grade, Coaching Club members are invited to become "apprentice teachers" in a summer basketball program for younger kids being held at the university and sponsored by Nike (see chapter 10, Cross-Age Teaching Programs).

The Energizers Club and the Responsibility Model

The second program we will visit is an after-school club that has met twice weekly for the past four years in the gym of an elementary school located in an economically depressed neighborhood in northwest Denver. The club, which is now in its fifth year, serves fourth- and fifth-grade Mexican-American boys and girls.

Early during the program's first year, the students selected the name "Energizers" to describe their club. The students are referred to the club for a variety of reasons. These reasons are perhaps best summarized by the principal: "All the kids are needy here, but the kids in the Energizers program are extra needy because of their behavior, indifferent attitude toward school, and lack of social skills." Many have troubles and fears that emanate from their own often violent urban neighborhood and, in some cases, disconnected, chaotic family lives. A few examples illustrate the challenges that these students present: Mercedes has experienced sexual abuse at home, harbors a considerable amount of anger, and is always threatening to quit the program; Victor has a veneer of toughness that induces him to goad others with unkind words or actions; John is shy but is prone to lash out at others at the slightest provocation; Edwin's mood swings mean that he is likely to be friendly and cooperative one moment but to disintegrate into tears the next, the perceived victim of others' injustice.

Although these students' attitudes and behaviors present huge management challenges, the program leader treats the kids not as remedial students but rather as resources to be developed. However, on occasions, their antics as well as their varied needs and behavior fluctuations require the program leader to "hang in there" with certain individuals.

Clear expectations for the program and a set of five explicit levels of responsibility (Level One: self-control, Level Two: trying, Level Three: self-direction, Level Four: caring, and Level Five: outside the gym) are infused into all activities and experiences, resulting in not only a clear purpose but a psychologically and physically safe environment. As we will see when we visit the club, the program focuses on competence and self-worth through individual- and group-oriented activities instead of highly competitive ones. Traditional sports such as volleyball, soccer, and basketball are introduced, but they are played within a cooperative value system that downplays winning and losing and encourages the inclusion of all, regardless of ability. Although the medium is physical activity, the message to parents, the school faculty, and the students themselves is that this is not just another sports program; instead, the focus is on the whole child. Children are empowered to take greater control of their lives in several ways: They become involved in their own development by setting goals as they participate in individual warm-ups, fitness activities, and group games; they contribute to the development of others by coaching and refereeing; and they contribute to the development of the program by giving their reactions to what they have experienced and by providing suggestions for what they would like to do in future weeks.

Self-Coaching and the Awareness Talk

We arrive as the end-of-school bell sounds and hurry to the school gym. As we observe from the sidelines, 16 fourth and fifth graders drift into the gym, put their bags and coats against one wall, and sign their names on a pad by the gym door. To warm up, the program leader tells them to practice the volleyball skills learned in previous lessons. As the children scatter to different areas of the gym and begin the activity, we observe how they are responding to the challenge of practicing the skills without direct teacher supervision. We notice that one boy is unable to resist the temptation of shooting the volleyball at one of the basketball hoops and then kicks a stray ball belonging to a pair of classmates. The program leader approaches him and asks quietly whether his actions were appropriate and whether he could have returned the ball in a different way. Realizing his error, the boy quickly apologizes to his two peers and adds that he should have passed the ball back instead of kicking it. Then he scurries off to ask another classmate if he can practice volleying with him.

As we look around the gym, we notice that some of the club members are playing volleyball against the wall, several practice the volley pass in pairs, and others play a game of "keep-away" in threes. For the most part, the program leader observes how his students are responding to the challenge of independently practicing the skills. From time to time, however, he takes the opportunity to engage in short, friendly conversations with several of them, asking them how they are doing and what kind of day they've had at school.

Five minutes later, the program leader calls the players into a circle for an awareness talk and, after welcoming them, congratulates them on the effective way in which they undertook the opening activity. He tells them that he understands that sometimes it is difficult to follow the instructions given by a teacher, especially when other activities and participants present more attractive options. He then reminds them of their five responsibilities in the club (self-control, trying, self-direction, caring, and outside the gym), adding that these are their responsibilities, that they are expected to take responsibility for their own behavior and learning, and that they will have many opportunities in the ensuing weeks and months to work on their own without direct supervision.

Fitness Activities and Reflection Time

The comments during the awareness talk serve as a bridge for the next activity, a fitness circuit that the participants perform once each week. The program leader asks the children if they can remember the three goals of the circuit. "To try your best" (Level Two), one boy volunteers. "To beat your own score" (Level Three), says a girl. Then after a few seconds of silence, another girl offers, "To be a good partner by encouraging them, counting their scores, and being honest" (Level Four).

The class divides into pairs, which then scatter to one of five stations that make up the circuit: a shuttle run, sit-ups, basketball chest pass, jump rope, and push-ups. On the program leader's command, half the participants perform each activity for 30 seconds while the others spur their partners toward increased effort and count their repetitions. When the 30-second period is completed, each student records her or his score on a card, which also contains the results of previous weeks' efforts. Next, the other participants perform the same activity while those who have just performed observe and count their efforts. Then the participants move on to perform the next activity on the circuit and continue to rotate until they have attempted all five exercises.

Having completed the circuit, many of the participants lie exhausted on the gym floor. One boy consults his card and says enthusiastically, "Today, I did better on the run, push-ups, and sit-ups!" His female partner responds excitedly, "I beat my score on the chest pass and jump rope!"

The program leader calls the participants into a circle and asks who achieved any of the three goals of the activity. Without hesitation, most participants say that they managed to accomplish all three. However, on reflection, a few admit that they could have tried a little harder, and one student confesses that he did not encourage his partner as much as he should have. The program leader reinforces the children's comments with specific advice about putting forth effort, setting individual goals, and encouraging each other and then praises them for the seriousness with which they approached both the three goals and the exercises themselves. He concludes his comments by reminding them how the three goals relate to the levels of responsibility.

Challenge Activities

The final part of the session is a jump rope activity. The program leader turns a long rope with one of the students and explains that the challenge is for every student to reach the other side of the rope by running through it without making any contact. He adds that if one student touches the rope, then the whole group has to begin the challenge again. After asking a few questions, the participants form a line and apprehensively watch the turning rope. Eventually a boy plucks up courage and sprints through the rope to the applause of his classmates. Next, a girl bolts through the rope and is greeted with a high five from the boy on the other side. Others run through successfully, but then one boy catches his heel on the turning rope. His efforts are met with a groan from the other participants as they realize that they will have to begin the challenge again. As they walk around the rope to the other side and reform the line, several participants suggest that the previously unsuccessful student should go first, and others instruct him how to time his entry into the turning rope and direct him to run faster. Nervously, he approaches the turning rope but his anxiety is quickly replaced by relief and satisfaction when he is successful on his first attempt. The other participants run through the rope and more high fives and even hugs greet them on the other side. As the final student dashes through the rope, her classmates cheer as they realize that they have achieved their goal.

The Closing Group Meeting and Reflection Time

As the cheers subside, the program leader calls the participants into a circle for the last time to process the activity. The student who touched the rope says that he felt bad when he heard the other participants' groans, but that he was grateful for the encouragement that he received from them before his second attempt. Several other participants admit to feeling nervous as they waited for their turn, and all admit to feeling pleased at accomplishing the challenge. The program leader asks the participants what they felt was the purpose of the activity. The participants' responses include, "to work together," "not to blame each other," and "not to give up." Next, they discuss how these issues relate to the children's lives in the classroom (a fifth-grade boy admits, "I could use a little more Level Two in math class") and outside school (a fourth-grade girl says, "I helped my mom with cleaning the kitchen—that's Level Four!"). Finally, the program leader concludes the session by asking them to reflect on their performance and attitude during the last hour. He reminds them again about what they are working on in the Energizers Club and then asks them to indicate with their thumbs (up = good, horizontal = OK, and down = needs work) the extent to which they carried out the first four levels of responsibility during the past hour.

Students' and Teachers' Evaluations of the Club

Students' and teachers' comments obtained at end-of-year evaluations provide insights into the program's impact. Here are some of the students' comments:

- "The program teaches us self-control and respect for other people."
- "The program taught me to control my temper, and now I don't lose it so fast."
- "In the program, people learn to like everybody."
- "When we were playing, we would get together and forget about our problems."
- "I learned to have faith in myself."
- "When I achieved my goal, I felt great."
- "I learned that we can do lots of things if we really put our minds to it."
- "After I leave this school, I want to come back and help you teach in your program."

The teachers also evaluate the program. Here is a sample of their comments:

- "It is great how you keep coming here every week."
- "I like the attitude you have toward the kids."
- "I have noticed a big difference in Luis. He used to be very shy in the classroom, but now he is more confident. I think this change has a lot to do with your program."

In an attempt to communicate the purpose of the Energizers Club to a wider audience, at the end of each school year one session is designated as an open house, and parents and other family members as well as school faculty join the children as they participate in the program's activities. Afterward, an informal discussion of the program takes place, and pizza and soda are provided using grant funds secured from a local foundation.

Martial Arts Club and the Responsibility Model

The third program we will visit is an after-school Martial Arts Club. The children and youth are African-American students in an elementary school located on the west side of Chicago. They reside in a destitute area where gangs and drugs are prevalent. The club serves up to 15 third- through eighth-grade girls and boys and meets once a week for one hour after school.

Like the two clubs previously described, the goal of the Martial Arts Club is to use physical activity as a vehicle for teaching kids to take more responsibility for their lives and to understand and be sensitive to the well-being of others. The main difference is the content, martial arts, which requires modification of the five responsibilities in the gym goals:

1. *Self-control*: As a club member, you are responsible for controlling your temper, which includes never trying to injure or make fun of fellow club members, especially regarding the martial arts techniques we teach.

2. *On-task*: As a club member, you are responsible for staying focused with the rest of the group on the day's activity. New skills sometimes feel awkward, which is normal, but you need to give your best effort and be willing to try new things.

3. *Self-directed*: As a club member, you are given opportunities to learn new martial arts techniques or become more competent with existing ones. You are responsible for working independently and learning how to set goals for yourself.

4. *Leader*: As a club member, you are responsible for helping others by taking on teaching roles and/or setting examples for other club members by demonstrating self-control, on-task behavior, and self-direction, which will all help create a safe and fun environment.

5. *True martial artist*: As a club member, you are responsible for trying these four responsibilities in school, at home, with friends, and in other life settings, and you especially are responsible for not misusing the martial arts skills you are learning. Physical confrontation is a last resort when all else fails to work. You are a representative of this club, and your everyday actions exemplify what this club is about.

The language used to express the responsibilities of the Martial Arts Club varies from the Coaching Club and the Energizers Club to help conjoin the program goals to the martial arts. In the Coaching Club, the second responsibility is teamwork. The students are already motivated to persevere, because basketball is a high priority in their world. However, working and playing as a team is not a priority. In the Martial Arts Club, the second responsibility is being on task. Martial arts lessons include many individual and partner skill drills, and being off task, for example, by pretending to be in a karate fight, is a continuous attraction.

The terms *leader* for the fourth and *true martial artist* for the fifth responsibility were created to help club members relate the club responsibilities to the martial arts.

Club Values and the Awareness Talk

I (Dave Walsh) am a university student who has worked in responsibility-based clubs for inner-city youth for the past five years, and I am now the program leader for this club. Two university students assist me. We arrive at the school 15 minutes before the day ends with enough time to greet the office aides, teachers, principal, and a few parents roving around the halls. We enter the gym as the bell rings and wait for the kids. On a given day, we may have 8 to 15 students whom we greet by talking about school, friends, and miscellaneous life issues. The kids rarely talk about martial arts until we start the day's activity. We have come to realize that the students who regularly attend the Martial Arts Club rarely come for the martial arts content but rather for the environment we have created. The club members have a sense of ownership of the club, for they know their voice is substantial and esteemed.

Instead of working on martial arts techniques before the class begins, one of the students finds a basketball that was left from the previous class and starts shooting at one of the basketball rims. Soon, a few others join without being asked or directed, and it is obvious that their actions reflect the values of the club. Tyrone, one of the smaller kids, gambols around the basket striving to get a rebound, while Rick, one of the older, more talented kids, easily pulls one down and gives it to him. Andreas, the most dedicated, knowledgeable, and talented club member, pulls a mat off the wall to practice tumbling, which draws Jimmy over to watch. Andreas says, "You wanna try?" Jimmy replies, "Sure, if you gonna help me." Andreas works diligently to get Jimmy to perform a back flip. We realize that the entire period could go on like this with everyone having self-control, working on tasks, and a few helping others get better. Now that 15 minutes have passed and it seems that eight students are all that will show up, I signal to the group that it is time to begin. One more shot and tumble are performed and the kids willingly sit in a circle for the awareness talk. April, my assistant, asks, "Next time when we signal to start, can we not take one more shot or one more tumble?" They agree that next time they will be ready to start when one of us signals.

The formal beginning of the club starts out with an awareness talk to remind the students of the goals of the club. This brief reminder helps the students focus on the club's purpose by reviewing their responsibilities. Paul, another assistant, asks the group, "Who wants to try explaining what this club is about?" Someone says, "Not laugh at anyone." A fourth grader says, "Don't hit anybody." I ask, "What if we're sparring?" (which is a martial arts simulation of fighting where light contact is permitted) and the fourth grader replies, "Yeah, then it's alright, I think." Some of the novice members look bewildered. As they ponder this question, Andreas takes over. He explains the five responsibilities to the club members and what they each mean in his own words. He especially explains to the confounded fourth grader, "We learn fighting techniques but you have to have self-control and only use them if there's no other option." Paul asks the group, "What are other options?" A seventh grader says, "Just walk away, it ain't worth it." April asks, "What if they hit you?" The seventh grader says, "Then you gotta do what you gotta do." The program leaders all stress nonviolence and promote peaceful conflict resolution. However, we also stress that it is the club members' responsibility to use good judgment about how and when to use their martial arts skills.

Leadership and Martial Arts Activities

I ask the group, "Are we ready to begin?" There are a few nodding heads and everyone stands up ready to go. The group remains in a circle but spreads out a bit for fitness and a review of martial arts techniques. For club members who have been in the club for at least two weeks, this is their opportunity to choose and lead an exercise for the group (Level Four). This part of the club is routine, giving small leadership roles to those who volunteer. The younger kids really enjoy getting in the center of the circle and leading exercises for the group. We have taught the group to target three main fitness areas: strength, endurance, and flexibility. The club members have learned that during the strength exercises (e.g., push-ups), each club member should exercise until overloaded rather than performing a set number of repetitions. During the flexibility exercises (e.g., sit and reach), participants stress nonbounce activity and stretching until taut. During the endurance exercises (e.g., jogging in place), members should perform a maximum of 60 seconds. The kids understand how to run this activity quickly, allowing even the least skilled kids to have some leadership roles.

Six basic striking techniques (e.g., kicking, punching, and blocking) are routinely performed so club members can achieve and then improve on a working form of each technique. The techniques were chosen from a variety of martial arts styles to fit our preference, but they could easily be changed. The basic techniques are also run by the students but require a firm knowledge of how to teach the skills. To teach techniques, a club member needs to be able to break them down for the fledgling members to understand. The club members remain in a circle while one member enters the center to teach either one basic technique or a combination of techniques. Any club member who demonstrates sufficient knowledge of the techniques and a willingness to take on leadership responsibilities is given the chance. During this process we walk around and help the students who need assistance.

The fitness and basic technique activities accomplish two things. They provide leadership opportunities (Level Four), and they require the rest of the group to listen and act on their peers' instruction (Level Two). Because these teaching roles are new to many of the club members, the session sometimes moves slowly, requiring us to proctor the activity so the participants are not bored with the day's activity. The kids learn to be sensitive to and understanding of their peers' attempts to teach, usually following their instruction willingly.

Andreas, the most dedicated club member as mentioned earlier, leads the group through a martial arts form (Level Four). A form is a pattern of martial arts movements similar to a dance or gymnastics routine that is taught in a step-by-step command style. At this time we move aside, allowing Andreas to take over the club, decide the group organization, break down and teach the form, and provide positive and corrective feedback to his students. Andreas is effective in his leadership and can maintain full control of the club for approximately 10 minutes.

Self-Direction and Wrestling/Sparring

The last physical activity segment offers the students a choice between wrestling and sparring. The kids pick which activity they would like to work on, usually splitting the group in two equal parts. Until this point, the students have not had any physical contact with each other. The two university interns provide leadership for the two groups. They start by reminding their group of their self-control (Level One) and self-direction (Level Three) responsibilities during this activity. In either wrestling or sparring, the students need to understand that light contact is allowed but self-control is essential. They also need to be self-directed, because it is impossible for an instructor or a fellow club member to direct every individual action.

At one end of the gym, two club members wrestle while the rest of the group watches and give tips to them. One spectator says, "Roll 'em over, put your weight into 'em!" Another says, "Go for her right leg, pull, pull!" After two minutes they stop to let others take their turn. The next match has a seventh grader wrestling a fourth grader, a definite mismatch. Without needing us to explain, the seventh grader sees this as a time for leadership and compassion and helps the fourth grader learn some basic wrestling techniques.

On the other side of the gym two martial arts sparring matches are going on at the same time. When sparring first began we would referee, but we soon realized the kids do not need a referee and that experienced club members can handle the job themselves. Sparring seldom gets competitive, and often the kids giggle and laugh about the experience.

The Group Meeting and Reflection Time

As the session comes to an end with five minutes left, we call the group back into a circle to reflect on the day. We want to find out what the club members thought of the day, both positive and negative. A variety of responses are given, including, "It was great," "I liked the sparring," "The wrestling was cool," and "Nobody got an attitude." One morose club member lets the group know that during his wrestling match, his partner was antagonizing him. The partner lets the group know that he was playing around and didn't mean to upset anyone. I remind the club members that everyone should have a good experience in the club and that taunting people reflects poor self-control. Paul asks, "Is there anything that we could have done to make this a better place to be?" Two comments arise: "I was bored during the warm-ups," and "I didn't get a chance to teach any techniques." We agree to come up with possibilities to resolve these issues for next week and also ask the club members to come up with possible solutions.

Reflection time concludes the session. At this time, the club members self-evaluate their day's progress in relation to their five responsibilities. Just as in the Coaching Club and Energizers Club, the club members indicate with their thumbs their exhibition of four in-the-gym responsibilities and one outside-the-gym responsibility. This is not a time to reprimand students for their self-reflection. Even on the worst of days, club members learn that honesty is respected and that lessons can be learned from "bad days." We view this process as a growth experience with teachable moments in which problems are converted into individual and group goals.

Student Evaluations of the Club

Here are some of the club member comments:

- "Since I been in the Martial Arts Club, I don't get in fights anymore."
- "Nobody got an attitude in here, even when we sparring."
- I ask a club member, "On a scale of 1 to 10 what would you rate the day?" The club member responds, "Infinity."
- "I liked how we all helpin' each other."

- "I do great in here, but not so great in school."
- "I'm a girl and my cousin said girls don't wrestle, I never wrestled before, I'm good."

The Martial Arts Club sometimes has visitors. A doctoral student who was investigating violence prevention programs (Eddy, 1998) told us that one of our seventh-grade club members, when asked, "Why do you come here every week?" replied, "'Cause they treat us like people here."

Extended Day Clubs and Youth Development

Think for a minute about what kinds of school-sponsored physical activity programs are typically available: intramurals, interscholastic sport, and in-school physical education. Youth agencies also offer some version of interscholastic sport along with open gym time and some instructional programs. In these various physical activity program options, where do kids have the opportunity, regardless of skill level, to belong to an organization over multiple years, receive a lot of attention, have a voice, share power with the instructor, and learn life skills and values? Sure, we say sport builds character, that what we learn on the playing field carries over to life. But do we practice what we preach? Do we have specific goals and strategies designed to teach life skills and values?

Extended day clubs offer an alternative to typical physical activity programs for children and youth. They don't meet all kids' needs, and they can't be developed without considerable curricular and organizational flexibility. But they can offer something different than typical physical activity programming. The clubs described in this chapter reflect the state-of-the-art criteria for youth program development and use the responsibility model. In so doing, they offer kids a safe place, a small community atmosphere, a chance to make important individual and group decisions, and an enjoyable way to learn life skills and values. And because the club concept is versatile, clubs can be developed in both schools and youth agencies.

For Further Study

DeWitt Wallace-Reader's Digest Fund. (1996). *Strengthening the youth work profession*. New York: DeWitt Wallace-Reader's Digest Fund.

These two volumes, Progress and Opportunities *and* Resource Guide, *describe the emerging field of youth development and a wide variety of resources for learning more about specific youth-serving agencies, program evaluation, and other aspects of youth work.*

Eddy, M. (1998). *The role of physical activity in educational violence prevention programs.* Doctoral dissertation, UMI dissertation services, Ann Arbor, Michigan.

Martha Eddy's investigation of a variety of physical activity programs that purport to prevent violence includes an evaluation of some responsibility-based clubs.

Terry, J.P. (Ed.) *CYD Journal: Community Youth Development* (Formerly *New Designs for Youth Development).*

This journal focuses on innovative and successful extended day programs with an emphasis on underserved youth. Subscription information is available by calling 202-783-7949 x3103.

Chapter 8

Alternative School Physical Education

Don Hellison, James Kallusky, and Jim Stiehl

The alternative school movement ranges widely, from affluent private schools to diversion programs for disruptive, truant, or court-referred youth. Some alternative schools, for example Central Park East in Harlem (Meier, 1995), became exemplars for the development of similar schools. Some alternatives piloted outrageous ideas such as individualized instruction that later became part of the traditional public school (albeit a small part). Many, however, were snuffed out after a few years, when the initial leadership departed or the current climate became less hospitable. The search for alternatives to the traditional public school continues, most recently in the form of charter schools.

The escalation of misbehavior and absenteeism in American public schools has encouraged the creation of more alternative schools that target youth whose needs are not being met. Many public school districts now support one or more alternative schools for underserved youth. The state of California requires that each public high school operate a "continuation school" for so-called at-risk students. Other alternatives are private schools that exist on grants often written by teachers in these schools, an exemplar being Open Meadow Learning Center in Portland, Oregon. Most of these alternatives serve high school students, even though it is clear that some kids are dropout-bound well before the ninth grade.

Alternative schools usually have several advantages in comparison with traditional public schools:

- Smaller school enrollment
- Small class size

- Student involvement for two or more years
- Teachers interested in working with kids who have not been successful in public schools
- Less specialized, more student-centered teacher roles
- Curricular flexibility
- Site-based management
- A sense of community in the school

I (Don) taught in three alternative high schools over a 10-year period and experienced all of these things. School size ranged from 40 to 100 students, and I never taught a class with more than 15 students. In general, teachers were more progressive, more interested in students as people, and more concerned about helping them than in public high schools (in my experience). Teachers helped to make school policy decisions, including the admission of students and the structure of each school day, and had considerable control over what and how they taught their classes. Yet each school seemed to have a clear purpose. As Raywid (1994, p. 28) put it, alternative schools take "their character, theme, or emphasis from the strengths and interests of the teachers who conceived them."

Teacher specialization is particularly strong in large public high schools. However, in 10 years as a part-time alternative school teacher, I taught physical education, history, and sex education; ran an after-school martial arts club; served lunch; interviewed incoming students and their families; consulted with parole officers; and attended endless teacher meetings to shape and reshape school policies.

These alternative school characteristics facilitate implementation of the responsibility model, as shown in the following examples:

- Small class size, a sense of community at the school level, and student-centered teachers all support the philosophy of putting kids first—that is, teaching the whole person, prioritizing the student–teacher relationship, and respecting students' strengths, individuality, voices, and capacity for decision making.
- Small class size facilitates the individualized and empowerment-oriented instructional strategies of the model.
- Less specialized, student-centered teachers will be more interested in, and supportive of, the model.
- Curricular flexibility permits the physical education teacher to implement the model without having to view teaching as a "subversive activity."

Raywid (1994) described state-of-the-art criteria for alternative schools. These criteria are strikingly similar to the state-of-the-art criteria for youth program development described in chapter 3 and shown in tables 3.1 and 7.1:

- Build on student strengths (see criterion 1).
- Empower students (see criterion 4).
- Keep the school and classes small (see criterion 8).
- Develop a local connection (see criterion 9).
- Operate separate from the system (see criterion 10).
- Be first and foremost student-centered rather than subject matter specialists (see criteria 1, 2, 3, 4, 11).

Studies of the resiliency of inner-city children and youth, which focus on those who succeed despite their environment, also support some of these criteria (Wang, Heartel, & Walberg, 1994). This support is particularly important, because resilience is in short supply among youth referred to alternative schools.

- Provide training and experiences in self-motivation and autonomy. Emphasize a personal sense of purpose (see criterion 4).
- Provide opportunities for success, task mastery, and problem solving (see criterion 1).
- Build on prior cultural knowledge rather than exploiting weaknesses (see criteria 1, 3).
- Create an atmosphere of belonging and involvement. Emphasize positive social interactions, and teach peer support (see criterion 8).

In short, the unique characteristics of many alternative schools provide fertile ground for the development of physical activity youth programs based on the state-of-the-art criteria for youth program development and the responsibility model.

Students whose needs are not being met by traditional public schools as reflected by poor grades, absenteeism, and misbehavior have a chance of being *Expelled to a Friendlier Place* (Gold & Mann, 1984). Such a "friendlier place," however, may well have no in-school physical education program, other than some recreational time. Faculties are small, and physical education expertise is not usually a top priority. As a result, volunteer physical education teachers are often welcome. Pete Mathiesen, for example, places selected Cal State

Chico physical education majors in continuation schools in northern California as part of a special program.

Alternative schools provide an opportunity to run a different kind of in-school physical education program. Here are some examples.

Visiting an Alternative In-School Physical Education Program

The following is an example of the kind of physical education lessons I taught while at an alternative school:

1. Self-direction time: It's fifth period. Kids drift into the gym. No one changes clothes. Some wander over to the equipment, take something, and with a friend or alone begin to practice. A few bump and set volleyballs to each other or against the wall, others shoot baskets, one jumps rope, and another kicks a padded shield held by another student. Still others sit, some by themselves, others talking and laughing together. I cruise around, taking role (which is easy with 15 students), talking to students who aren't active, giving feedback here and there to those who are. (My third period martial arts class has self-direction time built into the lesson. After a warm-up period, students gradually progress from teacher-directed drills to 15 minutes of self-direction time with a minimum of supervision.)

2. Awareness talk: When class starts, everyone saunters over and sits in a circle on the floor. I recognize those who were self-directed before class started and remind all students that they have made "personal physical education plans" that they could work on before class and that they can change these plans. Students are also quickly reminded that everyone has rights and feelings; that physical education is about giving it a try rather than excelling; and that if the class is to be successful, someone besides the teacher has to provide some leadership.

3. Fitness time: Everyone stands up, some begrudgingly, for fitness time. A cardboard box on the side labeled "fifth period" contains the students' fitness contracts. A few pull out their contract, glance at it, throw it back. Others start stretching or jogging or doing push-ups. (Even though they know that they need to raise their body temperature before doing anything strenuous, only a few do, so I make mental note to mention this next period.) A few go to the stage and are led through a set fitness routine by another student. I go over to a few who aren't doing anything. "It's choice time. Either your contract or up on the stage with Steven . . . or I can't give you any credit. I will still love you, of course."

Some smiles and giggles in response, and all but one kid reluctantly get up and go over to the box or up on the stage. I keep an eye on the clock. In a 45-minute period, 5 minutes for the awareness talk and 15 minutes for fitness still leaves 25 minutes for skill development and a game.

4. Skill development: This class meets three times a week for a semester. Skill development focuses on volleyball two periods every week for the entire semester, so that students can experience skill development and success in a game. (Almost all of these students have flunked physical education in public school, along with just about everything else.) Twice in the semester, a team of university physical education majors visit, so that these alternative school students can test their skills and see their progress. This also creates a team atmosphere in the class. As Joni notes, "We got to practice if we want to do well against the college."

Every Friday, different activities are introduced and, by the vote of students, continued or not on succeeding Fridays. Sometimes two or three activities can take place simultaneously, as long as students are self-directed enough to handle the independence. This semester-long volleyball with "open" Fridays is permissible due to the curricular flexibility of alternative schools.

Today it's volleyball, and the instructions are simple: "Do the progression with the set." This is part of a familiar routine, so students grab balls and begin setting, first to themselves five times (in a row if possible; if not, whatever they can do), then against the wall, then to a partner. Most work at it, a few talk and giggle. I wander around, giving cues to improve their form and gently reminding talkers to get started. Then, glancing at the clock, I say, "Okay. Quickly pair up. One coach, one player. The coach tosses the ball to the player who underarm passes it back five times. Coach should look for straight arms, lift with legs rather than swing arms, and hit ball at midpoint on arms. Go!" Again, this is familiar territory, so the pairs switch coaches, then get together and tell each other how well the partner coached (not how they played). Both of these drills take about 12 minutes; then it's game time.

5. The game: Two kids volunteer to coach. Their duties are to make fair teams (off to the side while others are practicing), to set the initial rotation, and to call time-outs for corrections in strategy or to deal with attitude problems. They also teach and help to monitor rule modifications, the most important one being that the ball must be hit twice before being sent over the net (except on the serve). Thirteen students are in class today, but one wants to practice on the sidelines rather than play, which is always a choice. As a result, both teams field six players. Sometimes teams have seven players, in which case the rotation

includes one station off the court. If a team has fewer than six players, I play. (This is another benefit of alternative school physical education; in public school classes of 30 or more, it was difficult to play while at the same time observing students who were playing in another game or doing another activity.) The game is still in progress when it is time for the group meeting.

6. The group meeting: Students are asked if any problems need to be dealt with. One student complains about not being able to complete the game. I ask who agrees with this complaint; two other students raise their hands. "Doesn't seem to be an overwhelming problem." Then I raise a concern about coming to class stoned. Everyone knows that school policy requires suspension for drug use, so there is palpable appreciation for being able to deal with this problem "off the record." I tell them that it is difficult to hide drug use in a physical education class, and everyone seems to agree with Beth Anne: "If it happens in here again, send them to Terri" (the school director).

7. Reflection time: Then students dig their journals out of the fifth period box and lie on the floor writing a paragraph about how they handled their four in-class responsibilities that day and whether they carried out any of these responsibilities outside the gym since the last physical education meeting. As they finish, they toss their journals and pencils back in the box and head out the door.

These excerpts from letters I received give some idea of a few students' evaluations of this kind of program a few years after they have left the school:

- "In your class you could always learn something . . . about how to deal and cope with everyday life and reality. Although your class was PE, I learned a great deal more [such as how] not to be quick to judge other people."
- "I honestly believe the one thing you personally helped me with was learning to control my temper, and that has really stayed with me."
- "I learned that it doesn't pay to put on an image of being tough."

Visiting In-School Physical Education in a Charter School

Arriving with a small group of college students, we notice that physical education for these 25 middle school students is already underway. Emphasis thus far has been on teamwork. In fact, teamwork is what sold our physical education program to the principal and several teachers in the first place. Whereas the school staff expressed only lukewarm support for a physical activity program, they were eager to include activities that fostered social responsibility. Results thus far have sustained their support. As a case in point, last week when two youngsters were beginning to fight at recess, a classmate intervened and helped resolve the conflict in a nonviolent way. When the principal asked about the incident, the 11-year-old "peacemaker" responded, "I learned about that in PE."

The first 15 minutes of this physical education class involves fitness time, which by now has become a familiar routine for these youngsters. As soon as students enter the gym, they select a partner and ready themselves for continuous movement time (CMT). A large sign next to the door reminds them of their gym-time teamwork agreements (e.g., include everyone, solve problems positively, honor others' differences, be a role model). Posted next to these are today's exercises, each with simple written instructions alongside a stick-figure portrayal. These same stick-figure images have been placed on the inside caps of tennis ball cans that are strewn across the gym floor.

Pairs proceed to a can of their choice, look at the image through a hole in the bottom of the can, and then perform the exercise during about two minutes of spirited music. Each time the music stops, pairs run to another can and, during a 10- or 15-second interlude, prepare themselves for the next exercise, which commences at the sound of more music. Today's CMT included some exercises concocted by students; until now all exercises were devised by the teacher.

CMT lasts approximately 20 minutes, followed by a five-minute awareness talk. Lately, a topic in many of these talks has been how to include everyone. Skills and interests vary widely in this class, so discussions have centered around issues such as ways of altering an activity so everyone is challenged appropriately; recognizing and openly discussing strengths that each player can contribute to the game; listening to everyone's ideas and learning to compromise; and persisting with a strategy, tactic, or effort in the face of adversity.

Having completed CMT and an awareness talk, the group now is engaged in skill development and game play. The teaching method being used is a tactical games approach (Griffin, Mitchell, and Oslin, 1997), which is a combination of skill and game play. Because teamwork is a key goal in this physical education class, the tactical approach was selected because it encourages students to solve problems and make decisions within a games context. Furthermore, because this approach is student-paced and game-centered, it also can entice students who previously have been discouraged from participating in physical activity, especially in team situations.

The youngsters are playing Tapu-Ae (Morris and Stiehl, 1999), a game involving two teams that score points by throwing a ball at the opposing team's milk carton, which is defended by a goalie. Players have different types of responsibilities (e.g., goalies protect cartons from being knocked over, shooters throw at cartons, rovers retrieve missed shots and pass the ball to their own teammates). Perhaps more important, each type of player must remain in his or her own designated area. Unlike some invasion games such as basketball, soccer, and hockey, players in Tapu-Ae cannot trespass into areas that have been designated for other types of players. In other words, players do not intermingle in one another's territories. This is a useful feature of the game because it promotes teamwork while minimizing players' concerns about being interfered with by opposing players.

A five-minute group meeting follows today's game. One player announces that, rather than hearing "just do it," she enjoys being encouraged to try her best and being permitted to make mistakes. Another suggests modifying the size of some playing areas while also designating one rover from each team to stray into the opponent's territory. After brief discussion among players, both suggestions are approved. Finally, the instructor mentions that next time he will ask for one volunteer from each team to serve as a coach. Each coach will receive specific instructions before the game.

Reflection time typically involves writing in journals. Today's class is an infrequent example of too little time to make journal entries. Some students seem disappointed, some not. A topic for today might have related to why they might want to be a coach, or what they expect from a coach. Almost always, however, they are asked to write a paragraph about how their performance compared against their gym responsibilities.

Conducting an Outdoor and Adventure Program in an Alternative School

Although chapter 5 is devoted to outdoor and adventure programs, the following example underscores the potential for promoting responsibility through outdoor activities in an alternative school setting. As with the previous charter school example, the responsibility model is modified to fit the needs, goals, and resources at our alternative school. In the program described here, the 25 participants (16 boys, 9 girls) attend an alternative high school that is predominately Hispanic (85 percent) and serves youngsters from low-income neighborhoods. For various reasons, the students in the school have not experienced success in the public school mainstream. Most of them now have a positive sense of the value of a secondary education and are working to acquire a high school diploma.

From the perspective of the school staff, one major obstacle that confronts many of the students in the school is the chaos in their lives (unstable family structure, drugs, gangs, poverty). Consequently, a primary school goal is to provide a learning environment that allows students to temporarily leave the chaos behind. The environment is safe, open, and caring, yet structured enough to permit each student to explore his or her potential as an individual and as a group member. Our outdoor program is designed to reinforce the school's goals, keeping in mind the youngsters' needs and capitalizing on available resources.

Two 15-week programs are conducted each year. The group meets on Friday mornings for two hours and sometimes for the entire day. Students apply to be included in the program, and 20 to 25 are selected by the school staff according to criteria such as school performance, ability to contribute to the program, and/or the likelihood of positive growth from the experience. Students can drop out at any time, yet few do.

The program is presented to students as a journey culminating in a multiday activity (mountain biking, winter camping, rock climbing, white-water rafting). It is portrayed visually as an expedition that will progress through a series of landmarks and milestones (depicted as road signs). With input from the group, the agreed-upon milestones for this journey, a weekend rock climbing camp, include

1. respect (operationalized as listening to others' ideas and opinions, communicating clearly, and taking care of their surroundings);
2. cooperation (understood to mean solving problems together, resolving conflicts appropriately, and looking for one another's strengths);
3. determination (taking risks and not being a quitter); and
4. sharing (helping others and sharing yourself with an intent to strengthen the group).

Although all landmarks are revisited frequently, sharing is the most risky for many students. It requires not only sharing joys but also fears and perceived weaknesses. Yet, when enough trust develops for students to share themselves fully with one another, the group is strengthened and individuals become much more self confident. All of the meetings take place away from the alternative school, and students have commented that because of this they feel less restricted and are free to be more themselves and not compelled to act in certain ways as when they are at school. Thus, we use a local playing field, the nearby university's climbing wall, a community gym, a challenge ropes course, and a mountain rock climbing site.

The group undertakes activities that promote the landmarks. Respect is initiated through games and problem-solving scenarios. The initiatives are designed to help youngsters enjoy one another's company while beginning to understand and honor each member's value and possible contributions to the group. Cooperation blends nicely with these activities and becomes the basis for underscoring communication, which is so necessary for success at the next activity, climbing at the artificial rock wall. During climbing sessions, the young climbers set goals and, with the support of their belayers and other group members, strive to achieve those goals. They learn knots, conduct safety checks on one another, and use specific commands (between the climber and belayer), which encourage effective communication and enhance the climbing experience. Determination is also highlighted on the climbing wall, where achieving personal goals is a product of individual effort and group support. These three landmarks are then reinforced at the challenge ropes course, another experience on our path to the rock climbing weekend.

Each meeting with the students includes a warm-up activity, an awareness talk (the plan for the day, review of the four road signs, and group goal setting), activities (the experience), individual journal entries (personal, written reflections), and a closure that includes a group debrief (verbal reflections to include how the day's experiences might be applied elsewhere). During this closure period, sharing is encouraged and nurtured. For these students, sharing one's thoughts and fears is sometimes frightening. As the group progresses through the landmarks, however, their willingness to share emerges slowly, thereby bonding the students and making them stronger, more cohesive, and more successful.

Because we operate away from the students' campus, one teacher from their school participates in our program. The teacher provides an important and necessary link between us and the kids. He assists by providing follow-through activities and discussions with the students in between our weekly outdoor sessions. His valuable participation also gives us insight about issues and events that might influence our ongoing plans for the group.

The Teen Parent Program

Some youth programs in physical activity are developed simply because students in alternative schools do not have access to physical education.

This was the case for 18 pregnant teenagers in Colorado at the time when I (James) was completing graduate school. While teaching math and physical education in one alternative high school, I discovered that the school district's pregnant teens were being educated elsewhere, in a house: yes, a two-story house that the school district had bought solely for the placement of pregnant teenagers. The students in this program had committed a wrongdoing according to the district, a wrongdoing that school administrators believed warranted placing them away from the general student population. These "relocated" students ranged from 14 to 18 years old. They were placed in an area of the city away from the high schools so that other young women would not imitate the behaviors that led to their pregnancies, a rationale that to this day I do not understand. They needed physical education credits to graduate from high school, yet they had no teacher to provide them instruction, so I volunteered. Using the responsibility model seemed more relevant here than in any other setting with which I had been associated.

In deciding to meet with the director of the teen program, who was the students' teacher for all curricular subjects as well, I made my first visit to the schoolhouse (literally). I was immediately taken back by the crowded facility—crowded, yet there were no books, no equipment of any kind, and barely enough chairs. These students were, in a word, underserved.

The director happily approved my proposal during that meeting, and I was to begin teaching the following week. The program would take place every day for an hour for the entire school year. I had no idea how to go about using physical activity with pregnant teens, so I did my homework—at the county hospital. I met a few times with a nurse who provided me with information on the dos and don'ts of activity for pregnant women. I learned a lot.

I began the program by getting to know the students. We sat upstairs and told stories about our lives for the first two days. I ended the week by introducing the responsibility model and transferring the information that I had gained from the nurse to the students. We did not do any physical activity that week. We did not have any equipment for activity, so I also spent that first week securing equipment from the university that I was attending and from other schools in the district.

I arrived at the program the next week with two exercise bikes and 20 aerobics mats. We did a lot of stretching on those mats that week (both inside the house and in the yard), and I taught the students how to take their pulse while on the bikes. It was important for the students not to attain a heart rate that was harmful to their pregnancy, so we did this routinely until all of them could regulate their heart rates with complete accuracy.

In the ensuing week, I secured a small donation for the program. I purchased a few volleyball and badminton sets and placed them in the backyard. After doing these activities for a couple of weeks, the students were ready to begin developing their own activity programs. Consequently, the students were now making choices between fitness (exercise bikes and stretching) and sports (volleyball and badminton). Their individualized programs went on for a while, but the weather in Colorado began to change (cold!), limiting the program to indoors.

To complement the responsibility model, we began to discuss aspects related to larger issues in the students' lives (Responsibility Level Five: outside the "gym"). Generated from these conversations were the notions of making a living to provide for their children and how the goals of the responsibility model could help them not only in securing a job but in finding a career. We explored occupations in a set of books provided by a guidance counselor from another school. We were still doing some fitness activities at the beginning of each session (they made me wear an empathy belly to simulate pregnancy so I would know what they were going through), but most of our time was devoted to our newly emerged theme, career development. This actually led to a few field trips, culminating in conversations between working adults and the students.

It was winter in Colorado, but realizing that we had to devote more time to activity so that the students were eligible for course credit in physical education, I acquired space in a junior high school gymnasium that was only four blocks from the teen parent house. I moved the mats and the bikes to the gym, and our routine changed again. Warm-up took place in our walk to the gym every morning, and basketball was added to our curriculum. The students now had more choices.

We finished out the year in the gymnasium. Most of them had had their babies by this time so we took the babies with us. We were late to the gym most mornings because the neighbors between the teen parent house and the gym were now stopping us to say "Hi" to the kids and, of course, their new babies.

Throughout the year, in the students' journals and during reflection time after each lesson, a strong interest in the responsibility model was evident. It made sense to them. They could easily relate what was going on in their lives to the goals in the responsibility model. It was making a difference not only in the way they treated others but also in the way they felt about themselves. Noticing that the students were constantly comparing this program with their previous experiences in physical education, at the end of our year together, I interviewed them. The following is what they said about the program in comparison with their other physical education experiences.

Participants' Perceptions of Traditional Physical Education and the Teen Parent Program

Three major themes emerged from the interviews concerning the students' feelings and perceptions of past physical education experiences. The first theme reflected that the teachers in their regular physical education classes determined experiences and goals for them. This is a common phenomenon in traditional physical education. When asked about the main differences between this program and her past physical education classes, Mary replied, "I don't know. I didn't really like my old classes. My teachers were jerks, always wanted things their way. It was kinda' hard when you couldn't reach their goals." Lara concisely commented, "They set the goals for us. We didn't have a choice or anything. We had to do what they said or our grade would go down. I didn't like it." Ana said, "I used to get mad because they set the goals for you and if I couldn't reach it, I'd give up hope and think I couldn't do anything."

The second theme, and in relation to a teacher-dominated environment, was that success was entirely based on performance. One participant revealed that not only did the teacher base success on performance, but her fellow students also reinforced this pervasive philosophy. Here is Ana's comment: "In PE before, they [her peers] would tell me, oh well, you're no good and you don't know how to do things, but in this class the girls don't tell me that I'm no good. They just say, 'you are going to do better today.'" Lara stated: "There [in previous classes] you couldn't play certain sports when you wanted to and, like I said, they set the goals for you, and here, we can reach our own goals. It doesn't matter if you are good or bad as long as we have fun, and we try, and put effort into what we do."

The third theme to emerge from the interviews regarding past physical education experiences was that no significant learnings took place. When asked what she had learned in her last physical education class, Krista simply stated, "Not anything I'd use today." Mary said, "Nothing really. I really didn't want to learn anything. I felt kinda' worthless in that class and didn't like what we were doing and I really didn't want to do anything. I didn't pay attention."

Participants' Perceptions of the Responsibility Model in Physical Education

Three major themes emerged from the interviews concerning the participants' thoughts about the responsibility model. First, activities were enjoyable, even when the participants were pregnant. Lara said, "I enjoy coming to this class." Krista stated, "I like it here; it's fun."

The second theme to surface had to do with the students' opportunities to relate their feelings to others and the teacher. "You give us a chance to open up and tell you about the way we feel," commented Krista. Mary then echoed, "When we have problems, you know, you sit and talk with us and help us solve our problems."

The last theme to emerge regarding general perceptions of the program was that learnings went beyond the subject matter with the responsibility model. I asked Ana, "What are the main differences between this physical education class and your old physical education class?" She replied: " [In here] I've learned a lot about everything and it's important stuff to me. . . . I only can't think about myself; I've got to think about my future, and my baby, and I get to do that here." Ana later went on to explain, "I've learned a lot about myself, and about PE, and about the world."

Behavioral Changes The most salient behavioral changes centered on the treatment of others. Ana stated, "I've learned a lot of stuff, like to communicate better with people, you know, we play the game to cooperate." She later said, "I learned to talk to people and cooperate, join together, and be friends." Mary said, "I learned that I can be a nicer person. I used to be, you know, mad and hatred. . . . I finally realized that, if I want to be treated nicer, I have to treat other people nice." She later explained, "Here, everybody treated me the way I wanted to be treated, like a person." Ana reinforced Mary's statement by saying, "I learned that you have to respect people, how they feel, and to never give up hope. To always try your best." The change was subtler for Lara. She believed that she had always been able to get along with her peers, but she said that she now got along better with, "people like you, you know, teachers."

Affective Changes Ana was one of the students to express affective changes due to the program. These changes focused on her self-esteem. Her comments, which were quite emotional (she was crying at the time), are worthy of a lengthy quotation:

> When I come to this class I feel like a human being and before I didn't because everybody always put me down and stuff. . . . I have a lot more self-esteem than I used to have. I used to, you know, not want to do anything because I didn't feel like I could do it and this class makes me feel that I can do things. . . . Talking is hard for me. It's hard for me just to talk to anybody, but when you are here, I can talk, especially if I need any help.

She later explained that her academic performance was enhanced by her experience with the responsibility model in physical activity. She mentioned that being able to talk about her problems with the other students and me allowed her to concentrate on schoolwork, instead of focusing on her problems throughout the day.

Students were not the only ones to notice such changes. The Teen Parent Program director pointed out, "They feel a sense of unity in there. In fact, I can tell the difference between the kids who go there to PE and attend all the time compared to the kids who don't attend. . . . There's a sense of teamness between those kids."

These quotes strongly suggest that the responsibility model can provide students with learnings related to what is actually going on in their lives. These interviews revealed that the students experienced many positive changes because of the responsibility model. This does not imply that any of these young women are less at-risk because of the program. It does, however, suggest that these students at least thought about their behaviors and feelings.

The students' thoughts also suggest that, at least for some of them, their experiences in the program provided them with a sense of effectiveness, which they transferred to their present school setting. In this regard, the Teen Parent Program director expressed the following:

> Well, I think that, in this type of physical education, these students have learned decision making. They are now setting goals for themselves. I think they have learned to interact with other kids better. . . . I think that when they go back to normal school they will have a better sense of how to act.

Many of the changes reported by these students may not be solely due to the teaching approach per se. Many of the students' perceptions may have been influenced by the difference in class size between public school physical education and alternative physical education programs. Other constraints in public school physical education may have contributed to the differences, or the young women's responses simply may be due to the attention they received in this alternative school setting.

The Walkabout Program

Though not necessarily located in an alternative school, the Walkabout Program had all of the characteristics and criteria of alternative school settings as outlined at the beginning of this chapter. This program for youth embraced these notions and created an environment that was, in a sense, a small-scale charter school itself. It did so by engaging 30 underserved youth from the State of Colorado in an eight-week educational summer experience. Students selected for this program were males and females, ranging from 16 to 19 years of age, who represented the low socioeconomic status and regional diversity that exist in Colorado. Representatives from the Governor's Job Training Office of Colorado, school principals, probation officers, and parents identified these students for the program. Most of the participants for this program were, at the time of their selection and ensuing recruitment, involved with gang activity, teen pregnancy, illicit drug use, and the juvenile court system. These youth were at risk of dropping out of school, unemployment, and, for that matter, dropping out of society. Walkabout was designed to prevent these social ills from coming to fruition.

Walkabout secured its roots from an academic model, Youth Opportunities Unlimited (YOU), first explored at St. Edward's University in Austin, Texas, in 1972. YOU served college freshmen of seasonal and migrant farm-worker families by providing them academic enhancement courses over a six-week educational experience. After the success of the program was noted, in terms of academic achievement of these college students, a similar project was designed for migrant high school students. Although academic enhancement was critical to the model, the addition of a work experience component greatly improved the design. Research and evaluation of this program indicated that this model would work well with any secondary school population, especially those considered to be at risk.

In 1988, the YOU conceptual framework was established at the University of Northern Colorado (UNC). This model combined education, work experience, and a wide range of supportive services in an intensive eight-week period; supportive services focused on health, wellness, and counseling. These factors, plus the requirement of living on campus, created a "total immersion" program for the 14- to 15-year-old students who attended. Implementation and evaluation of the YOU program occurred over a six-year period (1988-1993), with results showing significant academic enhancement and positive affective changes in its students. When James became director of the YOU program in 1994, the Walkabout program emerged.

Walkabout

The name "Walkabout" was chosen as a metaphor for the direction and goals of this "new" university-based program. Taken from an Aboriginal rite of passage, walkabout refers to a nomadic search for personal meaning in what is now known as the Australian Outback. During this journey, Aboriginal youth truly experience the world they live in. Filled with possibility and natural consequences, this physical and spiritual journey teaches adolescents the extent of responsibility and the value of social privilege. The walkabout is an adventure that ritualizes the departure from childhood dependencies toward becoming a self-reliant, contributing member of society.

Conceptually, the Walkabout program model was designed to celebrate the transitional stage of growth and development known as adolescence. Within the modified YOU framework, a summer residential program known as Walkabout emerged at the UNC. The broad purpose of Walkabout was to introduce success where it was often absent in adolescents: in vocational skills, in academics, and in personal and social growth and responsibility. Toward the goal of developing adult awareness and subsequent responsibilities, the Walkabout program consisted of four integral parts:

1. Academic enhancement
2. Work experience/career awareness
3. The Walkabout adventure
4. The responsibility model, which underscores other components

Typical Day in the Walkabout Program

The director and program coordinator relieve the dorm directors (one male, one female) at 6:00 A.M. and greet the students. Students wake up and prepare for the day, convening at the university dining hall for breakfast. The director facilitates a brief talk about our daily responsibilities, and at 7:45 A.M. the students scatter to their jobs. Most of the work experience component is located on campus (maintenance, clerical, mechanical, preschool), but one group of six students are driven to a local business to cover graffiti with murals they designed the week before. They are the artistic community service group. All students work for four hours and meet back at the dining hall by 12:15 P.M.

The four teachers and two academic tutors join the students for lunch and, after lunch, walk with them to the classrooms located in the Social Sciences Building on campus. The director meets with the entire group for 15 minutes, discussing and relating the goals of the responsibility model to both their morning's work experience and their upcoming classroom experience. The students then exit for their first class. They attend four class sessions, each 50 minutes in duration and with only eight students in each class.

After school, the students, teachers, and academic tutors go to the dormitory to rest or simply hang out. Four peer counselors (UNC college students) join them at 6:00 P.M. We all go to dinner for an hour and then the students are off to their dorm rooms for homework from 7:00 to 7:30 P.M. The teachers are there to answer specific questions, but all staff assist the students in their schoolwork.

The director then facilitates another discussion, using the responsibility model to guide the dialogue. This may last 10 minutes or, at other times, an hour. This is followed by evening activities, or choices. Programming in this area was designed to offer the students choices for the constructive use of leisure time. Offerings include such activities as basic guitar instruction, personal expression through different art media, Spanish language acquisition, community service projects, sports and exercise, and computer literacy.

The dorm directors show up at 10:00 P.M., as the students are finishing their evening activity, and lights go out at 10:30 P.M.

Outcomes

In cooperation with the local school district, all students who successfully completed coursework in mathematics, language arts, cultural studies, and physical education received credit toward their high school graduation. As a condition of this agreement, all students were required to attend (Monday through Friday) one hour of instruction in each of these academic areas. For each hour of instruction, the student–teacher ratio was 8:1, and two additional academic tutors were available throughout the program as needed. Because the Walkabout served some youth that were 18 and 19 years of age and were near the transition from high school to college, a higher education component was included in the design of the model. These students (6 of the 30) attended a community college for a special session of coursework throughout the eight-week residential summer program.

Work experience and career awareness were especially significant for the age group targeted by Walkabout. Each student in the Walkabout program was placed in a position of employment within the community or the university campus. Conditions of this employment required each student to arrive on time and exchange four hours of service for compensation. Throughout the period of employment, the Walkabout director evaluated each student for both conduct and work habits using the responsibility model. At the conclusion of the eight-week program, compensation was paid directly to the student at no cost to the employer through a grant.

In addition to the program emphases of academic enhancement and work experience, each evening was devoted to a number of individually selected activities (Responsibility Level Three: self-direction). Weekends were devoted to enrichment activities that could be accomplished on campus, in the community, or outside the community in other regions of the state. Students experienced museums, performing arts, professional baseball games, hiking, water skiing, and amusement parks.

As a culminating learning experience, during the seventh week of the program the students were involved in an outdoor adventure experience. Choosing from backpacking, technical rock climbing, or alpine mountaineering, each student spent eight days in a closely supervised wilderness setting practicing their newly learned skills. In line with the program theme (Walkabout), certain prerequisite skills for adventure served as focal points within the academic curriculum. Examples include basic first aid and adventure education in physical education, map and compass use in mathematics, and the social significance of the Aboriginal Walkabout in cultural studies.

Some of the students had a hard time taking such responsibility at the beginning of the program, but all showed signs of enjoyment and accomplishment by the end of the eighth week. We held a graduation at which their families and friends helped to celebrate their achievements, some traveling five hours to attend. There was not a dry eye in the house.

Walkabout's strategy for helping Colorado's kids was deceptively simple—giving youngsters worthwhile experiences within a support system that offered a healthy future and using the responsibility model for all operational aspects of the program.

Conclusion

Physical education is often neglected in alternative schools that target kids in trouble, because of the flexibility of the curriculum (physical education can be ignored), the issues students bring to the school (basic skills are weak), and often the lack of physical education training among the small staff of teachers. Yet, as we have shown, alternative schools provide attractive settings for putting the responsibility model into practice with underserved youth.

Our five examples also demonstrate the range of possibilities for putting the responsibility model into practice in an alternative setting. Whether you are interested in teaching in-school physical education, creating a summer "school," working with adventure or outdoor education, teaching leadership, or focusing on teen parenthood or other specific issues, the alternative setting might be the right fit for your program ideas.

For Further Study

Meier, D. (1995). *The power of their ideas: Lessons from a small school in Harlem.* Boston: Beacon Press.

A powerful description of a very successful small school in an underserved community.

Raywid, M.A. (1994). Alternative schools: The state of the art. *Educational Leadership, 52,* 26-31.

A succinct description of the strengths and potentials of alternative schools for underserved youth.

Chapter 9

Mentor Programs

Tom Martinek and Melissa Parker

It is Wednesday afternoon around 4:00 and Stephen Mathews is on his way to the Boys and Girls Clubs. Stephen is an undergraduate student from the local university who volunteers as a mentor. For the past year he has worked with Carlos Ortiz, who lives in Morningside Homes, a public housing complex. Carlos is 15 years old and the oldest sibling of a family of six brothers and sisters. The father left home when he was five years old and has not returned. Carlos took over many of the responsibilities of the home while his mother worked at a local fabric mill in the city. When Stephen arrives he finds Carlos waiting by one of the pool tables. Carlos breaks out in a big smile when he sees Stephen enter the club.

At first, getting Carlos to open up was not easy for Stephen. Fortunately, their relationship grew from session to session. Sometimes the two would just hang out together and shoot hoop. More recently, however, Stephen has convinced Carlos to set some goals for school. Carlos struggled throughout his school years and saw little value in getting good grades. Now he is in the tenth grade and still skipping classes, ignoring homework, being disruptive, and not paying attention in class. He feels that "hustling" girls and "just doing his thing" in school legitimizes his status among his peers and his neighborhood. Stephen learned that working with Carlos required getting him to deal with the norms of the school culture without disconnecting him from his own culture and value system. Now they are best friends, and Stephen has become a key figure in Carlos's life and his willingness to stay in school.

Mentors like Stephen are found in numerous settings like schools, detention centers, courts, churches, YMCAs, YWCAs, and community recreation centers. Through a mentoring relationship, volunteers like Stephen Mathews make a significant commitment of time and energy to foster academic, social, moral, and artistic growth in youngsters plagued by the ills of poverty. In Greensboro and Greeley, we have used mentoring as a way of augmenting our efforts to get youngsters to apply the responsibility values to everyday life. Here are some things we have learned.

What Is a Mentor?

The term *mentor* is derived from Greek mythology. Mentor was a loyal friend and advisor of the king of Ithaca, Odysseus. While Odysseus was off battling in the Trojan War, he made Mentor the guardian of his son, Telemachus. A strong bond between them grew as a result of Mentor's contribution to Telemachus's moral and spiritual growth. Since that time, the term has come to mean a wise and loyal advisor, teacher, or coach (Smink, 1990).

Mentoring has become the buzzword in many programs that attempt to give underserved kids the tools to overcome the many barriers caused by poverty. Mentoring requires that a significant adult work with a child or youngster. Mentors can play an important role in helping underserved youngsters overcome social and economic barriers created by poverty, racism, and neglect.

Mentoring can mean many things—from simply being a friend to motivating and equipping a youngster to competently interact with others and solve day-to-day problems. Other than creating a positive adult relationship, one of the most common aspects of mentoring programs is individual goal setting. Group goal setting is also used where the emphasis is on promoting group values and membership. An underlying assumption of goal setting is that by creating and achieving goals, youngsters will gain some autonomy and control in dealing with day-to-day challenges and setbacks.

What makes mentoring and goal setting work, especially in getting kids to be more responsible for themselves and their actions toward others? We have found that sound mentoring and goal setting require careful thought and intent. Our mentoring programs are all connected to their respective physical activity programs and the responsibility model described in the previous chapters. Although mentors and their students meet in the activity programs, they work together outside the gym on classroom behavior or academic goals that are guided by the responsibility model. Mentors facilitate this process and keep track of the progress.

This chapter attempts to put you in a better position to be a successful mentor, or to run a successful mentoring program. First, we provide an overview of what makes a good mentor. Personal qualities needed to establish and maintain an ongoing relationship with a youngster are highlighted. Second, we describe some of the things that good mentors do. Special attention is given to ways of connecting with your kid and to goal-setting strategies. Third, we discuss how kids typically respond to mentoring and goal setting. Fourth, ideas for keeping track of the mentoring sessions are suggested. The final section provides ideas for getting a mentor program started.

What Makes a Good Mentor?

Although most people feel that helping others is noble, not everyone can or decides to do it. Many people feel that they would not be very good at mentoring a youngster and therefore elect not to get involved. We also feel that mentoring is not for everyone. In fact, some mentors have done more damage than good. So how does one know whether he or she would be a good mentor? Here are some requirements that will help you decide whether mentorship is for you.

Be Comfortable With Kids

This is probably the most important quality for being an effective mentor. Being able to understand and appreciate their individuality, struggles, fears, joys, and indifference is a major factor in developing a "comfort zone" for working with underserved youngsters. Youngsters have great radar systems for picking up signals that the mentor is not comfortable with them. When this happens, youngsters may even blame themselves for making the mentor uncomfortable. This often makes the youngster reluctant to open up with the mentor. On the other hand, relaxing with the youngster will open doors for creating great dialogue and a sustained relationship.

Leave Values at the Doorstep

Like the youngster you are mentoring, you have acquired a set of values from your life experiences. In many instances, your values may be quite different from the youngster's. It is a good idea to leave your set of personal values at the doorstep, although this is not always easy. After all, your values have guided you well throughout life and are important to you. Similarly, the value systems of youngsters are also important to them. It is also true, for many, that their values have gotten them into trouble. In either case, you need to understand the youngster, which requires an open mind and listening ears. Imposing your own set of values will short-circuit the mentoring process. In short, the mentor can help youngsters get on the "right track" only when the mentor knows the track the kids have been on throughout their lives.

Be Patient With Kids

It is not unusual to hear mentors say, "My youngster is not talking to me," or "I don't think he wants me to be there with him; he doesn't like me," or "I am not doing a good job connecting with my kid." Oftentimes you will find that mentoring is a slow and difficult process. Having patience with the youngster is of utmost importance in the mentoring process. This means being patient with who he or she is and his or her occasional "screw-ups." Youngsters don't always bound into a mentoring session ready to talk about and set goals. In fact, we have found that some youngsters are very reluctant to be mentored and remain quiet for long periods of time—even for an entire year! Mentors often take this personally and feel that the youngster doesn't like him or her. This is usually not the case. Patience and persistence will eventually get the youngster to open up. After all, the youngster is still trying to figure you out. You have just dropped into his or her life and it will take time to get used to you (and vice versa). This is not to say that all mentor–kid matches are good ones. Some mentors and youngsters simply don't hit it off. But in most cases, youngsters want you to be there, especially if they feel that you really care about them.

Stay With the Kid

An important quality of good mentoring is staying with the youngster through the long haul. Mentoring is not a short-term commitment; you must be willing to commit at least a year in working with a youngster. Abruptly leaving youngsters creates an emotional letdown for them, and they often feel it is their fault that you dropped out. This can further crystallize their feelings of low self-esteem and inability to maintain a relationship. Consistency is a key ingredient in helping many underserved youngsters get a positive foothold in school and at home. Therefore, maintaining the mentorship for the long term adds some stability to their often unstable lives.

Keep Your Promises

Many of the youngsters you work with have had significant adults let them down in numerous ways. For instance, it is not unusual for youngsters to be forgotten and left waiting for parents to pick them up for a weekend together. Thus, broken promises by adults become all too common for kids whose parents struggle with their own problems. This is why it is extremely important that you keep the promises you make with your youngster. For example, if you promise to meet with him or her at a certain time on a certain day, be sure you meet this commitment. After all, getting kids to be responsible requires that you be responsible yourself. The child will eagerly look forward to that meeting, and not showing up will only further erode what little trust he or she has in adults.

Prepare for the "Ups" and "Downs"

Working with kids often places mentors in a position to deal with their own emotions. These emotions are like a roller coaster ride, fraught with periods of elation, satisfaction, disappointment, and self-doubt. Maintaining some equilibrium during the ups and downs of mentoring requires perspective and a sense of humor. Kids have their own way of interpreting and communicating things; their views of life are much different from those of adults. The best rule for getting the most from youngsters is this: Listen to what kids have to say, and don't take yourself too seriously. If you apply this rule, mentoring becomes a more positive experience for you and the youngster.

Being a Good Mentor

We believe that good mentoring serves two important functions: making a connection with kids and getting kids to set goals. For example, in Greeley, mentoring has been used to help youngsters with homework. Mentors (university athletes) set up a "study table" for Coaching Club members (see chapter 7) who are struggling with their schoolwork. The athletes also work with the youngsters at the club and encourage them to participate in the study table sessions. In Greensboro and Greeley, mentors work one-on-one to help youngsters set academic and social goals. They also take kids to various community events and centers where they can ice skate, in-line skate, bowl, browse through a mall, or watch sports events. Taking the kids to special places outside of their neighborhood provides opportunities to experience other aspects of the community that are very often inaccessible to them. "Hangin' out" with kids is fun because it gives you a chance to play and talk about different things.

Making a Connection

Establishing good rapport with the youngster is essential for developing a comfort zone in which mentoring takes place. During the first two or three meetings with your child, get to know him or her better and to see how things are going. For successful dialogue to occur, you must create an atmosphere that is informal and open. If kids do not feel comfortable to express themselves, you will have little chance of getting them to work on other things. You will find that some kids are really engaging and easy to work with. Others may be very quiet and will need special prodding. Staying with this type of kid will eventually pay off. Danish and Howard (1991) and we found that five important skills can be used to increase the interaction between you and your youngster: ice breaking, open-ended questioning, rephrasing techniques, nonverbal communication, and simple language.

Ice Breaking Several mentors have found that little fun activities can break down any barriers and initiate dialogue. Here are a few you can try:

- *Do magic tricks.* One mentor found that magic tricks worked wonders in getting kids to relax and open up. One trick he did, for example, was the "magic thumb" trick. In this trick it looked like the mentor's thumb came off! Youngsters were always fascinated with it. In fact, he showed them how to do the trick, so they could work on it. This turned out to be a great opportunity to begin goal setting with some of the youngsters. The mentor had some youngsters commit to practicing the trick so that they had learned it by the next meeting.
- *Share things about yourself.* Kids are very curious about you. Where do you live? Are you married? Do you have a boyfriend or girlfriend? Do you have any children? How old are you? Don't be afraid to share a little of your personal life with them. This helps connect them to the outside world. Besides, you are trying to learn a lot about them, right? Sharing pictures of your family, showing examples of your hobbies (i.e., baseball cards, arrowheads, etc.), and bringing baby pictures of yourself are but a few of the ways you can share a part of yourself.
- *Use e-mail to communicate.* One mentored youngster learned how to use e-mail via the school computer lab (in the library). The youngster and mentor began sending messages to each other. They even printed out their messages to share during the next mentoring session. It was a great way to get the youngster to open up. After all, kids love to send messages to one another—you are just doing it electronically.
- *Read a book together.* Some kids love to read books aloud to you. Some magazines like *Sports Illustrated* are of special interest to children and youth. We found that reading together is an excellent way to get kids to communicate and relate their own personal values. A good strategy is to ask them about certain things that occur in the book. Questions that focus on how they would respond to various situations often reveal fears, likes and dislikes, and indifference to their own life experiences. For example, one child was reading a passage from a book that illustrated how hard a mother and father worked at their jobs outside the family. It also showed how they were able to spend time with their children. The mentor asked the child if the story was similar to his family life. His extremely revealing response showed that his home life was dissimilar and that his relationship with his parents was quite difficult.
- *Play together.* Some of the youngsters whom we work with love to play sports, especially basketball. We have had many great discus-

sions while skating or over an informal "shootaround" or a friendly game of horse, bowling, or pool.

- *Go to events outside of school.* Kids love it when they can go with you to events in the community. For example, basketball and baseball games, concerts, and festivals have proven to be great venues for dialogue and connecting.

Open-Ended Questioning Open-ended questions cannot be answered by a simple *yes* or *no*. These questions force students to say more about what they are thinking or feeling. They can also serve as follow-up probes to single-word answers. Open-ended questions usually begin with the words *how* and *what*, as in the following examples:

- Lazelle, what kind of things would you like to accomplish this week?
- ReShonda, how are things going with your teacher, Mrs. Brown?
- Brittany, what are some ways you used the responsibility goals in your classroom?

To understand the nature of open-ended questions, it is helpful to contrast them with closed-ended questions. A closed-ended question can be answered with a *yes* or *no* or by other single-word responses. Usually these are questions that begin with *did, where, when, are,* and *will*. For example, the question, "Anthony, did you accomplish your goal this week in math class?" can only be answered by *yes* or *no*. Because a youngster doesn't have to say much to answer a closed-ended question, asking such questions may not start a discussion, especially when youngsters are shy about speaking out. Using open-ended questions requires practice to be effective.

Rephrasing Techniques The third skill is rephrasing what the student said. This is an effective way of affirming the student's response by showing you understand what he or she said. Rephrasing enables you to concentrate on the most important aspects of the student's comments. It involves restating in your own words what has been said. For example, if a youngster says, "I'd like to be a class monitor, but I am afraid the teacher won't think I am ready to be one," you might say, "So, you'd like to ask her to be a monitor but you're not sure whether the teacher feels you are ready to be one." You could also follow up with a question: "So you didn't like what the teacher said?" Using a questioning tone makes some kids want to share more.

Nonverbal Communication You have heard the old adage "actions speak louder than words." Nonverbal communication is incorporated into most of our interactions with others. In fact, it has been stated that nonverbal action accounts for over 90 percent of the meaning we convey during conversation with others (Good and Brophy, 1990). Think about how smiling, raising your voice, or wagging a finger help to emphasize a point. A nonexpressive mentor may appear to be bored. This will "turn off" students, causing them to become uninterested or restless. Your personality will be the "spark" that will ignite a good and lively discussion. Danish and Howard (1991) offered some tips for improving nonverbal communication during your mentoring session:

- *Eye contact.* Eye contact is one of the most important aspects of nonverbal behavior. There is nothing more distracting than talking to someone who is constantly looking away from you. What message does that convey? How involved do students feel when their teacher is always talking to the chalkboard instead of the class? An important rule is to always look the youngster in the eye when talking to him or her or when listening.
- *Body movement and posture.* Body movements include gestures and techniques that emphasize or clarify a point. Showing interest by proper posturing will go a long way in maintaining the interest and focus of the youngster. On the other hand, nervous habits or other movements can distract the student and decrease the effectiveness of the mentoring session. Avoid such things as chewing gum, playing with your hair, or tapping a pencil or your fingertips. Table 9.1 provides some *dos* and *don'ts* about body movement and posture.
- *Vocal quality.* This helps to communicate what you are saying as opposed to the content itself. Your voice should be easily heard by the student without interfering with other youngsters who are working. Also, avoid talking too fast or too slow. Try to maintain an even pace and vary the inflection of your voice (avoid using a monotone).

Simple Language It is important to use words that youngsters can understand. Remember, the youngster you are working with is not an academician. Using simple language prevents confusion and misinterpretation of certain words. Unfortunately, toning down the use of flowery words or phrases is not always easy to do—especially for university professors and students! Some ways in which words can be substituted for one another are given in table 9.2.

Setting a Goal

The most important role that mentoring plays is goal setting. Goal setting is the key to transferring the responsibility model to mentoring.

The youngsters whom you will work with probably need to establish some goal-setting skills to improve their academic, physical, and/or social performance. Goal setting should become an integral part of your mentoring sessions. Much of the youngsters' time is spent in different settings (i.e., school, clubs, home) daydreaming, wandering around the classroom or gym, bothering others, or working on learning tasks in haphazard ways. In short, the time spent in these settings is unproductive and often disruptive. Therefore, goal setting should focus on ways of linking the values kids have learned in settings where the responsibility model is used to other settings. Setting goals and working on them is especially important because of the potential for getting youngsters to gain some sense of control over their academic and social lives.

Table 9.1

DOs and DON'Ts About Body Movement and Posture

Do	Don't
Nod your head slightly to affirm that you are listening intently.	Have a "deadpan" look when listening.
Smile when the youngster has responded well.	Make facial expression of displeasure.
Sometimes pat on the child's head or shoulder. This is a good way of showing you care.	Physically separate yourself from the youngster.
Lean slightly forward to show interest.	Slouch in your chair and look bored.

Table 9.2

Substituting Words

Instead of using	Use
Contemplate	Think about it
Synthesize	Make up something
Recollect	Remember
Transfer	Try it out elsewhere
Inclusion	Don't leave someone out
Resolve conflict	Work it out peacefully

To accomplish this, encourage the youngsters to work on responsibility Level Three (self-direction and goal setting) and Level Five (transferring goals to outside the gym) of the club's responsibility model. When the student is ready to set goals, you should begin to formulate simple and reachable goals for the youngster to work on during the week. However, guidance for goal setting is essential. Blindly going into goal setting will only lead to frustration and a counterproductive experience for you and the student. The following steps are recommended to help establish direction for goal setting.

Step One: Determining the Type of Goal the Student Wants to Set This first step links the levels of responsibility to the goal being set. The protocol for goal setting is guided by the responsibility model discussed in chapter 3. Because the goals levels of the responsibility model are central to the content of our physical activity programs, it is important to use the same framework during the mentoring sessions. This helps to transfer gym goals to other settings. When you guide the student through this initial process, it helps to have the student select a goal from the responsibility model:

- Level One: Self-control and respecting rights of others (i.e., no fighting, respecting the teacher, no trash talk)
- Level Two: Trying to do my class work (i.e., doing homework, completing assignments, studying for tests, redoing assignments)
- Level Three: Being a self-starter (doing assignments without being told, creating and following a plan for studying)
- Level Four: Caring for others (helping a classmate with homework, asking the teacher to help, making someone feel better, spreading good rumors, resolving conflicts for others)
- Level Five: Using goals in the home (helping parents with work, doing your homework, being nice to other family members including pets, doing chores without being told, working on your plan).

Refer to these levels periodically during the goal-setting sessions to make the youngster aware of them. First, have the student select a level that he or she would like to achieve. Next, the student should try to identify a specific goal related to that level. Make sure the goal is realistic. Appropriate goals contain short-term outcomes and are within the youngster's social and academic capabilities. For example, getting a student to work on having "one clean day" is much more realistic than trying to get the youngster to be citizen of the month. Or getting the student to spend a certain amount of time on math problems in class or complete a homework assignment is much more reasonable than trying to get an A on a unit test.

Three important points will help you decide whether the goal is appropriately set (Danish & Howard, 1991). First, is it important to the youngster? The student should want the goal for him- or herself and not because other people want it. In other words, the goal should be important enough for the student to work on. Second, is the goal positive? Does it direct the student what to do, instead of what not to do? It also should create a picture in the kid's mind of what she or he wants to happen, rather than something that shouldn't happen. Finally, is the goal specific? The goal needs to be as specific as possible so that the student knows when the goal has been reached. Have the youngster ask, "How will I know that I have reached the goal?" If the individual can answer that question, then the goal is specific. Having kids write down their goal helps to solidify the commitment to reach the goal and allows them to see long-term progress.

Step Two: Establishing and Practicing Strategies for Reaching the Goal Once the goal is set, establish specific strategies to attain the goal. Make sure that the strategies are a good fit with the youngster's capability of reaching the goal. We have found that several strategies work well with different students.

The first strategy is the use of self-talk. Talking to oneself often helps to focus on a goal. Self-talk has been used successfully to enhance skill learning. It can also be used with goal setting. This does not mean that you simply ask youngsters to talk to themselves. Rather, you must help create self-talk dialogue that effectively addresses the problem (goal). For example, one mentor had a student recite a little phrase for getting through periods of frustration. Most of the time, the frustration was caused by having to rewrite an assignment. The student would shut down or act out when prodded by the teacher. To overcome the frustration the youngster would say to herself, "Don't be uptight, let's get it right." This helped her to identify her feelings and think of a more desirable response other than "bad-mouthing" the teacher. Here are a few one-liners that kids could memorize for self-talk purposes:

- You can choose not to help yourself, but don't take anyone with you (Level One).
- If people can get to you with their talk, they can control you (Level One).
- To get better, you have to pay the price (Level Two).
- When the air goes out of the ball, what are you going to do? (Levels Two and Three).
- Any fool can criticize, blame, and complain—and most fools do (Level One).
- Head first, fists last (Levels One and Four).

Personal planning through written contracts also works well. In these contracts, the youngsters have choices in the number and type of goals they want to work on. Table 9.3 illustrates a sample personal plan.

Sometimes verbal plans work well with youngsters. One youngster said she was going to work on not laughing at others. Although she needed some encouragement, she eventually became committed to her plan and was able to control her laughter toward others.

Some youngsters will want you to choose a plan for them. Try to nudge them into making decisions about their own plan. Ownership will help ensure follow-through by the youngster. Some kids may try to get out of following their plan. Encourage them to change their plan rather than not doing one at all. It is very important that youngsters commit to their plan so that they can make some progress. They need to value the plan because it is something they want to do—not what you want them to do!

Finally, students usually choose activities that fit their strengths—not weaknesses. This is okay because it will help harness the commitment we spoke of earlier. However, weaknesses should be addressed eventually, especially if self-image is to be improved.

Another mentor worked on getting youngsters to relax through mental imagery or what we call pretending things. She asked youngsters to imagine different experiences that would get them to relax and focus. Sometimes youngsters are agitated, abusive, or withdrawn because they are stressed by various events in their lives such as confrontations with a classmate or teacher, difficulty with a class assignment, abuse at home, or not feeling well. For example, the mentor had youngsters think about being a piece of spaghetti, which conjured an image of being stiff and brittle and then turning into a loose, drooping noodle. The idea was to help them to relax when tension arises. Here are some other images for youngsters to think about:

Table 9.3

Personal Plan

CHOOSE ONE OR TWO

My homework goal is to ________________________ (Level Three).

My goal for doing work in class is to ________________________ (Levels One-Four).

My goal in reading is to ________________________ (Levels Two and Three).

My goal in math is to ________________________ (Levels Two and Three).

My goal in social studies is to ________________________ (Levels Two and Three).

- Being at a beach or walking along a stream in the mountains.
- Being snuggled in a warm bed.
- Smelling your favorite food like pizza, turkey, dressing.
- Relaxing different muscles like fingers, toes, stomach, face, shoulders, etc.
- Floating on your back in a large lake on a warm day.
- Stepping into the batter's box and hitting a home run.
- Listening to your favorite music.

Find what youngsters like so that the image portrayed is compatible to their experiences and environment. Some youngsters, for example, may not have been to the mountains or the ocean; imagining themselves in these places may be difficult, if not impossible.

Another strategy is to have the youngster remove him- or herself from a situation that causes frustration and anger (a common problem for a lot of our club members)—in essence, a self-imposed time-out. This strategy was helpful for one fourth-grade club member who was always losing her temper in the classroom. One day, she was denied the opportunity to pass out some art supplies. Typically, this type of rejection would cause her to either throw stuff or just shut down. This day, however, she asked to go outside and cool off (self-imposed time-out). The teacher let her go into an adjacent room for 10 minutes. On returning she got back to work and was fine for the rest of the period. Over time she found value in the strategy and continued to successfully use it. Doing this gave her more confidence in dealing with future challenges.

Setting goals together also helps you gain a youngster's trust in the goal-setting process. That is, try setting your own goals when working with the student. The two of you can then check up on each other.

A final strategy is behavior modification. Behavior modification can be used with youngsters who continually lack the motivation to set goals. This is especially a problem with kids who are unable to control their outbursts or show respect for others. For example, behavior modification was used with one youngster who was always in trouble; previous goal-setting efforts were having no effect. He decided to see how many "clean days" (Level One) in one week he could garner. To facilitate the process, 2 × 3-inch goal cards like the ones shown in figure 9.1 were developed by the mentor.

The cards were given to the youngster's classroom teacher. She gave one card for each "clean day" that he attained. At the end of each week, the youngster showed the mentor how many cards he received that week. One card meant a school lunch together. Two meant lunch outside the school. Three or more meant a basketball game. Interestingly, the

GOAL CARD ONE

Monday

What a great start, kiddo!

GOAL CARD TWO

Tuesday

Keep up the good work!

GOAL CARD THREE

Wednesday

Don't stop at third base!

GOAL CARD FOUR

Thursday

Now you're in control!

GOAL CARD FIVE

Friday

Now you're a superstar!

Figure 9.1 Student goal cards.

cards became more important to the youngster than the lunches or game—he could get a clean day during the week and a card was reward enough! It is important that youngsters understand the contingencies that are used and how they relate to self-responsibility. Tokens such as goal cards and stickers (smiley faces) generally work well, especially when they are connected to something that is positive and that the youngsters like. Certificates, letters of appreciation, playing basketball together, having an extra mentor session, going to an outside event (e.g., baseball game), and being a team coach at the sports club are examples of rewards that can be used.

Because empowerment is central to the goal-setting process, behavior modification and use of extrinsic rewards should be used as a final resort. For some youngsters, even behavior modification approaches don't work. They should have what Hellison (1995) called the "right to exit." That is, they simply may not want to be mentored and therefore want out.

Step Three: Extending Goal-Setting Term Once the youngster has begun to reach short-term goals, you will want to encourage a longer term for setting goals. For example, the goal may be not to get in someone's face for two weeks, three weeks, and so on. Considerable variability may exist from youngster to youngster in terms of extending the goal-setting term. The term of the goal depends on how effectively the student established a system for gaining positive outcomes from short-term goal setting.

Step Four: Setting Goals for the End of the Year Eventually youngsters will begin to look at long-term possibilities in their goal-setting attempts. Establishing and reaching end-of-the-year goals are most potent factors in reestablishing positive self-concept and mastery over achievement outcomes. These factors also indicate a youngster's ability to change the quality of his or her personal and school life.

Giving Feedback and Goal Setting

Giving feedback is essential to keep the student on track during mentoring sessions. If feedback is to be effective, effort must be continually reinforced. Feedback can significantly augment the goal-setting strategies previously described. Effort feedback helps youngsters believe that success in reaching certain goals is accomplished by persisting, especially when they experience failure. However, simply telling the youngster to try hard is not going to do it! Alternative strategies for approaching learning tasks must be offered during the feedback process. The goal-setting strategies described earlier work well in doing this. Types of feedback statements that focus on effort are as follows:

- "You almost have it, Brandon. Keep working on your goal."
- "Toccara, try keeping the column of numbers aligned when doing these types of problems. Can we stay on this next week?"
- "Michelle, try paying attention while the teacher is talking. I know you can listen when you use the strategy we talked about last week."
- "Let's work on this one day at a time, Michael. If you do this, I think you can reach your goal."

Be sure that you are not negative or judgmental when giving feedback. Here are some bad examples of feedback:

- "I don't think that it is a good idea at all, it's really weird."
- "Your technique in doing these word problems is lousy."
- "You seem to get confused easily when the teacher gives you an assignment."

Here are some examples of effective feedback:

- "When I try to tell you something to help improve your reading skills, you turn away and ignore me."
- "I like how you tried to work well with your group. Let's try this for awhile and see how it works."
- I know this is something you want to do better at. Let's try one of the strategies we talked about last week.

The effect that feedback will have on students will largely be due to how sincere and believable it is. If the youngster sees that you are simply going through the motions, few if any positive outcomes will emerge. Making the right connection during the mentoring sessions will help you do this.

The closure of your mentoring sessions should be positive so that students have good feelings about themselves. Before leaving, tell the student when you are coming back, giving the youngster a definite time frame in which to work on the goal or goals set during your session. Be sure you keep the date; your youngster will not forget the date of your next visit. Not showing up will only reinforce students' lack of trust of adults who have all too often "left them hanging out to dry." If you are unable to make your appointment, let the student know ahead of time. Try to reschedule as soon as you can. You probably will feel great about some sessions and not so great about others. Having good and bad experiences is normal, so don't get discouraged. If you feel that you are losing ground with your student, review what you have done and see where things can be changed. Remember, you mustn't give up on these kids: Most likely, plenty of people have done that already.

How Kids Respond to Mentoring and Goal Setting

Kid's responses to mentoring and goal setting can vary from individual to individual and session to session. The variability in responses can be due to how the youngster is feeling that day, what's going on in his or her life at that moment (a trip to the principal's office isn't the best thing for getting a kid to focus), how the relationship is going with the mentor (some days are good and some are not), and other things about which we have no clue. Whatever the reasons, kids generally respond to mentoring and goal setting in one of four ways:

1. They refuse to set goals.
2. They set goals to please the mentor.
3. They set goals because they believe the goals will help them.
4. They set goals without help from the mentor or anyone else.

Refusing to Set Goals

Some youngsters simply do not want to set goals. For the most part, this reluctance is found at the early stages of goal setting. In fact, some youngsters refuse to set goals throughout the entire school year! Refusal to set goals is caused by various psychological and social barriers created by poverty. One of these barriers is the value system of the youngsters you are working with. For many, getting good grades, staying out of trouble, being a good citizen, or doing homework are not important items in their life. Instead, they have found that gang affiliation, playing basketball, flirting with boys or girls, surviving stressful family circumstances, knowing how to deal with their teachers and principal, and not being bullied by others are much more important.

Another barrier is dysfunctional home life. In general, there is much caring, nurturing, and concern among family members who live in poverty. Unfortunately, some families fall victim to impoverished living conditions. Children often learn to deal with the stresses of dysfunctional family life by emotionally disengaging themselves from adults. Developing a strong relationship between you and the youngster is extremely difficult, thus making goal setting an almost impossible task. It makes sense, then, that fostering renewed trust in an adult must be at the forefront of any mentoring efforts.

A final barrier is fear of choices. Probably one of the main culprits in getting kids to set goals is low self-concept. Lack of confidence prevents youngsters from choosing the right goal or using the right strategy. Because making choices is personal, it requires evaluation and commitment. Stiehl

(1993) wrote that helping youngsters acquire the free will to make good choices will depend on how you can get them to value the goals being set.

Setting Goals to Please the Mentor

There are also kids who set goals just to please the mentor, because they think it is what the mentor wants. Most of the individuals working with a mentor enjoy the adult companionship and want the relationship to continue. That is, many kids will "play the game" to look favorable in the eyes of the mentor. When goal setting is done in this manner, commitment to reach goals is oftentimes shaky, at best, and the youngster seldom uses strategies to reach the goals. Consequently, mentors become frustrated when goals are continually set and never reached. On the other hand, this form of goal setting should be viewed as an initial step in identifying sustainable goals in future goal-setting sessions.

Setting Goals Because They Believe in Them

Ultimately, we would like to have youngsters set goals because they feel the goals have value. If they feel that the goal is theirs (and not their mentor's), the probability that the kids will then work on the goal increases significantly. However, this takes time. Many mentors enter the goal-setting process with a faulty assumption that kids are eager to set goals and see the value in the process. Therefore, mentors need to enter the goal-setting process with the intent of "selling" goal setting. Once the youngsters believe the goals are theirs, the goal-setting process begins to be their ally in meeting future challenges head on.

Setting Goals on Their Own

Getting youngsters to set goals and develop strategies on their own is the final type of response. Autonomous goal setting puts youngsters in control of their lives; they become problem solvers and "do-it-yourselfers." They are able to apply alternative solutions to social and academic problems and use outside resources for help. The Boys and Girls Clubs, community recreation centers, churches, community colleges, nonprofit outreach groups, Big Brothers/Big Sisters organizations, and alternative school programs are but a few of the resources for young people seeking assistance.

Keeping Track of Mentoring Sessions

We suspect that because many of you have not mentored before, you will have many things to learn from the experience. The ideas presented in this chapter should serve as starting points for your work with underserved youth outside of the physical activity setting. Consequently, you will find yourself modifying or adding to the strategies described in the chapter. We feel that it is helpful to document any changes and/or additions that you make during your mentorship efforts.

One way to do this is to keep a journal. This can be done by simply keeping a mentor diary in a notebook. Or you can practice a more formal method of journal writing by using a specified format. For example, in Greensboro the mentor fills out a Mentor Journal Sheet each week (see form 9.1). Goals, strategies, and outcomes from the goal-setting efforts of the mentor and youngster are recorded and referred to in other goal-setting sessions.

In most cases you will be assigned to one or two youngsters to work with each week. Visits should last about one hour with each student. It is important to establish a meeting time with the youngsters so they know when to expect you. This ensures some consistency in the process. In school and other settings, locations such as the classroom, cafeteria, hallway, stage, swing on a playground, vacated office, or lunch table can be used during the mentor sessions. Sometimes you may find it useful to meet the youngster in alternative settings. For example, the mentors in both our programs have taken their youngsters to the university. Quite often the mentors shoot basketball or work in the computer lab with their youngsters and talk about how things are going and even set goals. Be sure that you have permission from a parent or guardian to take the youngsters to locations outside of the school setting.

We also believe it is a good idea to observe the youngster in the sports club setting before working with him or her. This gives you a better picture of how he or she is doing in the clubs and applying the levels of responsibility during physical activity. The youngster will also feel that the mentor is part of the entire program (not just the mentoring program).

Getting others (e.g., teachers, coaches, directors, parents, activity instructors) involved in goal setting is also helpful. For example, classroom teachers in each of our programs are asked to give feedback on how youngsters are doing on their goals. A Teacher Goal Card is filled out weekly by the teacher and given to the mentor (see form 9.2). The goal for the week and strategy are written by the mentor. Reviewing the Teacher Goal Card from the previous week tells you how the youngster has been doing. Later, this helps in the goal-setting process as well.

Getting Started

Setting up a mentoring program starts with the premise that a student needs something that an older person has: experience, status, abilities, and/or a caring attitude. Aside from this basic premise, there are

Form 9.1

Mentor Journal Sheet

Mentor's Name:____________ **Student's Name:**_______________

Teacher's Name:_________________________ Date:_______________

STUDENT GOALS

Last Week's Goal:

How Is the Student Doing on the Goal?
(If the student is not doing well on the goal, ask him/her why.)

Next Week's Goal:
(How will the student work on the goal? That is, what steps will the student take to achieve the goal? For example, will she or he use self-talk, refocusing, self-imposed time-out, etc.?)

Mentor Reflection:
(How is your relationship with the student? Describe any concerns you have. What specific strategies are you using in your session(s)? What things have you done to improve the relationship?

Form 9.2

Teacher Goal Card

Goal for the week
(levels & specific goals)

Strategy

How did the club member do in working on the goals?

How did the club member do this week in class?

Comments
(pleasant surprises/things needing work)

variations in mentoring programs. Schools and communities are as diverse as the people in them. We believe, therefore, that no single program will work for all schools and communities. Each program must be tailored to meet the specific needs of those they serve. Research on mentoring is consistent: When mentoring is done with clear goals and purposes, the chances for success increase significantly (Martinek & Hellison, 1998; Testerman, 1996).

For us, a golden rule of effective mentoring is that someone who shows real concern for a youngster can have a significant positive effect on his or her self-esteem. We have taken this idea a bit further: Mentoring can be the "bridges" between the gym and the school, neighborhood, and home. It is a way for getting kids to apply the values of responsibility to other settings. To do this well, mentoring should be guided by ideas that work with a majority of youngsters. For the past seven years we have run mentoring programs that have been guided by the personal and social responsibility goals presented in the previous chapters. We have found that common elements of planning and implementation are necessary for success.

Tom's and Missy's Seven Points for Planning and Implementation

- *Program Compatibility.* The program should be connected to the goals of the club. This helps to ensure that the values and goals of responsibility are applied to other settings. It also provides a coherent framework from which goal setting can be done. Goals should also be determined by the youngsters so that a sense of ownership is fostered.

- *Administrative and Staff Commitment.* There must be support from administrators and staff of schools and community programs. In school-based programs, principals, assistant principals, guidance counselors, district administrators, and teachers must provide input and assistance. Community program directors and staff must also be involved in planning mentoring programs. These people also serve as valuable resources for selecting and monitoring students.

- *Pilot Program.* The first step should be a pilot program. Plan on starting small. Working out problems early will help avoid unwieldy and disastrous outcomes when the mentoring program is expanded to a larger scale. Learning how to match mentors with kids, evaluating program outcomes, gaining access to the youngsters, and developing effective mentoring strategies are a few of the things you can "iron out" before full-scale mentoring takes place.

- *Selection and Matching.* Mentors and kids should be carefully matched. Improper matches can lead to frustration by both. Several steps can be followed in the selection of mentors. The first step is to recruit mentors. This can be done by announcing the need for mentors in classes throughout the university, by posting flyers, by placing ads in the campus newspaper, and by "word of mouth." The second step is be sure that the individual cares about kids and is willing to stay with the youngster for the long haul (at least one year). Many of these kids have had adults drop in and out of their lives for years. Dropping out of the program midyear disappoints the youngsters and makes them feel that another adult has given up on them. Preliminary interviews of potential mentors help to determine if the individual is right for the program and vice versa. A third step is to have the mentors attend club sessions at least three times. This gives them a chance to see the youngster in action. It also gives the kid a chance to work with his or her potential mentor before the match is confirmed. A final step is to ask if the mentor assigned to him or her is okay. We have found in some instances that youngsters prefer to choose their mentors. They gain ownership in this matching process, thus providing solid footing for future goal setting.

- *Training.* This essential step should include familiarizing the mentors with the responsibility model goals and the type of commitment expected from them. It is a mistake to assume that because a person is caring and enthusiastic, he or she will make a good mentor. Training must be geared to specific problems experienced by underserved youth, as well as different styles of communication. Procedures for accessing the youngster from class or other settings should be described along with evaluation procedures. When possible, teachers, community staff, administrators, and parents should be invited to the training sessions.

- *Monitoring.* The program should have scheduled meetings throughout the year. This helps to monitor progress and results and to resolve emerging problems. This also provides an opportunity for the mentors to share their experiences and gain ideas from one another.

- *Evaluation and Revision.* Developing a plan to assess the impact of the mentoring program is essential. Data collection can be qualitative, anecdotal, and quantitative. The data should also correspond to the program goals. For example, if one goal is to get the student to improve self-control and respect for others (Level One), then the number of office referrals made should be recorded. The program director can learn how the youngsters are responding to the mentoring sessions by having the mentors, teachers, community staff, and parents provide feedback. Such feedback also helps in future funding efforts. For mentors, feedback from teachers and parents can yield important information for planning future mentoring sessions.

Final Thoughts

Despite its advantages, planned mentoring should not be considered an independent program. As many of those who work in dropout prevention programs know too well, there is no immediate cure or single approach to resolving the crisis of our underserved youth. Mentoring should work in conjunction with other programs, ideas, and strategies for helping underserved youngsters. This is why we strongly encourage you to use the responsibility model's values as the basis for developing and running your mentoring program. This makes your program more holistic and effective in helping youngsters to be productive human beings. Although other values can be linked to mentoring, the responsibility values have served us well. We hope this will be the case for you—good luck!

For Further Study

Grossman, J.B., & Garry, E.M. (1997, April). Mentoring—A proven delinquency prevention strategy. *Juvenile Justice Bulletin*, pp. 1-6. Washington, DC: U.S. Department of Justice.

This issue provides a great overview of the various mentoring programs operating across the nation. Data from these programs are given along with important guidelines for those who wish to start their own mentoring programs. Addresses for obtaining important information about these programs are also included in this issue. Subscribing to Juvenile Justice Bulletin *is highly recommended.*

Martinek, T., & Hellison, D. (1998). Values and goal setting with underserved youth. *Journal of Physical Education, Recreation and Dance, 69*(7), 47-52.

This article encourages teachers, youth workers, counselors, coaches, and volunteers to rethink how traditional models for goal setting may be modified to fit the needs of underserved youth. Specific barriers related to environments and belief systems of inner-city youth are explored. Guidelines for setting goals are also suggested.

Testerman, J. (1996). Holding at-risk students: The secret is one-on-one. *Phi Delta Kappan, 51*, 364-365.

Knowing the secrets of getting at-risk youth to reestablish themselves into the mainstream of schooling is a focus of many mentoring programs. This article provides some valuable information that solidifies efforts of mentoring programs in assisting youngsters who struggle in schooling. A nice overview of research supporting the efficacy of one-on-one mentoring is offered.

Chapter 10

Cross-Age Teaching Programs

Nick Cutforth and Tom Martinek

Today more than ever we are hearing that there should be a connection between school and the world outside, and that children should be engaged in and connected to real-world problems and issues. Related to this belief, and in the wake of daunting new societal challenges, there has been much conversation among teachers, administrators, community leaders, politicians, and officials of social agencies at local, state, regional, and national levels about the importance of giving young people the opportunity to provide service to others. Many believe that young people are citizens in the making and that preparing students to be responsible citizens should be a more prominent goal of public schools.

Young people have a natural desire to be helpful, but too often youth is a period of emptiness and a time of waiting. In the past, opportunities to engage in a service-oriented activity were usually limited. Service learning provides young people with the opportunity to actively serve their communities through such projects as building parks, working with the homeless, rehabilitating existing homes, and tutoring (Haas & Lambert, 1995). Now, most states encourage service learning programs in all levels of schooling, and some states even make service a requirement for graduation.

We believe that the physical education profession should respond to the service learning emphasis. When you were young, perhaps you volunteered for organizations such as the Special Olympics or the YMCA. If so, you will appreciate the potential of physical activity programs to provide meaningful service experiences for young people. In this chapter, we illustrate the potential of physical activity programs to give young children and youth the opportunity to provide a service to others. We will show how youth learn leadership skills, including the development of critical thinking, negotiating, and decision making. Many of the children we work with are regarded as "problems" and are the focus of preventive and remedial programs. However, we believe that these children need to feel valued, needed, respected, and acknowledged. We also believe that behind their unpredictable behaviors are immense human resources and qualities. When young people engage in meaningful service experiences involving real-life purposes and consequences that address the needs of others, they experience the joy of reaching out to others.

What Are Cross-Age Teaching Programs?

Perhaps you teach in an extended day program and have grown attached to the young people in your care. You hope that they will stay in school against all the odds, and you wonder how you can maintain contact with them during their middle school or high school years. Or from an academic perspective, you wonder whether the experience of teaching younger children will improve young people's visions of their "possible futures" (McLaughlin & Heath, 1993). You wonder whether such a teaching experience might influence these young people's vocational and avocational possibilities. Perhaps if they taught younger children for an hour or two each week, for instance, some of them might consider coaching a basketball team at their church or in a youth program, or even entertain thoughts of attending college to become a teacher.

Cross-age teaching programs provide middle and high school students with the responsibility of teaching sports and recreational skills to grade school children. In Denver, Greensboro, and Chicago, cross-age teaching programs have evolved from extended day programs developed and taught by university professors and their graduate students, and these programs are the focus of this chapter. In Denver, middle school students who were themselves in the Energizers Club (which you read about in chapter 7) when they were younger return to their former elementary school for an hour each week to teach their younger peers in the after-school program. In Greensboro, high school students who have participated for several years in an after-school sport club similar to the ones described in chapter 7 travel to the University of North Carolina at Greensboro campus once each week to teach nine- and ten-year-olds from local Boys and Girls Clubs. In Chicago, past and present members of the Coaching Club spend five weeks of their summer vacation teaching eight- and nine-year-olds enrolled in a summer sports camp at the University of Illinois at Chicago.

These cross-age teaching programs contain similarities and differences in structure and focus, while sharing the same purpose of extending the notion of responsibility through leadership opportunities. The responsibility model provides direction for the programs; however, the terminology differs slightly to reflect each program's content (basketball in Chicago and Greensboro, and a variety of individual and team sports and fitness and challenge activities in Denver). Cross-age teaching programs are a logical next step for many young people because such programs require young people to assume responsibility not only for themselves, by punctually arriving at the extended-day program each day, but also for others, by instructing younger children.

Teaching and Leadership Options Within Cross-Age Teaching Programs

We refer to the teachers and program leaders in cross-age teaching programs as apprentice teachers. Cross-age teaching programs can take various forms depending on the amount of teaching and leadership responsibilities that the apprentice teachers assume. Several possibilities are described next.

Teaching Part of the Lesson

Here, one or more apprentice teachers are responsible for teaching part of a lesson. For example, one apprentice teacher teaches a tag game to the younger students as an introductory activity, or another may do warm-up exercises. In addition, all apprentices are required to assist program staff in teaching daily activities. Usually, this involves working one-on-one with a student, monitoring a small-group skill practice, leading a small-size game, coaching a team, or providing input to the closing reflection activity.

Teaching at One of Several Stations

This can be done in one of two ways. In Denver, each apprentice teacher is given responsibility for teaching at one of several stations on an activity circuit. For example, one apprentice may teach passing skills, another dribbling skills, and another shooting as part of a basketball or soccer circuit. The younger students rotate around the circuit, and the apprentice teachers teach the same activity repeatedly, perhaps as many as six times in a session. In Greensboro and Chicago, apprentice teachers are paired up and teach a 15-minute basketball lesson several times to the younger children as they rotate around the stations. The children are divided into four groups, and there are four stations each consisting of half a basketball court and manned by a pair of apprentice teachers. Each group visits each station for 15 minutes of basketball instruction; thus, each pair of apprentice teachers is responsible for planning and teaching a lesson four times each day. The children remain at their final station to participate in a brief group meeting and reflection time session (as in the responsibility model lesson format in chapter 3) in which the apprentice teachers solicit the children's views about their experiences and to what extent they carried out the responsibilities of the responsibility model.

Teaching Assistant

Here, the director of the program introduces activities during the lesson and then turns over responsibility to each apprentice teacher to monitor a small group of younger students as they undertake the activity. For example, during the fitness circuit that you read about in chapter 7, an apprentice teacher could be in charge of a station and ensure that the students perform the activity and record their outcomes.

Teaching a Small Group

With this method, each apprentice teacher teaches activities to the same small group of students for the entire lesson. In Denver, the apprentice teachers often work with the fourth and fifth graders individually and in small groups. For example, one apprentice teacher may teach volleyball skills to her group, while another apprentice teacher may be responsible for teaching jump rope skills. Also, during basketball or softball games, they may act as a player or coach.

Teaching a Large Group

Here, one or more apprentice teachers teach the entire lesson to all the students. Clearly, this represents the ultimate test of teaching and leadership responsibilities for the apprentice teachers. However, after several years of experience, some apprentice teachers are capable of assuming responsibility for introducing and teaching a skill, challenge activity, or team game, and then conducting a reflection session.

Essential Components of Cross-Age Teaching Programs

The Denver, Greensboro, and Chicago programs possess four core elements that must be present if cross-age teaching programs are to be successful: orientation and training, teaching opportunities, reflection, and recognition:

- Orientation and training involve the apprentice teachers in planning the teaching activity.
- Teaching opportunities occur when the apprentice teachers teach activities and provide both skill and responsibility model feedback to the younger children.
- Reflection includes activities such as individual and group discussions as well as journal writing that enable apprentice teachers to relive or recapture their teaching experience to make sense of it, learn from it, and develop new understandings and appreciations.
- Recognition is the vehicle that acknowledges the impact of the apprentice teachers' contribution and celebrates individual and group accomplishments.

Orientation and Training

Even the most experienced teachers know that teaching skills take time to develop. The same is true for the apprentice teachers. They do not have any specific training in leadership and pedagogical skills, and they need to be prepared to teach the younger children so that they can be confident, organized, and effective teachers. Furthermore, apprentice teachers, unlike adult teachers (presumably), don't have the maturity or experience to independently develop and reflect on their teaching.

Providing specific training promotes a smooth transition from attending an extended day program to teaching young children. However, we have found that even if you already have a Coaching Club and your students are used to coaching their peers, the transition from a player–member to a leader–teacher of young children can be a formidable one for apprentice teachers, some more than others. Therefore, the apprentice teachers need ample opportunities to become comfortable with their new role.

In Denver, apprentice teachers attend Project Lead—a training session one hour each week to practice the teaching activities that they will use with the younger children later in the week. At these training sessions, Nick shares activity ideas and options with the apprentice teachers by actually teaching them and inviting them to make suggestions. There are several benefits for the apprentices when they experience these activities as learners who will soon be teaching them: They experience some of the same challenges the younger children are likely to experience; they begin to realize the importance of providing challenging activities for all ability and aptitude levels, including using several balls instead of one during practices; and they appreciate the value of giving positive feedback and encouragement to the younger children.

In Greensboro, apprentice teachers attend two training sessions conducted by staff members. The graduate students who work directly with the apprentice teachers throughout the program attend as well. Unlike the Denver program, there are no follow-up sessions during the year. Instead, a university student "helper" monitors each lesson and meets with the apprentice teachers afterward to discuss what was taught, what went well, and what could be improved next time.

In Chicago, training of the apprentices is less structured. When the program began five years ago, minimal presession preparation was balanced by up to an hour spent evaluating the session and preparing for the next day. Since then, Don has built more time into the Coaching Club for peer coaching and for the more experienced members to coach in a club for younger members.

Teaching Opportunities

The apprentice teachers experience several of the teaching options previously outlined, including teaching part of the lesson, teaching a skill practice as part of a station's activity, being a teaching assistant, teaching a small group, and teaching a large group. In Denver, the apprentice teachers teach a variety of individual and team sports as well as fitness and challenge activities to 20 fourth and fifth graders for an hour each week. In Greensboro's program, apprentice teachers follow a similar schedule and are responsible for teaching basketball skills and the responsibility model to about 25 nine- and ten-year-olds from local Boys and Girls Clubs. In Chicago, the apprentice teachers are responsible for providing basketball instruction to 40 eight- and nine-year-old boys and girls enrolled in a summer camp for an hour a day for 21 days over a five-week period.

Reflection

There is a great deal of variability in the way apprentice teachers work with youngsters. Thus, cross-age teaching programs should contain structured opportunities for the apprentice teachers to receive feedback on their teaching and to think, talk, or write about what they did and saw during their teaching activity. The end of the program session, after the younger children leave, is an ideal time for the apprentice teachers to reflect on their teaching.

One way to promote this reflection is to give written and oral feedback on the lesson just taught. Of course, this requires that you find ways of monitoring the apprentice teachers while they are teaching. Rather than trying to observe every teacher in a single session, watch two or three teachers each day and schedule time to meet with them either individually or in a group. Helping them with such things as giving clear directions and feedback, arranging equipment, dealing with disruptive students, modifying tasks, or just getting their students to be responsible enhances their confidence and ensures a positive learning experience for all. Although these elements should also be covered in training sessions, such monitoring and feedback help the apprentice teachers improve their teaching skills.

A second way to facilitate feedback and reflection is to assign a helper to one or two apprentice teachers. For example, in Greensboro, an outside adult (usually a graduate student) helps the apprentice teachers in planning (if they want help) and gives feedback about the session. The helper meets with the apprentice teacher at the end of each session. If graduate students are not available, peer coaching can also be used when apprentice teachers are paired together (like in the Denver program). In peer coaching, apprentice teachers can observe each other's lessons and then give feedback. Guidance for giving feedback should be provided during the initial training sessions. In either case, it is important for the feedback to be positive as well as constructive; confidence building must be at the forefront of all sessions.

A third way to ensure reflection is to hold group meetings during which the apprentice teachers reflect on their teaching experience and consider their effectiveness and contribution to the program. Here the program staff serve as facilitators, guides, mentors, and friends. The apprentices learn from one another by discussing their teaching experiences, identifying issues, obtaining information, comparing assumptions, solving problems, and determining the most effective and feasible course of action. Among the issues discussed are the teaching strategies that are or are not working and the challenges presented by individual children. We have been particularly heartened by the apprentices' ability to listen to constructive criticism and to respond by improving their teaching (see, for example, Cutforth & Puckett, 1999).

Whichever approach you choose to generate opportunities for reflection, your goal should be to create a sense of community as the apprentice teachers and program staff identify and grapple with problems they confront and make plans for subsequent sessions. We have found that discussions often focus on individual children who are presenting discipline problems, on pedagogical issues such as how to prevent boredom and off-task problems, and on the need to be enthusiastic and excited about the activities. Such discussions lead to a common bond among program staff—both adults and apprentice teachers. These reflective thinking processes also enable the apprentice teachers to solve problems collaboratively and to make effective decisions.

Recognition

It is important that the apprentice teachers receive recognition for their service activities. In Denver, Project Lead apprentices are recognized in several ways: They receive clothing from Adidas as well as University of Denver notepads, caps, and wallets; they are given publicity when the program is covered in the university newspaper; and twice each year they are treated to dinner at a neighborhood restaurant. In addition, each May they visit the University of Denver, where university students show them the residence halls, the library, computer laboratories, and recreation facilities and treat them to lunch in the university restaurant.

Greensboro's apprentice teacher program provides warm-up outfits and gym shoes donated from Adidas and weekly dinners at the university's cafeteria. The apprentice teachers get to "rub shoulders" with the university students and, in a certain way, become part of the university culture. On occasions, university staff have helped the apprentice teachers with homework and given them access to the university's computer facilities. Other forms of recognition have been through the local news media and newspaper and in an ongoing column in a program newsletter that is distributed four times a year.

In Chicago, a pizza party is held at the end of the program at which the participants are thanked personally by the director of the university summer camp; they receive Nike clothing, a letter of recognition from the program director, and a free pass to the university recreation facilities. Also, they have received media attention in the university paper, the alumni magazine, and on a local television station.

Impact and Outcomes of Cross-Age Teaching Programs

So what do apprentice teachers experience and learn in cross-age teaching programs? What are their perceptions of themselves as teachers and leaders? How do the programs contribute to their overall development? The extent to which the potential benefits of cross-age teaching programs are realized depends on the program's quality, the nature of the teaching activity, the characteristics of the apprentice teachers involved, and perhaps most importantly, the nature of their personal experience in teaching and in their reflection on that experience.

For several years, Nick, Tom, and Don have documented apprentice teachers' attendance, their teaching competence, each program's successes and struggles, and the possible impact of the program on their development (e.g., Cutforth & Puckett, 1999). Findings indicate that cross-age teaching programs have the potential to

- extend learning beyond the traditional school setting into the community;
- improve the apprentice teachers' leadership skills, particularly their self-esteem, maturity, personal competence, and self-efficacy;
- improve the apprentice teachers' attitudes toward adults;
- provide opportunities for problem solving and higher order thinking skills; and
- improve the apprentice teachers' attitudes toward academics.

Extending Learning Beyond the Traditional School Setting Into the Community

The kinds of responsibility given to apprentice teachers in cross-age teaching programs are ones that they rarely see within the confines of the school setting. These programs provide consequential activities that capture the interests and talents of young people who in their school careers are often characterized to varying degrees as behavior problems, poor attendees, and low achievers. Such students often experience school as a frustrating place, a place that is fragmented from real life, where they fail and where no one cares for them. These young people can thrive when they assume a position of responsibility, participate in an activity that relates to real-world experiences, and help others. Indeed, it is likely that these benefits will be most marked for those youth whom schools have traditionally found the hardest to reach. The teaching experience can impact dimensions of citizenship, particularly the apprentices' sense of social responsibility for others, attitudes toward being active in the community, and connection to others.

Overall, participation in the programs has sparked an awareness in the apprentice teachers that they can contribute to other people's lives. Rather than prolonging their dependence on adults, undermining their self-esteem, and crippling their capacity to care, the apprentice teacher program regards participants as competent, capable, and quite able to contribute to their world. The apprentices' regular attendance shows that they find the experience worthwhile. Several apprentice teachers are beginning to see an alternative future for themselves and are realizing that their lives are not hopeless.

Improving Apprentice Teachers' Leadership Skills

The experience of teaching young children can develop perceptions of personal significance and belonging, personal capability and mastery, and personal influence. The apprentice teachers become aware of the ways they can help others. Although they experience some of the joys and the frustrations of teaching as they provide instruction to youngsters, over time they can observe their actions positively affecting a person or group.

During the early program sessions, the challenge of teaching young children is daunting for all apprentice teachers. They are nervous each time the younger children walk through the gym door, and they worry about meeting the challenge of engaging particularly difficult children. However, as the programs continue each day or over several months, the apprentice teachers begin to relish the opportunity to reach out to others. As one apprentice said, "They [are] little kids, you can't get mad at the little things they do. You have to work with them to bring them along. You got to take time to teach."

The apprentice teachers' performance improves throughout the duration of the programs and they begin to take ownership for teaching the responsibility concepts they themselves experienced when they were in the extended day programs—as one apprentice put it, "teaching the kids what I learned." After several years in the Chicago program, a number of apprentices have clearly made the transition to teacher. Indeed, they show heightened levels of effectiveness: Their lesson content is sequential and challenging, their communication style is purposeful yet empathetic, they understand the nuances of their students, and perhaps above all, they are confident in their ability to make a difference in the skills and attitudes of the young children in their care.

Furthermore, the young children appreciate the apprentice teachers. Typical comments from them include, "They [are] nice," "They help people," "They [are] young," and "They be nice to people because they help you shoot, they show you how to do defense and stuff." Such comments reinforce the apprentice teachers' awareness that they are making a valuable contribution to the young children's lives and their satisfaction about the role they are playing. They also illustrate the reciprocal nature of service—the lives of both parties are improved or empowered as a direct result of the experience.

Improving Apprentice Teachers' Attitudes Toward Adults

Earlier we discussed how participation in teaching experiences and structured reflection time can lead to a common bond among apprentice teachers and program staff. Furthermore, feelings of connectedness can arise from the high degree of support and collegiality in the apprentices' relationships with adult program leaders. A sense of community quickly emerges as the apprentices identify and grapple with problems they confront, make plans for the next session's activity, implement their plans, and reflect on their actions. Contributing to this sense of community is the tendency of the apprentices to "hang out" with the program staff after the meetings. In Greensboro and Chicago, the setting is the directors' office, whereas in Denver it is in the gym and in program staff's cars on the way home. These informal occasions, characterized by much laughter and gentle ribbing between the apprentices and program staff, illustrate how mutual respect and involvement of all participants are key to service learning experiences.

Opportunities for Problem Solving and Higher Order Thinking

As we have seen, cross-age teaching programs should provide opportunities for apprentice teachers to provide input into program development and figure out what kinds of service they can provide to the young children. Reflection enables the apprentices to collaborate on problem solving and teaching strategies and to overcome the challenges of teaching. Often these conversations are quite sophisticated, reflecting the apprentice teachers' increasingly mature attitudes toward their role. As the apprentices gain in experience, they plan their own practices and become aware of the need to challenge the wide range of abilities present in the class so that children do not become bored and off-task (Cutforth & Puckett, 1999).

Simultaneously, they learn that they have to be enthusiastic and to "get into the activity." As one apprentice said, "They are going to be as excited as we are about it." Thus, apprentices use both moral reasoning (learning to think about why boredom occurs and why the young children act in certain ways) and ethical decision making (the "should" part of modeling enthusiasm).

Thus, in addition to providing a service for the children in the physical activity programs, the apprentice teachers develop and learn analytical skills, moral acuity, and social sensitivity through their critical assessment of and collective response to authentic problems. The apprentices' ability to listen to constructive criticism and to respond by improving their teaching is heartening to the program staff. The apprentices' actions illustrate how service experiences can empower young people to succeed and, more particularly, how positive results can occur when students are given opportunities to be responsible and participating members of a community.

Improving Apprentice Teachers' Attitudes Toward Academics

Feeling a sense of connectedness with caring adults has the potential to affect how apprentice teachers feel about school and academics. When the cross-age teaching program is connected to a university setting—through the presence of a university faculty member or graduate students, or location at the university campus, or both—exposure to and an increasing degree of comfort in the university environment can help the apprentice teachers appreciate the value of higher education and can raise aspirations to attend college (Cutforth & Puckett, 1999). In Greensboro and Chicago, regular visits to the university reinforce the apprentices' emerging perceptions of what is possible beyond high school. University faculty and staff treat them "like adults, not like we [are] at school." In Chicago, having a pass to use the university recreation facilities emphasizes their growing sense of responsibility and maturity. The cumulative experience of taking a 10-mile bus trip each day to the university on their own, interacting with university personnel, and assuming a leadership position has taught them not to be intimidated by such surroundings. Referring to the role the program director has played in their lives, a female apprentice teacher said, "He [tries] to teach us [to] have a good education; we can do some things if we get an education."

Although the Denver apprentices only visit the university once a year, their knowledge of university life is enhanced by their weekly interactions with graduate students and their professor. They hear about and become interested in the graduate students' work and come to understand their routine as well as the commitment required. Perhaps most significant is the apprentice teachers' expectation that they can go to college if they work hard and stay focused on their goals, and this helps them see the connection between doing well in school and living successful and personally meaningful lives.

Thus, we are suggesting that the apprentices' familiarity with the university environment can generate a vision of their possible futures. Several see college education not in terms of a product that is beyond their reach, that is, in relation to long-term enhanced career opportunities, but rather in terms of the process in which they can participate, meaning that college is hard work but can also be fun if you act responsibly.

The Neighborhood Scholar Program

The Neighborhood Scholar concept is simple: Anyone who participates in one of the entry programs (extended day clubs, outdoor adventure program, in-school physical education), follows this experience with membership in a cross-age teaching program, and then graduates from high school (no small task in some underserved neighborhoods) is eligible for some kind of postsecondary educational support. Funding college for underserved youth who graduated from high school was first made popular by the I Have A Dream Foundation. The term *neighborhood scholar* is meant to honor kids in the neighborhood who have achieved academically as well as in taking responsibility for themselves and others.

The Neighborhood Scholar Program has been piloted in Chicago, thanks to a grant from Nike as well as a collaborative agreement with the Chicago Workforce Development Partnership. The participants are called Nike Scholars, which has the advantage of linking a term attractive to the kids with one less attractive. Nike Scholars can receive funding from an interest-bearing gift from Nike for postsecondary education, whether community college, four-year university, or trade school. They can also take advantage of a number of opportunities offered by the Chicago Workforce Development Partnership. These include free-of-cost college-level training and job placement in such fields as manufacturing, biotech, and human resources. For example, opportunities in manufacturing include entry-level technician jobs with benefits that require only one semester in a two-year college certificate program. Continuation in the two-year college certificate program earns advancement to a skilled technician position for at least double the wages. Continuation to a four-year college degree leads to either technical supervisor, salesperson, or engineer with another boost in wages. Students who pass a qualifying exam can take up to two free-of-cost college credit courses while still in high school, and a few are participating in this program.

In Chicago, high school seniors now in their eighth year as former Coaching Club members and current participants in the apprentice teacher program have already learned about and applied the idea of taking responsibility in basketball and to some extent "outside the gym," have coached their peers, and have taught younger kids what they have learned. The Nike Scholar Program broadens their opportunities beyond the physical activity setting. Physical activity fades as the program focus, and is replaced by citizen and career education. Before the advent of the Nike Scholar Program, citizen-career guidance was limited to

- discussions about taking the responsibilities outside the gym,
- university student leaders who themselves came from underserved neighborhoods and therefore provided role models for the kids, and
- emphasis on youth development as a career or avocation as the result of cross-age teaching experiences and discussions about professional and avocational opportunities in youth work and

coaching, conducted by youth leaders like Don who have little in-depth knowledge about any other careers.

Challenges Facing Program Leaders

We hope that by now you realize the potential benefits of cross-age teaching programs for the apprentice teachers. However, we also hope that you understand that successful cross-age teaching programs and effective apprentice teachers are not created overnight. Many challenges face the program leader and staff, and three of the most common are discussed next.

Perhaps the biggest challenge, especially in the early stages of the cross-age teaching program, is making the apprentice teachers aware of their leadership role, particularly the need to take charge of their teaching activity. As we said earlier, the transition from player–member to teacher can be difficult. It is not unusual to see lazy, disorganized, or unplanned leadership by the apprentice teachers, which results in children standing at their station waiting to begin the activity while their teachers are talking among themselves or shooting baskets rather than teaching.

Another significant challenge facing program directors is to temper the competitive nature of some of the apprentice teachers, some of whom seem to be obsessed with the need to prove themselves during games with the children. They become intensely competitive and usually dominate the activity by scoring baskets or points and playing aggressively, thereby losing sight of the purpose of the activity. In short, they are more concerned about their own sporting prowess than the children in their care and have resorted to being a student in the program rather than a program leader! However, other apprentice teachers (perhaps those more confident in their physical ability) do not exhibit such behavior and focus more on the development of the young children rather than their own performance. One way to address this challenge is to regularly discuss the problem and to provide time to improve the apprentices' sport skills during orientation and training sessions. We have found that over time, this sense of responsibility to the younger children emerges and remains steadfast. Several of the Denver apprentices' awareness of their skills and understanding of children just a few years younger than themselves has meant that they are able to connect with their students in ways that often the adults are not. As one of the graduate student helpers in the Greensboro program noted, "I saw Rayshone change from being a 'camper' to being a 'camp leader.'" In Chicago, the apprentice teachers who have been with the program for five years exhibit a degree of professionalism beyond their years.

A third challenge is the need to reinforce the apprentice teachers' teaching skills. Their effectiveness varies considerably, with some being considerably better than others at planning practices, being assertive, and motivating students. Some apprentices are so effective that they require little supervision; however, the performance of others varies from day to day and they need to be monitored more closely. Among the most common weak areas are lack of positive feedback, being too negative, being unassertive, and, in some cases, teaching as they are taught by traditional "role out the ball" physical education teachers. The most difficult apprentices are those who are still prone to extremes in behavior and attitude—some even have disagreements with other program leaders, to the point that they cannot work with each other.

Addressing the Challenges

We offer two pieces of advice for program staff to deal with these challenges. First, you need to adopt different approaches with each of the apprentice teachers to ensure that they will be at their best for the children in their care. For example, with some apprentices it might only be necessary to confirm that they are prepared for the session's activities; however, it is necessary to check in with others regularly to determine whether they feel like being program leaders and to ensure that they are mentally prepared to lead the session in a responsible, inclusive way.

Second, the program staff need to decide how much autonomy to give the apprentice teachers in planning their sessions. Although we have a strong commitment to democracy and community and a belief in empowering young people, this approach can present problems at times, particularly when apprentices are not as prepared as they should be or resort to autocratic teaching methods, which, clearly, are not in line with the philosophy of the program. Regularly we witness drills in which two or three students are active while other children wait patiently in line. In such instances, the staff are in a predicament. Although they want to give the apprentices ownership of their teaching, they also want to ensure that learning is both fun and relevant for the children. Such occasions have to be addressed in the reflection sessions. Usually the staff and apprentices provide their views and reach some consensus about the need to be prepared to teach so that all kids are involved. The degrees of support provided by program staff can range from gentle suggestions of how to "jazz up" a practice when not all children are as active as they can be, to admonitions to take a different approach either to content or toward individual children. Constantly we grapple with ways to improve our apprentice teachers. On the one hand, we want to offer constructive criticism to help them improve their pedagogical skills and relationships with children. Often all that is required is a gentle reminder about their responsibilities and what they are capable of. But occasionally it is necessary to intervene and take charge of a session to model and affirm positive teaching behaviors. On the other hand, sometimes we are concerned that too harsh criticism might frustrate certain apprentices and that they might leave our programs. We don't want the cross-age teaching experience to be like the negative aspects of school, and the question sometimes becomes, "How much 'toughness' can I get away with before the apprentices don't come?"

The following list summarizes what the apprentices need to internalize to be effective: Be positive, take charge, communicate, know your students' names, and don't stand around. To keep these principles and the program values at the forefront of the apprentice teachers' mind, they can complete the evaluation form (see form 10.1), which prompts them to reflect on their daily performance and attitude.

Conclusion

This chapter has shown how physical activity settings and cross-age teaching programs in particular possess considerable potential as service learning environments that can engage youngsters in responsible and challenging activities for the common good. We have found that the leadership opportunities given to the apprentice teachers have enabled them to be responsible and participating members of their community. The connection with others is what the apprentice teachers find most appealing about the teaching experience. Rather than being viewed as dependent on adults, the apprentice teachers are regarded as competent and capable with much capacity to care. We believe that more middle and high school students could be trained in basic teaching techniques and could provide assistance in elementary schools, homeless shelters, and recreational programs in their communities.

For Further Study

Cutforth, N.J., & Puckett, K.M. (1999) An investigation into the organization, challenges, and impact of an urban apprentice teacher program. *The Urban Review*, *31*(2), 153-172.

This study draws upon qualitative and quantitative data to describe the implementation of the Chicago apprentice teacher program described in this chapter.

Form 10.1

Apprentice Teacher Self-Evaluation Form

Name:____________________________ Date:______________

1. Were you on time today? *Yes*___ *No*___

2. What percent of the time did you provide leadership for the kids?

*All of the time*___ *Most of the time*___
*Some of the time*___ *None of the time*___

3. What percent of the time were your kids active *(doing something related to the program)?*

*Almost all the time*___ *Most of the time*___
*Less than half of the time*___

4. How positive were you with the kids?

*A lot*___ *Some*___ *Not much*___

5. How many kids' names do you know?___

PART IV

Leadership, Evaluation, and Outcomes

In part IV, chapter 11 outlines essential attributes that program leaders should possess, and chapter 12 provides program leaders with a variety of tools to determine the effectiveness of their programs. Chapter 13 revisits the authors' programs through the eyes and voices of kids, university students, and professors.

Chapter 11

Leadership

James Kallusky

Physical activity programs for kids have a long tradition of contributing to the development of important skills, including leadership. Leaders come in all shapes and sizes and indeed have varying missions and goals, and different leaders find different ways to positively impact society. We can find leaders flourishing in the most ordinary places.

Kayla's involvement with various physical activities offered through her local Boys and Girls Club has provided her with a sense of purpose; she is now in college planning a career in nonprofit management and wants to start her own organization, focusing on after-school programs for youth in Vancouver. Although Kenny was not a talented player, he has forever and unceasingly loved basketball. As a kid, he was involved with numerous basketball programs and now volunteers as a coach at his local Youth Basketball Association. These individuals are exhibiting leadership skills partly because of their involvement with positive youth programs in their home communities and partly because of their desire to interact with youth.

The ultimate purpose of the responsibility model is to enhance leadership qualities in youth and guide youth in positive directions so that they take on leadership roles. In using physical activity to teach self and social responsibility, the model offers kids the opportunity to become leaders within the program first, and then encourages them to transfer these skills into the real world (see chapter 3). However, the program leader (hopefully you) will have a lot to do with bringing this concept to reality. The ability of the responsibility model to positively affect a kid begins with the program leader and his or her ability to lead.

Program leaders directly influence the program and its participants. This is fairly obvious, but what one does as a program leader is critical to the effectiveness of this influence. Being aware of this is central to good leadership and is the focus of this chapter. But what do good program leaders do? I will answer this question and provide a set of qualities that are imperative for those who wish to use the responsibility model effectively and to its full potential, ending with a plan of action for you to start your own program. But first, I will discuss (superficially, because whole books are devoted to leadership and hundreds of scholars have examined leadership theory and practice) the concept of leadership and describe one theory of leadership that I have found effective in implementing the responsibility model.

Exploring Leadership

In seeking common denominators of successful leadership, we find two problems. First, there is no definition of the quintessential leader; a study of history provides us with this insight. Second, one cannot necessarily emulate those who have been perceived as leaders, much less expect to obtain the same results. Because of this, it is necessary to create one's own sense and style of leadership that will be embraced by program participants. Therefore, on the whole, leadership is an individualistic endeavor.

Leadership is also misunderstood. There is often a false conception that if you are not presently a leader, you cannot be one. The old adage about "leaders are born, not made" is preposterous. Leadership qualities can be found in everyone. When leadership is viewed in this way, individuals are liberated to find their gifts, talents, and skills that can guide them to successful leadership.

Second, the word alone conjures up visions of greatness on a worldly level: Gandhi, Mother Teresa. This is a false conception as well. Many leaders at the community level are contributing positively to the world by making a difference in the lives of others. Teachers and coaches may be the best example of this.

Last, performing leadership effectively is often thought of as a single-recipe dish; that is, there is one correct way to appear and to conduct yourself if you are to be a successful leader. This is a false conception, too; there is more than one way to cook a chicken, and there is more than one way to lead.

I want you to consider some ideas as you think about what it means to be a program leader. First, leadership is about action. Action, in relation to the responsibility model, is directly tied to the prosperity of program participants and, for that matter, the betterment of society. The goals and strategies of the responsibility model are intended to be the foundation for this action and change. Second, leadership is process oriented. One must be willing to attempt new approaches to leadership to find what works best. In that light, leadership behavior becomes flexible and without stringent rules. And third, in light of youth programming, leadership is a two-way street, in that program leaders strive to be good leaders and also to impart leadership to others, in this case kids. Therefore, leadership is not circumscribed as power for oneself and a means to dominate. Rather, it is a way to empower others and allow them to become leaders in their own environments.

In regard to these leadership issues, it should become clear that one who feels incapable of leading a program should learn to think otherwise. The potential to develop leadership skills is in everyone.

Servant-Leadership

There are numerous theories of leadership, but for the purpose of this text I will limit the focus to one. The most appropriate theory (for me, anyway) for use in combination with the responsibility model is called servant-leadership.

My contact with servant-leadership begins with a story that will introduce the theory's intentions and meaning. In 1989, I had just completed my bachelor's degree in physical education, thinking that I wanted to teach in the public schools. This desire was flattened after I attended my first course in a credential program. In that course, I observed what was actually taking place in physical education in the public schools. I found that few of the teachers seemed to take real notice of the students. I am not implying that the teachers whom I observed did not care about their students. Nevertheless, not many teachers seemed to have a strong impact on their students. In general, the teachers seemed more concerned about class procedures than anything else. Many of the teachers I observed appeared to give order precedence over learning.

The students in these classes were voiceless and apathetic. Very few of them seemed to be enjoying the time they spent in physical education, let alone growing as individuals. I knew then that I did not want to be a part of what I was observing, so I went back to school. In doing so, I met Don Hellison. This meeting changed my world. As he explained his work to me (as described in chapter 3), I became increasingly excited. Especially interesting to me was that what he was effortlessly explaining seemed right; it seemed real. It made sense. Perhaps in some way Don was exhibiting his leadership skills to me.

It wasn't long after that meeting that I starting working with Don in one of his programs. Through all of this, I began to find meaning in both physical activity and, more importantly, in my work. In many ways, my newly found career was transformed into a calling. Unlike so many other experiences I had had in working with kids, this one allowed me to begin to uncover what I valued. This concept is what made me realize that I wanted to do the same for others: that I would serve them in a way that allowed them to discover their calling.

I never started a program, thereafter, without trying my best to serve the kids in the program. I learned as much as I could about them. I let them learn about me. I put them first and the program second. Moreover, realizing my place in the big picture as related to the overarching purpose of my programs, I put myself last. This is the bedrock of servant-leadership.

Simply put, servant-leadership theory is based on the idea that the leader is first a servant. Therefore, a servant-leader is a person whose sole purpose in being associated with an organization or program is to serve others (Komives, Lucas, & McMahon, 1998). Servant-leadership may be summarized as follows: A servant-leader leads in order to positively change the setting from which the service is provided and to make a difference in the lives of those being served. Such leaders do not engage in youth programs for personal gain, be it money or prestige. They dedicate themselves to strengthening communities by providing a platform from which program participants can then become leaders in their own lives and communities. Subsequently, a servant-leader approaches youth programs by putting his or her own needs aside and putting the needs of others first.

Increased levels of unemployment, crime, drug use, gang activities, and community breakdown, particularly in inner-cities, have generated a legion of social, emotional, physical, and ultimately survival challenges for youth living in these areas. The call for servant-leadership possibly has never been greater. An appropriately tailored activity program that uses the responsibility model within the scope of servant-leadership can help youth who face these problems to focus on positive human qualities and, inevitably, positive change.

Certainly, the responsibility model is based on the notion of providing service to others and to society in general. This is why it is imperative that anyone who attempts to practice the model clearly understands servant-leadership. Ultimately, the goal of both servant-leadership and the responsibility model is "for those who are served to grow, to become more knowledgeable and empowered, to gain interdependence or independence, and to become servant-leaders themselves" (Komives et al., 1998, p. 45).

Leadership, the Responsibility Model, and You

Your authors have described themselves as program leaders in discussing their work in chapters 5 through 11. This title, however, is not one that any of us takes for granted. Being a program leader is a very important undertaking and is one of the most meaningful things that we do.

Drawing on your personal characteristics to find such meaning may be the first step in becoming a good program leader. Much of what will make you successful as a program leader will come from within; thus, clarifying your own values and beliefs first will help guide you in your initial experience as a program leader. Conceivably, you can begin this journey by thinking about the ways in which you would like to be treated as a human being and then extrapolating those findings to how you will attempt to treat program participants. If you find that you value obedience and control, then perhaps this work is not for you. The strategies of the responsibility model are in direct contradiction to those values.

In addition, your personality will have much to do with the way you are perceived. This is true in any realm of life, but especially when you are in a leadership position. Clearly, personality is central to one's ability to effectively lead. Again, questioning yourself, specifically your actions, beliefs, and conduct, is a good starting point.

What is your tolerance level for inappropriate behavior? What will you do when it occurs? How will you react when it's time to celebrate a group's accomplishment? Are you capable of pulling yourself together for the welfare of the group after a rotten morning? Do you truly value the goals of the responsibility model? The answers to these questions, as well as others that you deem important, will help to define the connection between you and the spirit of the responsibility model and, let us not forget, servant-leadership.

Being a Good Program Leader

If you are interested in the well-being of youth, you probably already know at least one kid who could use your help. What would it take to get something extraordinary accomplished to help that child? Could you accomplish this task? If so, you are well on your way to becoming a good leader, because program leaders are constantly faced with the challenge of making such decisions.

Leadership Skills

Leaders are, in fact, the primary decision makers in regard to initiating, creating, and sustaining the program environment, which are the foundational components of programming. Every decision the program leader makes will affect the appearance and feeling of the program. The responsibility model will guide many of these decisions, but, in part, the decisions that you make as a program leader will come simply from who you are and will have much to do with the physical activity environment that you will create.

Eventually, you will arrive at conclusions that beckon you to modify the responsibility model to fit the specific needs of the kids whom you are working for. I strongly encourage you to heed this call. Changing the model is part of being a good program leader. You will know what is best for the specific program environment and must make appropriate changes to maintain a successful program.

Constructing a program where kids have a chance to learn and grow is essential for its success. To provide kids these opportunities, the program leader will have to construct a sense of belonging for youth. All successful youth programs provide an atmosphere where kids feel that they are part of something special. This is the pillar of good programming. The feeling of belonging, so important for youth, will probably be the most critical element in establishing a successful program.

Have you ever been in an environment where you did not feel welcomed? I imagine that you have. I also imagine that you did not necessarily want to participate in that environment. The same occurs when youth enter a program that does not feel inviting. This is the first thing that I consider when starting a new program. I do everything in my power to make sure that kids feel comfortable. I greet them. I attempt to learn something about them early in the program. And I treat them with respect.

The program leader must create this sense of belonging in the program and ensure that it is a place where kids feel wanted. Some kids meet the need of feeling wanted by joining gangs or by taking part in other detrimental activities. Yet when youth are provided with positive outlets, they tend to flourish. Good program leaders provide kids with this alternative by building environments where youth want to be and where youth are given opportunities to blossom.

This feeling of belonging is fostered by the program leader's ability to develop a positive rapport with the kids in the program. Therefore, an essential ingredient to creating a sense of belonging for youth is based on some very basic principles of relationship building. One way to amplify positive relationships with youth is by treating them as individuals, with individual needs, weaknesses, and strengths. A good program leader always views youth as unique and worthwhile individuals; good program leaders listen to kids, understand kids, and give kids dignified experiences.

Out of this sense of belonging, youth will feel respect for one another and a sense of responsibility toward those they feel connected with. The consequence of our society's failure to create places for youth where this occurs is seen in the many troubling stories associated with adolescent behaviors. These behaviors, whether reported in a research study or on the nightly news, make a strong call for programs similar to ones described in this text. A good program leader is committed to helping ameliorate these problems.

Positive Leader Qualities

Of all the characteristics found in successful program leaders, five have been particularly important for my youth programs.

Vision: A Focus That Extends Into the Future Vision is often referred to as an ability to bring an idea to reality. Indeed, this is an important aspect of developing youth programs and performing good leadership. Good program leaders have an idea of where the program is headed, and they know to what extent certain elements of the program will naturally unfold.

Although the concept of vision seems straightforward and is easily understood, having good "vision" is not simple. A program leader who has a keen sense of vision begins by relating all issues of the program to the larger picture. In doing so, the program leader brings relevance to the program by taking cues from the overriding aspects that surround youth today.

A good program leader might begin this process by figuring out how the program relates to the larger overall organization or site in which the program is operating. Then, the program leader relates the organization's purpose to the overall needs of the community. From the community level, the program leader then attempts to make ties to an even larger picture, society. Subsequently, the program leader makes decisions for the program that are based on a greater vision.

Consequently, the program operates on what can be perceived as a trilevel reflection system: from program to organization, organization to community, and community to society. The good program leader also reverses the system, relying on hints from the larger picture to influence the nature of the program itself. For instance, if you are leading a program where the majority of your participants are performing below expected grade levels, it is not likely that many of the kids in that community are graduating from high school and even less likely that any are seeking higher education. A good program leader will discern the problem and may even begin to implement a tutoring program in combination with the activity program.

Finding Charisma in Common Qualities One of the most noticeable traits associated with leadership is charisma, the special quality that gives an individual influence, charm, or inspiration. Leaders are often defined as charismatic persons who inspire and influence others. Charisma is usually viewed as a trait that some are born with, an innate facility to communicate with and appeal to others. However, I think that charisma can be acquired to a certain degree.

We all have the potential to become charismatic leaders (or at least to enhance the elements associated with charisma). Good leaders heighten their sense of charisma by being receptive to the different characteristics and needs of people. This entails having empathy for others. When one makes the effort to walk in another's shoes and truly understand what motivates others, others tend to look to that person for guidance. It is important for program leaders to remain genuine in their offerings. Genuineness is an important aspect of charisma, not necessary, but helpful in magnetizing program participants. Being a genuine program leader tells kids that you are a trustworthy person whom they can rely on for assistance.

If a kid tells me that she is having a problem and I say, "Listen, if you want to share the problem with me, I'd be happy to listen and it will only be between you and me," I am implying that she can trust me, and I know that she is only going to trust me if I am genuine. If I am faking it or if I do not follow through with my promise of confidence, she will most likely notice and distrust my intentions to advocate for her.

Caring is another significant factor in one's charismatic development. In fact, I would dare to say that a sense of caring is the single most important characteristic that youth look for in program leaders. Young people mostly remember those adults in their lives who genuinely cared for them. People also tend to be attracted to others who care about them. As another author of this book (Jim) recently said to me, "Kids seldom care how much you know until they know how much you care."

Modeling: Leading by Example If a program leader expects youth to change their lives through experiencing the responsibility model, then the program leader must act responsibly. This means maintaining your self-control, respecting the kids, exploring new things with them, and supporting them. A good program leader adheres to this standard.

Adaptation: The Chameleon A good program leader is like a chameleon. Chameleons adapt to their environment, and good program leaders are constantly adapting to their environment and to the young people they are serving. When someone says, "Things are different now," they are most likely correct; nothing remains the same. Change is a significant part of life and will play a significant role in your program. Good leaders create positive change in their programs. They do not rely on what they have done in the past to keep a program moving forward. They only use the past to create the future.

Believing in Kids One of the oddest and most ignorant stances adults sometimes take with youth is that, because of their age or behavior, kids cannot exhibit leadership skills. There is no reason to suppose that youth are incapable of providing leadership in a program, and there are plenty of stories about young people who are demonstrating leadership. Unfortunately, we as a society prefer to hear about the inadequacies of youth today. We do not have to look beyond the nightly news and daily newspaper to see these stories.

Our misconceptions about youth are possibly built on lopsided, top-heavy information. Yet good program leaders see beyond headlines and trust in kids' unseen abilities. Good program leaders focus on reality and view young people as potentially able leaders for their programs. This outcome is inherent in the responsibility model and should not be stifled by misleading suggestions from outside sources.

Taking Action

After examining the characteristics that lie within you, and after concluding that your beliefs and strengths are compatible with the responsibility model, you are ready to act. Hellison and Kallusky (1999) recommend an action plan that follows a simple four-step progression: start smart, start small, start, don't stop.

Start Smart

Conceptualize your vision of the program, and then acquire pertinent information by reading and talking to those who do work similar to your idea. You may possibly even collaborate with others who have a shared interest. The point here is to do your homework. What are you going to do with the youngsters? How will you accomplish your plan?

It is important to begin with an idea you have a passion for. It is not recommended that you plan an eight-week program focusing on an activity or concept that you do not care much about. Likewise, choose content that provides you with a high level of comfort; choosing activities that you are unfamiliar with at the beginning of your programming endeavor will only make the program more difficult to implement.

Start Small

Don't try to change the world. Try your idea out in one program that you think you can handle. It may be best to start the program with 10 to 20 participants. Starting small will allow you to try different things without laboring over logistical issues. Moreover, small groups are naturally easier to manage, and the positive contributions that you make to the program (and, in some incidences, the mistakes) are easier to detect.

Start

If you have been seriously thinking about this type of work as you have read this text, quit hovering. Nothing comes from thinking alone. At some point, one must get involved. This is really the underpinning of leadership in regard to youth work and the responsibility model. But where do you start?

There are many places to search out if you want to become involved in physical activity programming. Many local nonprofit agencies such as the YMCA/YWCA and the Boys and Girls Club offer after-school programs. These type of agencies are looking for volunteers in youth programming, and chances are you may be asked to take a leadership role from the outset. Schools also offer physical activity programming for youth, especially at the elementary school level. It may even be feasible for you to request a specific group of kids to implement the responsibility model with, daily or only one to two days per week.

Other places to explore are churches, childcare centers, departments of parks and recreation, universities, and various local youth service agencies. As you begin your inquiries, you may find dedicated and diligent people carrying out programs in your community. In that case, you may want to join them in their efforts. If no one else is doing this type of work in your community, the first step may be yours.

Yes, first steps are frequently intimidating. A prevalent belief is that leaders are not fearful. In my case, however, nothing could be further from the truth. As you venture out to initiate a new program, remember that each one of your authors still admits to a sense of nervousness and, sometimes, even fright when starting a new enterprise with kids; it is a huge responsibility.

Don't Stop

There is no doubt that you will face obstacles early in the program. Certain situations (participant misunderstands the purpose of the responsibility model, staffing problems, logistical problems) will most likely make you wonder why you are there in the first place. My suggestion, in a word: persevere.

Perseverance is the ability to face adversity and overcome obstacles. It stems from one's determination and ability to solve problems, definitely derivatives of your leadership abilities and qualities. Unfortunately, in many instances, you cannot plan on the obstacles that you will encounter as a program leader. Sometimes they are just set before you. For example, you arrive for the program and the space that you reserved is occupied. What do you do? Do you cancel the program for that day, or do you quickly locate another space and briskly plan a different activity? What do you do when a kid in your program experiences a death in the family? Do you go through the routine of the program, or do you find a way to discuss the issue with the kid? These are some of the issues that you will have to resolve.

To persevere over such obstacles, it is best to take notice of what I like to call the "daily private victory." These are the small things that happen in the program, the little details, which you should take pride in or even celebrate. They are too numerous to mention here, but they can be as trivial as having all participants in the program arrive on time. There will be many incidences to applaud.

The message of this section is simple: Do not give up. Good program leaders do not give up on kids. This work is laborious and perplexing at times, but the rewards are well worth the effort. Good program leaders occasionally become heroes, and there is nothing trivial about that.

Staying On Track

The important role that leadership plays in youth programming, especially in the cases of underserved youth, needs to be stressed. Programs that keep leadership issues at the forefront of their agenda provide a positive counterpoint to the alienating and disempowering environments that surround many young people. Nevertheless, youth programs too often overlook these issues.

I can conclude that program leaders give of themselves to offset this problem. To do so, those in leadership roles might say, "I am here to help guide you and to provide you experiences so that you can illuminate yourself and help others grow along the way." This can be a taxing quest. Nonetheless, kids need guides who prepare the way for them so that the road they walk is paved with dignity. Nothing honors youth more than to have someone by, and on, their side; good program leaders, with as much enthusiasm as they can muster, are always there for the kids. This is the ultimate duty of the program leader.

Carrying out responsibilities associated with leadership is not easy. Providing leadership for youth and transferring leadership to youth are precipitous tasks. Furthermore, leadership is an ongoing process, and as you change, so will your values and beliefs, and so will the needs of the young people whom you serve. Here are some questions to help you keep focus based on Covey's work (1991); they should be used as a self-check device for implementing the responsibility model.

- Is my purpose based on proven principles that I currently believe in?
- Do I feel that this work represents the best within me?
- Do I feel direction, challenge, and motivation when I implement the responsibility model?
- Am I aware of the strategies and skills that will help me bring forth the goals of the responsibility model?
- What do I need to do now to be where I want to be tomorrow?

For Further Study

Frick, D.T., & Spears, L.C. (Eds.) (1996). *On becoming a servant-leader.* San Francisco: Jossey-Bass.

Frick and Spears bring to life many of Greenleaf's unpublished essays and personal diary entries that relate to servant leadership in this fascinating read.

Greenleaf, R.K. (1977). *Servant leadership: A journey into the nature of legitimate power and greatness.* New York: Paulist Press.

This collection of Greenleaf's lectures and articles on how to lead by serving others underscores the nature of leadership as a covenant of service.

Jaworski, J. (1996). *Synchronicity: The inner path of leadership.* San Francisco: Berrett-Koehler.

Synchronicity *is the story of Jaworski's personal journey toward a defintion of effective leadership and is designed for anyone seeking to reflect on and improve their own leadership style.*

Chapter 12

Program Evaluation

Tom Martinek

Evaluating the processes and outcomes of programs for underserved youth is, like teaching and coaching, a messy business that does not always follow a step-by-step blueprint. Often the line between instruction and evaluation becomes blurred because both activities require observing, asking questions, and trying and retrying things. Once programs begin, however, people need to evaluate them to pave the way for change and improvement. Evaluation involves collecting information about program activities, characteristics, and outcomes. For this information to be useful, some kind of plan must be devised that fits the goals of your program. The purpose of this chapter is to explore ways that youth development programs such as those described in this book can be evaluated. The key is to identify processes and outcomes that will be useful to those directly involved in the programs—teachers, youth workers, university faculty, and university students. Both traditional and nontraditional methods will be described, along with various data sources (e.g., questionnaires, interviews, observations, journals). In addition, the chapter provides specific ideas that will enable you to evaluate your own programs.

Why Do We Evaluate?

Probably one of the most important reasons we evaluate programs is to improve them. The programs described in the previous chapters undergo continual change because we see that some ideas are not working or that the program's goals are not being met. Very often evaluation occurs on the spot because something needs to be fixed quickly. When things are not working because of poor matching of kids, unclear directions, coaches who are too competitive, or inappropriate learning tasks (too difficult or easy), immediate attention is required. Because we believe that evaluation is ongoing in all we do in the clubs, being able to address on-the-spot problems requires careful attention or what Kounin (1970) called "withitness."

Other changes are linked to long-term observation, where patterns (some good and some not so good) begin to emerge. This type of evaluation tends to be more formal and requires careful and systematic analysis of the program's operation. For example, in one of the Coaching Clubs in Greensboro, office referrals were tracked throughout an entire school year. The data were organized around each nine-week grading period. Changes across the periods indicated how certain program goals were being met, especially those that focused on self-control and respect in the school setting (Martinek, McLaughlin, & Schilling, 1999). In general, evaluation results have been used in programs to

- assess need,
- document how well a program is working,
- determine how participants view the program,
- show the usefulness of a particular approach,
- examine how certain parts of the program (e.g., mentoring, apprentice teaching) are working, or
- provide information for modifying program goals.

Assumptions About Evaluation

Evaluating programs that use the responsibility model is difficult. Often we have struggled with some ideas that seem to work and also with those that have failed miserably. Getting it right takes time—sometimes years! Whether evaluation is done in a traditional or nontraditional way, the meaningfulness of the data relies on basic assumptions. Knowing these assumptions is critical in developing any kind of evaluation scheme, because they provide the guideposts for interpretation and application. Here are five assumptions that have guided all of the authors' evaluation efforts over the past several years:

1. There is commitment to making a difference.
2. There is no one way of doing evaluation.
3. Evaluation does not have to be done by outsiders.
4. Findings are useful to stakeholders (kids, youth leaders, coaches, teachers, etc.).
5. The program is running smoothly.

Commitment to Making a Difference

Evaluating a program should result in making a difference in kids' lives. This type of commitment needs to be at the forefront of any evaluation plan. Without this commitment, the evaluator will assuredly short-circuit the process of tying the findings to program improvement. Motives vary for doing program evaluation. Some individuals evaluate because there is a need to be accountable—no argument from us on this one. Programs based on the responsibility model are often met with skepticism. Therefore, some program directors may feel they have to provide evidence that something is happening; they have to prove that kids are becoming more responsible! Others feel that funding agencies will want "hard data" to fund programs or because they want data to publish. Unfortunately, such motives often leave kids out of the picture. If kids are going to be the benefactors of responsibility-based programs, they must come first. This assumption encourages the staff to remain connected to the youngsters throughout the evaluation process.

There Is No One Way to Evaluate

Many people feel that they have to select a single best design when evaluating a program. Perhaps you were taught in your measurement class that there is one best design. We guess that the reasoning behind this is that for every problem there is a single best answer. However, we must account for many complex factors when examining programs for underserved youth. Creativity enables us to attend to the multiple roles, values, and situations inherent in youth work. Consequently, there is no best way to design or conduct a program evaluation. Michael Patton (1987) argued that maintaining "rigor" in design will lead you away from evaluating what is useful to the staff and the kids in your programs. A scientific or technical approach leaves little room for looking at the genuineness of any program because it attempts to mold and define the program to fit a model of how things should be evaluated. Therefore, modifying and matching evaluations to the uniqueness of the program enable one to be responsive to the needs and interests of those who play and work in our programs. Rather than being faithful to some model, we must be faithful to the characteristics of the program (Patton, 1987). We need to adopt a "real world" view so that we are able to recognize and deal with a multitude of choices and decisions in the evaluation process.

Evaluation Is an "Inside Job"

The authors of this book not only plan programs, but actually work with kids who attend them. This places us in a good position to know what, who, and when to evaluate. It also puts us closer to information derived from evaluation. Outsiders who are not intimately connected with the program are often unable to effectively translate their findings to the situation. That is, outside evaluators are often unfamiliar with the social and economic constraints of the program's setting, the varied dispositions of the kids in the program, and personal values of the individuals running the program. Some of our colleagues in the sciences (e.g., physiologists, psychologists, biomechanists) would argue about potential biasing because they believe we are too close to our own data! We believe, however, that having biases is not necessarily bad. After all, why shouldn't we be biased, especially when it comes to working with underserved youngsters? Why shouldn't we deliberately look for things that we have struggled with in our programs? We know the types of information we already collect, such as journal entries, informal and formal observations, and other anecdotal records from individual and group discussion. If we truly want the evaluation strategy and the findings to relate to what we do with our kids, then we must be involved with the development, delivery, and application of the evaluation program.

Data Are Useful to All

Evaluation data are important and must be useful both to those who run the programs and to youngsters. Program staff should be able to make sense of the data so they can adjust the program. Likewise, youngsters and others (parents, teachers, mentors, volunteers) should benefit from the products of evaluation. Many types of data are available to the program evaluator. Deciding what to use will depend on the goals of the program and the feasibility of obtaining the information from participants and other data sources. No matter what kind of data are available, it would be foolhardy to gather information that was not useful or interpretable to those who run the programs. This requires that the results of any evaluation effort be communicated in a way that all parties can understand.

The Program Is Running Smoothly

Until the program is running relatively smoothly, traditional evaluation methods are not very helpful. That is, there is little to be gained in doing pre and post measures until the program leaders clearly know what they are evaluating! This is not to say that informal, ongoing evaluation isn't a must—it is vital to providing positive day-to-day experiences for kids. Unfortunately, there is often a rush to put a traditional evaluation scheme in place at the beginning of a program. A design is created, measures are selected, a timetable is established for data collection, and analysis procedures are predetermined. However, this type of traditional planning is not very useful in the long run. A main reason for this is that it takes time to get the program right. There are many "bumps in the road" that have to be dealt with before one knows what to evaluate. One of these bumps is getting kids to understand the purposes of the clubs. Program leaders continually use various trial-and-error methods and some kids don't attend regularly. Another bump is not using effective teaching strategies, or selecting the wrong strategy to use. Kids bring varied and unexpected dispositions into the gym, requiring on-the-spot changes. In short, those who are just starting programs need to approach evaluation with a clear understanding of what they are doing.

Evaluating Youth Programs

The remainder of this chapter describes evaluation approaches through examples of programs that have used the responsibility model with underserved youth. The examples show various evaluation designs and tools for collecting information about each program. The examples are to serve as guides for developing your own ideas for evaluation.

There is always a tendency to compare programs to a set of standards or criteria such as those presented in chapter 3. This is a legitimate way of describing the quality of programs. However, another way is to look at specific outcomes or what kids gain from participating in a responsibility-based program. This chapter attempts to do both without adhering to any set of criteria for either process or outcome measures. Although programs described in the text use the responsibility model, they differ in the ways of using the model and determining its effectiveness. Each example includes a description of

- what is being evaluated and why,
- the data collection process and analysis,
- the results, and
- the lessons learned from the evaluation process.

The examples are presented in progression starting with traditional approaches and then ending with nontraditional, creative forms of evaluation. In each example, one or multiple approaches are emphasized to provide you with detailed information for use in your own programs. An overview of the five examples is presented in table 12.1.

Table 12.1

Overview of Evaluation Programs

Description	Evaluator(s)	Topic	Methods	Findings	Application
TRADITIONAL MODELS					
Chicago Coaching Club	T. Cummings (1997)	Club impact on future school performance.	Participant and control group comparisons.	Dropout rate decreased, no differences were found for grade retention and absenteeism.	Strong link between being in the club and staying in school.
Chicago Martial Arts Club	P. Wright (1998)	Club impact on conflict resolution skills.	High- and low-attendance group comparisons.	Conflict resolution skills improved.	Program promoted positive values and leadership.
LESS TRADITIONAL MODELS					
Chicago apprentice	N. Cutforth & K. Puckett (1999)	Impact of apprentice teacher program on leadership and commitment.	Descriptive study of veteran club members who participated in a summer apprentice teacher program.	Some kids were effective teachers and showed strong commitment to club values.	Apprentice teaching appears to foster leadership and commitment to club values.
Greensboro veteran club members	T. Schilling (1999)	Describe why kids "stay with" the club over time.	Descriptive study of how kids view commitment and what factors influence levels of commitment.	Program structure and environment, relationships, and personal characteristics influenced commitment.	Including fun activities and clear goals, giving students a voice in the program, and developing relationships.
CREATIVE MODEL					
Greensboro sport	T. Martinek, T. Schilling, & D. Johnson (1999)	Self-designed case study of club members and their ability to transfer.	Matrix analysis of data obtained from participant portfolios.	Some goals were met both in gym and classroom; transfer of goals was indicated.	Transfer of club goals needs to be focus of club and mentor programs.

Example One: Comparing School Outcomes Using Club Members and Control Groups

Teresa Cummings's (1997) study of "graduates" from a basketball Coaching Club at a Chicago elementary school (see chapter 7) is an example of how a traditional program evaluation looks. The study focused on the impact that the club experience had on the graduates' attendance, grades, and dropout rate. In essence, Cummings wanted to know whether the club experience was a significant factor in future school performance.

Using an experimental-control group design, Cummings compared a control or "nonparticipant" group with former club members. Both groups were made up of kids with similar backgrounds. She analyzed data by graphing group differences (percentage dropping out) and using statistical techniques for looking at absenteeism, grades, and retention. Past evaluation of clubs had been qualitative and provided various images of how the program was working for kids and staff members (Debusk & Hellison, 1987; Mulaudzi, 1995). However, quantitative evaluation of dropout rate, retention, grades, and absenteeism had not been done during the program's six-year tenure.

Cummings found a notable difference between the two groups, with none of the club members dropping out of school as compared with the nonparticipant group, which had a 34 percent dropout rate. She also found no significant difference between the two groups for grade retention and absenteeism. In other words, club members and nonparticipants repeated a grade and were absent about the same amount of time.

Cummings's evaluation suggested a strong link between being a basketball club member and staying in school. Unfortunately, there was no way of determining whether being in the club was a reason for staying in school. Knowing this would help determine whether there was an actual cause-and-effect relationship between club participation and dropout rates. Qualitative research via interviews would help in determining this. In presenting this to program staff, Cummings stressed the importance of doing some sort of qualitative follow-up (i.e., interviews) to identify the reasons for staying in school. Although keeping at-risk youngsters in school is an important goal for many programs, it was not a major goal in Hellison's early inception of the responsibility model. Rather, he wanted to focus on getting kids to feel good about themselves, clarifying their strengths and identity, and giving them purpose in life.

Example Two: Comparing Aggression Levels Using Subgroups Within a Martial Arts Club Program

Paul Wright's study (1998) of a Chicago middle school Martial Arts Club is another example of a traditional two-group design. Paul evaluated two groups of students based on their attendance records at the club; no actual control group was used. He focused on the number of aggressive acts by students and their responses to confrontation. The students were from an elementary school located in the northwest part of Chicago; all were participants in the Martial Arts Club described in chapter 7. The teachers were becoming concerned over the increased amount of fighting among students at their school. In addition, physical and verbal confrontations were becoming more extreme, sometimes involving the use of weapons. Some teachers had been assaulted by students.

Wright was trying to see whether the frequency, types, and causes of conflict and the use of conflict resolution skills were related to attendance in the Martial Arts Club for the previous two years. Unlike Cummings's use of independent groups, club members were divided into three groups based on their attendance records during the past two years. Wright felt that students with low attendance rates could serve as a control group. He was especially interested in how the club members were able to stay away from conflict in their schools and neighborhoods.

He found that a variety of circumstances sparked conflicts. Examples of situations leading to conflict were basketball games, classroom disputes, stolen property, gang-related problems, and sticking up for someone. The highest number of incidents were the result of actions during basketball games (e.g., fouls, ball hogging). Outside the school, incidents such as being jumped or attacked by rivals and fighting with friends and relatives were also frequent, indicating that the participants' natural environment was violent and unsafe.

Wright also created a conflict resolution scale that categorized the types of conflict resolution skills. He found that participants who had the lowest attendance fell between violent and aggressive on the conflict resolution scale. Students in the middle attendance group were neutral on the conflict resolution scale. The group with the highest attendance were more assertive and peaceful on the scale, in terms of conflict resolution, than the other two groups.

One concern with using this scale related to categorizing responses that contained two or more types of conflict resolution. For example, one of the youngsters and a friend were assaulted one day. The youngster first tried to walk away but eventually physically defended himself after being attacked. He then left and called on some of his friends to help him retaliate. Although he started out as being assertive, the scenario ended with revenge. Because each student was only assigned to one conflict resolution category, Wright decided to maintain consistency by assigning the students according to the most extreme behavior. This may not have allowed us to see the whole picture. Therefore, it may be useful to include another category referring to the youngster's initial response.

Although club attendance and conflict resolution appear to be related, causality could not be inferred. This study used a descriptive design rather than an experimental one. It is possible that students who already have positive values and conflict resolution skills are drawn to the club and stay with it over time. Similarly, some students may not commit to the club and stop attending because the club values and their own values do not match. Thus, rather than serving as the impetus for changing values, the club may serve as a supportive and reinforcing environment in which youngsters can comfortably accept and act on their own sense of right and wrong. This may be different from what they encounter in their natural environment.

Example Three: Examining the Social and Psychological Outcomes of an Apprentice Teacher Using Journals, Interviews, and Questionnaires

Nick Cutforth and Karen Puckett (1999) evaluated a specialized program called the Apprentice Teacher Program. The program was designed to give urban youngsters the opportunity to teach basketball to young children attending a summer basketball camp. Unlike Cummings's and Wright's programs, this one focused on one group of 11 kids. Both quantitative and qualitative methods were used to extract information about experiences in this sport camp for younger kids. This program was a nice example of how quantitative and qualitative data could be combined in the evaluation process.

All of the students were in or had been in the before-school Coaching Club previously described in Cummings's evaluation program. Their responsibilities were to teach basketball and the responsibility goals to approximately 40 eight- and nine-year-olds from a nearby housing project for an hour a day, four days a week, over a five-week period.

The evaluators used informal observations, entries from a personal journal kept by the director, and interview responses from the director and apprentice teachers before and after the program as the main data sources for the evaluation. In addition, the director took attendance of the apprentice teachers and graded (i.e., A, B, C, D, F) their effectiveness each day.

An important aspect of this evaluation was that the evaluators knew the teachers and had worked with them in previous years in the

Coaching Club. This rapport help considerably in getting the apprentice teachers to respond with candor during the interview and thereby increasing the validity of the data.

The evaluators concluded from their data that the "core" program staff consisted of eight reliable teacher apprentices, the program director, and the graduate assistants. The journal entries and interview responses of the director indicated that the greatest challenge was to make the apprentice teachers aware of their leadership role, particularly the need to take charge of the sessions. Some teachers were organized and seemed to get down to business teaching skills and motivating the children. However, some teachers needed to be checked consistently throughout the camp to be sure they were prepared for the morning activities. Others simply needed confirmation that they were on track. The evaluation data showed that training in managing student behavior and teaching basketball skills was needed. It was also concluded that ways to dilute the competitive edge of some of the teachers needed to be explored.

The evaluation scheme of Cutforth and Puckett provided a nice baseline of information for the Apprentice Teacher Program. Overall, the evaluation showed that the program increased the apprentice teachers' awareness that they could contribute to other people's lives. They also knew that they had done something good that summer and began to see an alternative future for themselves. This appeared to foster an eagerness to stay with the program and be a part of it the next year.

Example Four: Using Interview and Q-Sort Techniques to Look at Commitment to Program Goals

Tammy Schilling's (1999) evaluation program looked at "veteran" club members of University of North Carolina at Greensboro's Project Effort (see chapter 10). Because the program originated with participants in an elementary school in a poor area of Greensboro, the program staff were interested in seeing why club members stay with the program into their high school years. Therefore, the purpose of Schilling's evaluation program was to determine program involvement and commitment over the length of the program's history (i.e., five years) through the participants' perspective.

Schilling chose a case study method that allowed for an in-depth look into the experiences of individual participants. Data collection included individual and focus interviews and a card-sorting task. The focus group interview involved asking questions to all seven of the participants as a group. Schilling used this method because she wanted to ask them about barriers (e.g., gang involvement, school activities) to program commitment and to compare their own and the staff's commitment levels. She felt that the participants would be more likely to answer the questions honestly and to elaborate on their feelings in the supportive presence of the other kids, rather than by themselves.

For the card sort, Schilling took main themes (e.g., "learning new activities" and "having a mentor") or ideas from the participants' responses in an earlier interview and asked them to rate the relevance and importance of each theme with respect to their personal involvement. The card sort allowed Schilling to look across the program participants and note the aspects that were consistently most and least important to the participants' involvement.

As with the other studies, it was essential for Schilling to use multiple data sources to find out about the participants' program commitment, particularly because the program participants were youngsters. Therefore, she interviewed the parents/caregivers to get their perceptions of their child's program involvement and commitment. Two of the program leaders were also interviewed. The leaders developed commitment profiles for each participant that included things such as commitment ratings of factors most important to the participant, change over years of involvement, parts of the program that they like/dislike, and examples of the participant transferring the goals of Project Effort outside the gym.

The analysis consisted of two phases. The first phase included the development of historical profiles and the card-sorting task. This information provided a backdrop for subsequent information regarding the participants' commitment.

The second phase consisted of a content analysis that included the identification of main data themes (i.e., meaningful quotes) from all the participants' data regarding commitment. Schilling also examined which themes were validated by the parent/caregiver, leader, and/or focus group data. Finally, a cross-case analysis was conducted, which allowed Schilling to look across the cases of all five participants to note similarities or interesting trends.

The results suggested some considerations for program development. The participants noted that important factors related to their program involvement were opportunities to try out new activities and participate in specific activities (e.g., basketball, swimming), having fun, having a voice in how the program runs, staying out of trouble, and having program goals. The participants also perceived that their commitment across a multiyear period was influenced by program structure (e.g., type of activity), program environment (e.g., having fun), relationships (e.g., with staff and other participants), and personal characteristics (e.g., lack of alternative options for participation). The results reinforced what research has consistently shown—make it fun and they will come! However, it was clear that participating in fun activities was just a part of the big picture. Developing close relationships with other participants and the staff members and being given responsibility and leadership opportunities were also central components of the participants' commitment across time.

Example Five: Evaluating Program Outcomes Using Matrix Development From Journal Entries, Interview Responses, and Informal Observations

In this evaluation program, a more "creative" approach was used by me along with Tammy Schilling and Dennis Johnson to find out whether the goals of a program were being met. By creative, I mean that a self-designed strategy was used, one that strayed from traditional methodologies. The strategy focused on the development of a matrix that helped the evaluators look at how each club member was meeting goals. A main issue with the staff was to find ways of organizing and interpreting an ample amount of information that was collected during the program. Again, Project Effort was the program being evaluated. The evaluators were particularly interested in seeing how well the values learned in the sport club were being applied to the classroom and elsewhere.

We developed a participant-goal matrix (Demos, 1989; Van Tulder, Van der Vegt, & Veenman, 1993) to organize and interpret student portfolios. The portfolios included informal notes taken by staff, journal entries, and end-of-year interview responses. The matrix allowed staff to see how each club member performed in relation to the values and goals of the club. The matrix also enabled us to see how well the club members transferred the values and goals of the responsibility model to the classroom setting.

All of the information was placed in a student folder that served as the portfolio. Using a specified procedure, a matrix was created from the contents of the portfolio. The matrix allowed the users to compare common and contrasting patterns. The procedure consisted of first having staff review all the data (journal cards, mentor journals, etc.) collected for each student. After each student's portfolio was reviewed by a staff member, a code was assigned to each program goal for the gym and classroom settings. For example, a student was coded for showing self-control and respect for others as these items related to the two settings. Then the student was coded for trying things out, and so on.

A student was coded with a plus symbol (+), an asterisk (*), or a minus symbol (–) for each goal category. A plus meant that the student demonstrated that goal most of the time. An asterisk meant that each goal was demonstrated some of the time. A minus meant that each goal was demonstrated little of the time. All the staff evaluators reviewed and coded each student. Table 12.2 provides a sample of the matrix.

The data showed that the youngsters were able to acquire a degree of persistence at learning tasks in the gym and classroom. Their ability to set some goals and respect others in the gym setting also appeared to be augmented by the program.

The club members struggled, however, to transfer some of the club's values to the classroom. For example, goal setting was a persistent problem for the kids. Likewise, incidences of self-control, respect, and caring for others were not as high in the classroom as in the gym. The evaluators felt that this inability to transfer the values of the gym to the classroom also partially reflected a lack of ownership in the values of the club.

Principles Learned From the Evaluation Process

All of the leaders discussed in this chapter have applied certain principles for evaluating their programs. Some of these principles are common for all evaluators, and some are unique to the setting. In all cases, they reflect the essentials for conducting program evaluation: use of control groups, accessing various data sources, organizing and

Table 12.2

Program-Goal Matrix

	Personal responsibility				Social responsibility				Ownership
	Effort (trying things out)		Self-direction (set goals)		Self-control		Caring		Ability to transfer
Student	**G**	**C**	**G**	**C**	**G**	**C**	**G**	**C**	**G to C**
Rayshone	+	*	+	–	+	+	*	*	M
Lateesha	+	+	*	+	+	*	+	*	H
Leonard	*	–	–	–	+	–	–	–	L

+ Showed most of the time. * Showed some of the time. – Showed little of the time. C = classroom; G = gym.

analyzing data, and understanding limitations of applying results. We hope you can apply some of these principles to your program.

Principles Applied to Using Control or Comparison Groups

Some individuals feel that if you don't have a true control group, you cannot find answers to your questions. However, Wright showed that with a little creativity, you can compare different groups of kids within one program and discover possible relationships between the variables of interest (e.g., conflict resolution skills, referrals). By simply selecting kids with low attendance, he was able to establish a so-called control group.

Cummings's study presents a cautionary principle in the traditional use of a control or comparison group. It is important to recognize the difficulty of using a control group of underserved youngsters. This is especially problematic when the participants are volunteers; that is, they choose to come to a program. Trying to control for prior achievement, grades, socioeconomic status, or other factors does not account for the obvious motivational levels of the kids who elect to participate in the clubs or the teacher, principal, and perhaps parents who urge them to attend. The most common solution would be to randomly assign all the kids who wanted to be in the club to the program or to a "waiting list" group. This assumes a large number of kids want to be in the club, which may not always be the case. The waiting list or control group supposedly becomes equivalent to the treatment or program group.

Although this strategy seems sound from a pure research perspective, there are two problems with it. The first is an ethical concern: What happens to the kids on the waiting list? Are they to be ignored or put on hold just for the sake of research? The second concern relates to more practical issues regarding group comparisons. It is extremely difficult (if not impossible) to determine a "true control" group in this type of work. Although poverty, racism, and societal indifference are common denominators among underserved youth, each youngster brings into a program circumstances and daily experiences unique in severity and scope. They also bring in various levels of adaptability that allow them to navigate through a social system fraught with economic and geographic barriers. Thus, looking at how and why individual kids respond to the club becomes extremely important. This is not to say that group comparisons cannot highlight possible causes. However, making comparisons, such as those in Cummings's evaluation, must be done with caution and insight into the true meaning of any differences found or not found.

Principles Involved in Using Various Data Sources

Where can data come from for program evaluation? This critical question often leaves evaluators scratching their heads. There are a multitude of data sources, and describing each one would exceed the page limitation of this text. However, we can offer several principles about accessing certain data sources described in the previous studies.

One data source is school records. Of course, accessing these requires clearance from administrators, kids, and parents. However, these data can be quite useful in determining overall school performance. School records can augment much of the qualitative information acquired by other evaluators of the various clubs using the responsibility model. However, the accuracy of measures such as grades, dropout rate, and absenteeism depends on the diligence of those who keep student records (i.e., teachers, school and central office staff). Computer retrieval systems are helpful but only to the extent to which data are carefully entered into the data bank.

Another source for data is questionnaires. Some questionnaires can come from previous work or can be devised by the evaluator. You will often find yourself stuck in the evaluation process when you cannot find any literature, scales, or past examples regarding what you are trying to find out. At these times it is particularly important to use pilot work to get a feel for what is going on and even to create your own scale for measuring or categorizing responses. Wright used pilot work to create a conflict resolution scale that allowed him to use categories that made sense for his work and the club participants. He found that the scale had to be brief and worded so the kids could understand.

Journals are another big source of data. Participant-observers like program directors, staff (mentors, teachers), and kids (i.e., see studies by Cutforth & Puckett, 1999, and Martinek, Schilling, & Johnson, 1999) are encouraged to keep personal journals. Journal entries usually include such things as feelings about what happens in the club, how kids are doing, and impressions of staff performance. The entries are an important data source for evaluating many segments of the program. Journals can include quantitative assessment (i.e., grades of performance) as well as narrative data. The narrative entries help to embellish the quantitative data. As demonstrated by Martinek, Schilling, and Johnson (1999), portfolios can be developed to provide profiles on how each club member is doing. The portfolios can contain journal entries from mentors, teachers, and staff who work with the youngsters in different capacities.

A final data source used in these studies was interview responses. Cutforth and Puckett (1999) and Martinek, Schilling, and Johnson (1999) applied several principles to maximize the information gained from interviewing kids and staff members:

- Practice your interviews. This helps you avoid pitfalls such as poor phrasing and prompting, inappropriate questions. Although many texts provide some guidance on how to conduct interviews, these guidelines don't always apply very well with underserved kids.
- Employ a "multiple meeting" approach. Use information from previous meetings to prepare for the next meeting. This provides coherence among the various sources of information. Multiple meetings also mean that you must fit into the schedule of those you are interviewing.
- Consider parents' perceptions of their child's involvement in after-school clubs. Parents provide a much richer picture of how the values are being transferred outside the club setting.
- A wonderful by-product of interviewing kids is the extended experience of working with the club members. There is much value gained in the time spent with kids during data collection; you learn more in the extra time spent in the car or playing basketball than you normally do in running the club.
- Kids and parents should be interviewed by individuals who know them. A trusting relationship between the interviewers and the interviewees is a must if responses are to be believable. In the programs described in this chapter, the interviewers had worked with the youngsters in the clubs, thus establishing a positive rapport with them.

Principles Applied to Organization and Analysis of Data

The organizing and analysis of data can take many forms. The decision on what method to use will depend on the type of data collected and how you want to use them. Charts, biographies/stories, case studies, tables, metaphors, and themes are but a few of the ways in which qualitative and quantitative can be organized (Patton, 1987). As you become more experienced in evaluating programs, you will develop a broad repertoire of methods. Many evaluators have used a combination of methods to analyze and present their findings. For example, Cummings (1997) found that simply graphing dropout rate for both groups was all that was needed. One could then simply "eyeball" the graphic differences. On the other hand, statistical analyses highlighted group and time differences for grade retention and absenteeism.

In Cutforth's and Puckett's study (1999), attendance data, participant interviews, and the director's impression of how the apprentice teachers were fulfilling their teaching roles were interconnected to provide a true view of their commitment to the program. Schilling (1999) organized her interview and journal data around themes and categories that helped to explain effectiveness and commitment of veteran club members. Both presented their information through case descriptions. Each case provided an in-depth and unique characterization of each club member's sense of commitment to the responsibility model and the clubs.

Finally, information is often gathered throughout the course of the program. Martinek, Schilling, and Johnson (1999) organized the data into student folders or portfolios. At the end of the program, data from each portfolio were transformed into a participant-goal matrix. This matrix format requires that a simple but useful rubric be developed so that material can be evaluated. The rubric contains basic guidelines for assigning a value or code to the portfolio content. The participant-goal matrix allows users to look at how each club member did during the year. The matrix provides a general picture of how the program impacted the club members' values and their ability to transfer these values to the classroom setting. Pre and post measures do not have to be used with the matrix analysis. Rather, an overall assessment based on the content of each member's portfolio can be derived from this strategy.

Principles Applied to the Use of Information

The main premise of this chapter is that program evaluators should be concerned with how program leaders, kids, and policymakers will use the processes and findings. Three main principles guide this utility emphasis. First, utility must be in the eyes of the beholder. That is, utilization means different things to different people in different settings, and it is an issue to negotiate between evaluators and users. Knowing the needs of the program leader, the kids, and perhaps the community will clarify how the information can be used.

A second principle is that the users of the information should be identified. They are to be real, visible, specific, and caring human beings—not general or abstract audiences, organizations, or agencies. And finally, the evaluator must react, adapt to the unexpected, and interact with all those who will benefit from the findings. Design and redesign, focus and refocus, analysis and reanalysis, and interpretation and reinterpretation are all part of this process. The interplay of these processes will ensure a tighter bond between utility and user. I hope the ideas presented in this chapter will enhance your understanding of how evaluation can be meaningful and useful.

For Further Study

Alkin, M. (1990). *Debates on evaluation.* Newbury Park, CA: Sage.

This book provides frank and provocative views about evaluation. Alternative conceptions of evaluations are offered not only from researchers but from practitioners as well. The book gives rich insights on how evaluation should be approached and important implications for evaluating youth development programs.

Martinek, T., & Hellison, D. (1997). Service-bonded inquiry: The road less traveled. *The Journal of Teaching in Physical Education, 17,* 107-121.

This article describes a new approach to evaluating programs in school and other community agencies. The approach allows evaluators to expand the boundaries of scholarly inquiry through the integration of scholarship and service.

O'Sullivan, R. (1993). *Programs for at-risk youth—A guide to evaluation.* Newbury Park, CA: Corwin Press.

This book provides an excellent overview of various types of programs for at-risk youth. Examples of evaluation models are provided to help school personnel evaluate programs designed for at-risk students.

Patton, M. (1987). *Creative evaluation.* Newbury Park, CA: Sage.

This book describes various ways evaluation can be done in a creative and user-friendly manner. It shows the reader how to evaluate by using a variety of concepts, techniques, communication skills, and teaching methods.

Chapter 13

Program Outcomes

Melissa Parker and Nick Cutforth

The least one can say about what we do is that we are passionate about it. Our work and our beliefs drive us and provide meaning, and we are committed to them. In short, we believe in our work. One could just as easily ask why we believe. What makes it worth doing? Our collective answer would be that it does some good, that it makes a difference in the lives of children and youth. One could then justifiably ask, how do we know?

The following case studies (stories) are a glimpse at some of the outcomes of our work. They tell us that our work makes a difference. You might say that quantitative data would provide a more believable answer. Numbers would convince more people. A member of my dissertation committee once asked me, "Are there things that cannot be measured through behavioral research?" The response (from another committee member) was "yes—nonbehavioral events." Though certainly behavioral responses are clear in our work with kids, we largely deal with events that stem from the internal states of children, youth, and leaders. The nonbehavioral events are important to us.

We deal with children and youth, and these are stories about children and youth and the program leaders and teachers who work with them. Numbers take away the humanness of the answer; with numbers, the uniqueness, the richness, the personality of the person—the child, the leader—are lost. All you have left is an impersonal statistic to match a generic entity that is evaluated according to its logical character (Martinek & Hellison, 1997b) (and when did you see an underserved youth who functioned with "logical character"?). In other terms, the simple question of whether Joey improved *x* amount from the first day to the last day is answered without any detail or explanation. These types of answers, for us, are boring at the least and more importantly don't answer the whole question. We have decided that qualitative information, as in our stories presented here, tells us whether what we are doing is worth doing. This information is enough for us; you have to make your own decision about what is worth doing and what kind of evidence you need.

As you might well imagine, our outcomes are mixed. We have glowing successes and dismal failures mixed with tentative breakthroughs. Of those, the successes seem very small and the failures always loom large, but we have learned that we mostly have small successes, and that success is measured in very small achievements. We will share some of these successes in the following stories about kids, college students, and professors. You decide if it is enough.

Kids

The kids are the reason why we teach the programs. As we saw in chapter 1, their lives are complicated, often tragic, but sprinkled with joy. We hope our programs contribute to their joy and purpose in life.

Is That Why Your Eyes Are All Red?

Sophie was a student in our fourth/fifth-grade physical education class. At 10 years old, she weighed about 150 pounds and was about five feet four inches. An African-American girl, she came to us with a self-proclaimed "attitude." She was accurate about that. Not afraid to talk, she would tell us when she didn't want to do something and when she wasn't going to do something . . . which was most of the time and most of what we did other than basketball.

The school was a charter school with a population of 50 percent Hispanic (Chicano) and 50 percent African-American students. Forty percent of the students did not speak English as a first language. The students had limited physical education before we arrived and never from a specialist. Sport, or more accurately basketball, was a street medium for them whether they had any skills or not. One of the goals of the school was to create responsibility, but the faculty went at it very differently than we did. They taught compliance to rules, standing in straight, quiet lines, and not making mistakes when it came to behavior. In fact, if you acquired too many reprimands you were dismissed from the school. Sophie wasn't very good with this compliance and made lots of mistakes. She was on her third strike.

The class met outside on the blacktop in south central Los Angeles. Our goals for physical education were to teach personal and social responsibility while at the same time to expand the activity base of these students beyond basketball. One of the things that we learned early on was that sometimes new content was uncomfortable for the kids and not something they took to readily. Hence, our class guideline of "just try it" was put to the test. Basketball was the only sport (other than jump rope), and basketball only involved individual trick skills. Hockey was "stupid" and "felt dumb." Students didn't know how to turn double dutch. They had never held a tennis or racquetball racket and thought them most useful as weapons. When we took them to a swimming pool, some wouldn't even go in the water; others only went in if someone held onto them, but then we were showered with the screams and giggles of pure delight that emerged from the new experience.

Sophie was a special case. She would stick with content about 10 minutes (if we were lucky) and then go sit down or talk to her brother and cousin, who were in the kindergarten class that shared the playground with us. We would allow her to sit or talk, then after about five minutes go and get her back, constantly talking to her and expanding her time limits of trying new activities. We were making progress and each of us began to accept and trust more of the other; except when her classroom teacher joined us for physical education. The classroom teacher did not accept our little give-and-take system and was constantly trying to force Sophie back into the class. Sophie at this point couldn't discriminate between the inconsistencies, and we would lose a week of progress after each of those instances.

Although Sophie was getting better about trying new activities she wasn't comfortable with, she still settled arguments by yelling, swearing, and fighting and did not know how to deal with frustration or, for that matter, anything that didn't go her way. One day we were in the cafeteria, after setting up for fitness stations, and we were waiting for the remainder of the class. The group was loud and several times had been asked to calm down. Most did; however, Sophie kept running around the area, climbing on the railings, and chasing Rosie. We were using a progressive time-out system, and Sophie was told to take a time-out. She ran out of the cafeteria into the courtyard, and then we didn't know where she had gone. She was found about five minutes later in the girls' restroom and was panic stricken that we were going to send her to the principal, which meant being sent home and expelled from school. Instead we talked, and Sophie actually began to let us in and to talk to us daily at school and often by phone at night. At least for us she never ran away again. Though she would still sit out when she needed to—most often of her own accord—she was with us.

Although Sophie had worked out this relationship with us, she wasn't making much progress with her peers. One day after we had been there about three months, Sophie and Rosie (a friend with an attitude equal to Sophie's) ended up jumping double dutch with Ben. Ben was one of the students Sophie had the least patience with. He was a Middle Eastern boy about half her size. His physical skills were minimal. She had already fought him twice that year (and won handily). Whenever they were near each other, you could feel the tension and simply waited for something to happen . . . and it was always "Ben's fault." How Ben even ended up jumping rope this day and how they ended up together we have no idea, but there they were and things weren't going well. You could hear Sophie across the playground telling Ben that he was "dumb" (and a couple of less flattering adjectives). The next thing I (Missy) knew Sophie had thrown the rope down and said she was going someplace else. The student teacher with them had no clue what to do. I talked to Sophie, asking her why she was leaving. "It's no good. Ben can't turn. I'm goin' to 'nuther rope." I asked, "Didn't someone teach you to turn?" "Yeah." I stated that Ben would never get any better if someone didn't teach him and we would always be in this situation. With a disgusted look on her face, she looked at me, said, "Here, take these," and handed me her two ends of the rope. She walked to the other end and kindly and gently stood behind Ben, took both his small hands in her big ones, and guided him through the rope turning. She explained that he had to have rhythm to turn (something that didn't come naturally to him, in her opinion). When she thought he had it, she would begin to relax her grip and then tighten it again when he couldn't keep the rhythm. After about three minutes she determined that he had learned well enough and came back and took the ropes from me. Rosie was jumping and there was a bad turn. Sophie said, "Sorry, my fault." They went for a while longer, and she said, "Good job, Ben." I couldn't take it anymore and walked away; she had never before uttered such words. At the end of class that day as students were filling out journals, I told Sophie I was proud of her for helping Ben and not fighting. I told her, "I was so happy that you almost made me cry." She responded, "Is that why your eyes are all red?"

After that day, Sophie became my inseparable friend. When we brought students to the university for the day, the big tough kid held my hand all day as we toured campus. I am no longer at the school or in Los Angeles, but Sophie writes, most often telling me of the parties she attended over the summer or other things to rouse my attention, but she writes. And whenever I suffer from seasonal allergies, I always think of why my eyes are red.

Sophie's growth is certainly very conditional. I have little hope that in two years without constant reinforcement and guidance that Sophie will not be "in trouble." She is not yet able to discriminate on her own about how to behave and she is still easily guided by her peers, but for one bright and shining moment we knew that Sophie had learned something about responsibility. It is a clear indication that programs with youth must be developmental and must view success in very small steps. Not all stories have happy endings, but they show glimmers of hope, if even for a short while.

You Listen To Us

Juanito was a sixth grader when he first entered the Coaching Club, a before-school basketball program. He was an English as a second language (ESL) student with Spanish as his first language. He spoke English well enough but wrote at about a second-grade level. He was a gifted athlete, especially for a kid who had never played organized sport. He was good-looking and street tough . . . quite macho. He came to the Coaching Club voluntarily and never missed a 6:30 A.M. meeting.

The Coaching Club's purpose was to develop personal and social responsibility through basketball. Juanito's basketball skills rapidly progressed and his responsibility skills with us were never an issue. His behavior was fine (even on the quiet side), he practiced on his own without prompting, and he helped others—especially the younger kids in the program. He would take these kids under his wing. He came early, helped set up, taught others, and was polite. He even started joking with us. We loved having him with us in the morning—he was the model team member. Yet, at the same time he was constantly being suspended from school for a variety of offenses, most of which involved being disrespectful to teachers and disrupting class.

During this same time, Juanito was in a class taught by practicum teachers from the university. It gave us a good chance to observe him in another setting. One day, while conducting warm-up exercises, the teacher told the students to do 15 push-ups. In response, Juanito sat on the back row and did none. The next class another teacher phrased the same request as, "Do as many push-ups as you think you need to get stronger." Juanito hesitated. The teacher in passing, almost under his breath, said, "You don't have to do any, but you can keep those skinny arms." Juanito did 52 push-ups. It was during this class that we also learned of his inability to read or write English.

He was an enigma to us. We loved having him in the Coaching Club. He had character and personality and was a delight. But every teacher in the school had problems with him and labeled him as hopeless and apathetic. When discussing the program at the end of the year, we asked, "How come you are so good in here and so bad in school?" He looked at us, hesitated, and with great conviction said, "Because you listen to us."

The story didn't end so well. Juanito stuck with us another year, but in the end the school won. Juanito is now in alternative school for trying to start a fire in the boys' locker room and for bringing a knife to school. He doesn't speak to us. When he sees us he hangs his head and looks the other way.

Juanito is one of those heartbreaking failures. The answer for him was so easy—respect him and help him and he would do the same for you. It happened in one isolated area, but we weren't able to make that transfer outside of a gym at 6:30 in the morning. The system won; Juanito had had his chance and didn't take it, and he was no longer their concern.

It's Fun Teaching Them the Right Thing to Do

Francisco was 13 years old and lived on Denver's predominantly Mexican-American northwest side with his mom, stepdad, and younger brother. His biological father committed suicide by hanging when Francisco was nine; Francisco found him upstairs in the bedroom. His mom was very supportive of her children and her efforts were reinforced by Francisco's stepdad.

Francisco entered the Energizers Club as a fourth grader in the fall of 1994. He was referred to the program because of his short temper, low self-esteem, and consequent behavior problems in the classroom. Francisco's basic agility and ball skills were not helped by his excessive weight. Often during his first year in the program, he was reluctant to participate in activities. Sometimes he would refuse altogether and pout from the side of the gym; at other times he would participate by going through the motions. A photograph of a reflection session during the summer of that year shows the youngsters sitting in a circle talking with Nick and his graduate students. Francisco, however, is sitting alone with his head down a few yards outside the circle, seemingly listening to the conversation but not participating.

The following year, as a fifth grader, Francisco became a more active member of the program. His physical skills grew, and consequently his self-confidence and level of participation increased. As he matured socially, emotionally, and physically, he was inspired by three former members of the previous year's program—then sixth graders at the neighborhood middle school—who were the first youngsters to assume the role of apprentice teachers. He remembers the nice way they treated him: "They were fun because they told us how to play and helped us do lots of stuff that I was having trouble with." Perhaps this appreciation sparked an awareness that he could contribute to the program when he went to middle school.

Five years after his initial visit to the Energizers Club, Francisco is an eighth grader at the middle school and the most senior apprentice teacher in Project Lead. He is a reliable and valued helper and regularly teaches the fourth and fifth graders in small groups, coaches teams, assists in settling disputes, and even disciplines individual students on occasion. Most of the time, the children respect him, listen to him, and take to heart what he says. Often his purposeful approach and ability to relate to the younger kids amaze the program staff. As he says, "Sometimes information has different meaning to younger children when it comes from someone closer to their age than from an adult."

Francisco enjoys teaching the younger children some of the same concepts that he himself learned and thinks that the program is "fine because it teaches kids how to work with partners they don't like and are sometimes mean to." For Francisco, the best part of the program is playing games, getting exercise, and working with other people—as he says, "I like helping those fourth and fifth graders because it's neat for me and them."

However, along with these perceived benefits, Francisco's involvement also brings several challenges. His biggest frustration is when the children misbehave and their actions suggest that they don't "buy into" the goals of the program. "When kids get out of control," he says, "we talk to them, make them sit out, and take time out to help them." Nevertheless, on occasions Francisco quickly becomes exasperated and he admits that he tends to get irritated with some kids. "When they mess around I feel like I want to leave the program. We're trying so hard but sometimes I feel like we don't have any control." Then, after further reflection and a wry smile, he remarks that these occasions remind him of his own "short fuse." We have been heartened by his ability to reflect on his teaching style and to incorporate these reflections into subsequent dealings with the kids.

Although Francisco enjoys the challenging role of apprentice teacher, he isn't blind to the weaknesses of the program. For example, in an end-of-year interview, he put forth ideas about how the program could be improved: "Give the kids more free time. The activities should be more varied. We could use the scooters to teach a cooperation game. They would teach them to trust each other." Turning to possible enrichment activities for the apprentice teachers, he says, "You should take us to the Denver Natural History Museum."

Francisco does not receive any financial reward in return for his hard work and dedication: "Yeah, we get track suits, but that's not why I come." When asked why he shows up regularly he quickly responds, "I want to teach and have fun." Then he adds, "I come to the program to stay out of trouble. If I wasn't here I'd be selling candy or something, probably getting in trouble, getting in fights." He likes the way the apprentice teachers interact inside and outside the program. "We talk about the program, how it's working and who's in it." When his friends ask him why he "works" in the program, he tells them, "It's fun teaching the kids self-control. Even though some of them are bad, it's fun teaching them the right things to do."

Francisco's regular attendance as an apprentice teacher shows that urban youngsters need association with relevant activities and that they will respond positively to activities that promote autonomy, self-confidence, and self-determination. Francisco has grown in maturity and is a competent and popular leader. Although nearing the end of his time in middle school, he is committed to continuing his involvement in Project Lead while in high school.

University Students

Students in our classes, especially physical education majors, have a hard time accepting our approach. Coming from a sport background, they often equate the development of responsibility with the ability to conform to and follow rules set by a domineering coach. They are taught to be tough and not give an inch. Jody was one of those people.

Jody was a 25-year-old undergraduate student finishing her teaching credential while also teaching physical education in a small private school. She had been a highly competitive collegiate basketball player, was a skilled athlete, and was headstrong and opinionated. She loved working with kids and saw physical education as a place to transmit her love of sport. She had the two of us (James and Missy) for the majority of her teaching classes; within a six-month period, she had two theory classes, a practicum experience in the elementary school, her own teaching situation, and three practicum students from the university at her school. She, in essence, was a student, a teacher's aide, a teacher, and a mentor teacher all at the same time.

She thought the philosophical ideas that James espoused in class wouldn't work in the real world and that the practical strategies that I

(Missy) proposed were completely illogical. And she openly told us so. Yet, at the same time she listened and thought and didn't completely write us off.

The practicum course she had with us was an experience as a teacher's aide in physical education at the charter school in south central Los Angeles—a place where she hesitated to leave her car on the street long enough to teach a 30-minute class. But she came—once we convinced her that there was a gated lot for her car. Her responsibilities were to assist individual fourth- and fifth-grade students during their physical education lesson, after I had presented the initial task. Silently she struggled with the structure of the class. You could see it in her face as we addressed the class. Managerially, she thought kids had too much freedom. They could get water as they pleased and go to the restroom when they needed to. They didn't have to stand in lines, and they called the teachers by their first names.

Instructionally, she questioned most everything that happened. Kids came to class and began practice by reading the first task posted on the wall; some did this better than others and some always had to be prompted. Kids were allowed to choose their own partners as well as their own equipment. Kids worked in small groups with about every group doing a different variation of the task. And in terms of content, we were not teaching large-group traditional games and sports but rather the skills that lead up to them in small-sided games. In short, we contradicted her way of thinking and operating and teaching. She would talk to us vehemently after class and write pages in her journal, but during class and with the kids she never deviated from what the teacher asked or wanted for the kids. As much as she disagreed or questioned it—she clinched her teeth, bit her tongue, and was the model assistant teacher. But we heard about it afterward.

Her questions never ceased. After every lesson she would ask me questions. "Why did you let kids choose their own partners when it took more time?" (In other words, I wasted time.) "Why did you spread equipment out before class and let kids get it themselves when you had to call them back at least three times for running or leaving before you were finished talking? Why did you have them in small groups spread out all over the playground when it was easier to see and control them in one single group? Why did you force new content on them when all they liked was basketball? Why? Why? Why?"

Then one day it began to happen. Jody was the lead teacher (I was out of town) and she was determined to stick to what I wanted to happen. Not quite sure of herself in this situation, she stuck to content that she knew and the kids liked—basketball. She planned forever and developed a remarkable lesson that involved students stretching on their own and then making choices between four different kinds of basketball situations: a highly competitive game refereed by a teacher, a recreational basketball game where you called your own fouls and minor violations were okay, an "Around the World" game, and a court where you could just practice skills. She had another university practicum student as an assistant. Her journal says the rest.

> I gave the students the responsibility to stretch for two minutes. All of the students were stretching when Adam (the other practicum student) began giving loud and firm instructions on how to stretch and what stretches to do. Later in class two students came to me with a concern over Adam's officiating the game that was to be called by the students. After a short discussion with the students, I realized Adam was wrong and that we were sending mixed messages. We needed to give students the chance to take responsibility for their own thoughts, actions, and behaviors. In closing, I am not dogging Adam; I was just concerned with the signals we were sending the children.

From that point on, Jody still questioned everything but now in terms of how what we did helped students take responsibility and how well it worked. She started to analyze situations on her own, not just question them. In fact she wrote,

> I overheard the classroom teacher telling her aide that she was amazed at how well the students [Missy's students] listened [in physical education]. She was saying how Missy never yells, blows a whistle, or struggles to get the students' attention. I could be wrong, but here it goes: I think through respecting the children, and having expectations the students' behavior naturally improves. Through stressing personal responsibility and personal development, students want to participate. Missy, what's your secret?

Jody began to pick up the subtleties in teaching that communicated mixed messages or lack of respect to students. For example, she recognized that the way one of her practicum students "talked down" to elementary students communicated a lack of respect to them. Once she realized what was happening, it was just another skill to teach, and as with sport skills, she could analyze what I was trying to do with amazing clarity. She became my sounding board. She possessed the uncanny knack to develop physical education tasks that taught complex motor skills while at the same time developed responsibility.

A recurring theme in Jody's journal was how uncomfortable students were in trying a new skill. "I also noticed that the children were timid with the hockey sticks. They were extremely comfortable with basketball." Yet, she picked up on the fact that students were becoming more comfortable learning new skills and sticking to it—"I noticed that the children were timid with striking, but they stuck with it and learned a new skill. If I compare this class with the floor hockey class, I can see a vast improvement in the children's self-confidence level." Or, "Some of the lower skilled children had a difficult time making the hard, fast, clean V cut. However, with guidance even the lesser skilled students improved. I noticed that even Cindy stuck with the skill. This is a vast improvement from six weeks ago." Interestingly, Jody was writing about the changes she saw in children but was also subtly writing about herself learning new skills as a teacher. She was expressing her desire to try new strategies with her kids, her uneasiness in doing so, and the fact that she had to stick with this method if it was going to work.

And so she began to take the things from the charter school to her school. First she started with managerial tasks. "I have also made the big jump, letting the older kids (third, fourth, and fifth grades) decide when they need a drink and when they have to use the restroom." Even more developmentally, she prevailed with those ideas even when they were not as successful as she hoped. "Right now, I think they are taking advantage of this new privilege [the restroom and water], but they will accept the responsibility and everything will run semi-smooth in a couple of days." Later (actually quite quickly), she progressed to instructional propositions, all the while assessing the results with amazing astuteness. For example, a second-grade class got to choose what they wanted to do—these four "girly" second graders chose basketball.

> I thought they hated basketball. I asked them why they chose basketball; they told me that they liked basketball a lot but they were embarrassed because all the other kids were playing and were a lot better than them. But today, they got to choose what to work on and they got to practice at their own pace. What a wake-up call for me. Why did I not think of this earlier? A competitive situation or set standards or single activity class limits participation to the athletically gifted. However, now my classes are still challenging to the advanced, but exciting, encouraging, and welcoming to the average and lower skilled children.

Her journal ends with a situation at her own school where a large, strong, yet babyish and immature fifth-grade boy had been bullied and ultimately got in a fight. The child had a series of behavioral encounters with other students and teachers. The administration's concern at this point was either to expel him or to suspend him. The parents begged the school to keep him, because no other school would take him—no one seemed to focus on the child. Jody wrote, "I realized that I totally put the children first and the administrative staff second. This was the first time in teaching that I was scared for my students and myself. Clint could have hurt someone badly. Instead of punishing him, I think we need to find out why it happened, so that it will never happen again." As Jody said about Cindy earlier, six weeks before that would have never happened.

Not all prospective teachers end up like Jody. Jody is now an ally to children. Many teachers can't leave behind their preconceived beliefs that teachers have to control kids. Jody's waking up, as she calls it, was because her eyes were open and she was looking, even behind the gruff exterior of telling James and me that we were out of our minds with these ideas. She hung in there and we hung in there, and Jody's teaching was changed because she was open to change, was willing to try, and stuck with it.

College Professors

At the same time, Jody had not acquired her teaching beliefs and methods from the back of beyond. She was teaching as she had been taught and as she was taught to teach. Those of us entrenched at the university pass on a lot, many times without questioning it. We just seem to do it—like being in a rut. Tom was one of those people.

Tom and I (Missy) crossed paths once or twice a year at the American Alliance for Health, Physical Education, Recreation and Dance (AAHPERD) or the AERA (American Educational Research Association) convention. He always had a paper to present and was always dressed in a sports coat, khaki slacks, a preppy shirt, and a tie. He presented the relaxed, casual academic look. We exchanged greetings and shared a few common experiences, as he taught at my undergraduate alma mater and I at his. But beyond that I was never quite sure what to say to him. I didn't understand all the statistical analysis of his research, and although I knew it was important, especially the concept, I was largely dealing with children and potential teachers of children and wasn't sure how it all fit together or simply didn't want to take the time to translate his work into what I was doing. Whatever, he was a nice person and I always felt there was something else he had to say, but I was never quite sure what it was. I remember leaving conversations with him having the feeling that something was unfinished, though I had no clue what.

We had all known Tom for years. He was one of the most prominent physical education professionals around. He had a research life balanced between pedagogy and sport psychology. He adapted the term "learned helplessness" for the field of physical education. He published furiously. For 18 years he pursued traditional research projects looking at teacher and coach expectations, how they are communicated, and how they affect youngsters' self-perceptions and behavior. He was a quantitative researcher who brought respect to the fledging teacher research in physical education. He was successful. He had tenure and was a full professor in a Doctoral I institution and had a long line of successful graduate students. In short; he had made it in higher education. Life was good (or at least it looked that way to all those who try to make in the academic world).

Then one day in late 1994, out of the clear blue, he called Don Hellison and asked if he could spend a semester working with him in Chicago. Don, wondering why (but suspecting Tom needed a reason to return to his native Chicago), said "okay." I can actually remember Don calling and saying, "You'll never guess who wants to come to Chicago when you leave. I wonder why?"

The need to return to Chicago was not Tom's reason for wanting to work with Don and his programs for underserved youth. Tom admitted to being haunted by a nagging question about what he had committed his life to for those 18 years: "How can I use this stuff to make a difference in kids' lives?" He began to find his answer to this question by venturing down a road that combined his need to make a difference and a need to pass something different on to his undergraduate students with his research. His answer has made all the difference to a multitude of kids, teachers, administrators and students in Greensboro, North Carolina, and in Chicago.

Since his six-month stint in Chicago, Tom has returned to the university where he spent the past 20 years. It is the same university where he "made it." Yet, now it is a new place for him. His work has a decidedly different character. He works largely in one middle school implementing programs for underserved youth. In addition to the standard sport programs that we have talked about, Tom has developed mentoring programs that are designed to help kids take the skills learned in the gym to the outside world. He works with teachers, principals, and graduate and undergraduate students. He has developed a mentoring handbook and summer programs for kids.

Additionally, his research has changed, and he has questioned the entire scholarship model and expectations of higher education. He is no longer conducting research simply to present at AERA or AAHPERD but research that can be used to change the lives of kids. For example, instead of papers such as "Motor Ability and Instructional Contexts: Effects on Teacher Expectations and Dyadic Interactions in Elementary Physical Education Classes" (Martinek & Karper, 1984), he now writes such papers as "Fostering Resiliency in Underserved Youth Through Physical Activity" (Martinek & Hellison, 1997a). He has publicly called for an expanded conception of scholarship at the university that includes the integration of service and scholarship (Martinek & Hellison, 1997b). One of his reasons for promoting such inquiry is that the traditional research paradigm has proved itself irrelevant for changing practice in schools and youth programs. Tom has come to integrate his beliefs, his teaching, his scholarship, and his service into one. With it he has developed a passion that seemingly changed his life.

Today Tom still attends AAHPERD and, at times, AERA. Now, however, his dress is different—his trusty Loyola sweatshirt (and khakis) and even sweats have become his attire. You will find him more often talking to teachers and students than in research sessions. He still publishes feverishly but now it is about how to better the world for kids. Although he is busier than ever, he is not frantic. In the middle of the rush there seems be a calm in his life, a stabilizing force. He has more energy. He is focused on something that drives him in a positive way, not driven by the requirements of the university. Now there doesn't seem to be enough time to talk about all we have to say. And I, for one, can honestly say that I am glad our paths have again crossed, not just in meeting but in working together for kids. He has added depth, diversity, and richness to all five (Nick, James, Don, Jim, and Missy) of our lives. Life is good for him and for us.

Endings

These stories tell us what we need to know. They give us hope. They sustain us in the darker times. They are what we do and why we do it. Just one Sophie, one Francisco, one Jody, one Tom, and yes, one Juanito offers hope. They are our children, students, and friends. We do hear them cry; we see them struggle. We try, in part, to answer their cries and add clarity to their struggles. For us it is enough. For us it is worth doing. In the end, you have to decide for yourself—what is worth doing?

For Further Study

Howe, Q. (1991). *Under running laughter.* New York: The Free Press.

Quincy Howe is a university professor who returns to the public school to teach. Yet, it is not any public school but Leake and Watts, a residential facility for underserved youth. The book, with seriousness, humor, compassion, and depth, recounts his experiences—successes and failures—in working with the kids in his classes. This is a must-read for anyone who has struggled with trying to make learning relevant for kids who don't value education and in trying to teach to issues larger than content.

See also For Further Study from chapter 2.

Epilogue

Challenges

Tom Martinek

No amount of skill or care on the part of those engaged in youth development work will eradicate the problems of underserved youth. Racism, drugs, violence, poverty, and lack of resources are root problems that will not disappear quickly. What we can do, however, is demonstrate the value of these young people and empower them by providing choices for better decisions about relations in schooling and "doing the right thing." The authors of this text believe that getting kids to gain a positive perspective on their lives and society can begin with programs that empower and value them.

For those who want to become involved in this kind of work, we have offered our own 70 years of experience in service learning and youth development programs. We have also suggested some guidelines for doing this kind of work and for developing and implementing specific programs. Although we have various views of what seems to work, we have found that there are some constants that need to be present if any program is to succeed.

Personal values are probably the most important of these constants. Valuing kids, their voices, and struggles is necessary if programs are to work. How these values are acquired is unclear. We have stressed throughout this text that all of us operate from a common set of values based on the responsibility model. And yet, the six of us have acquired these values in different ways. One of us has spent more than 25 years of his professional life trying out ideas to help kids buffet the social ills of the underserved. Others have developed these values through their exposure to graduate school coursework and personal involvement in youth programs. One has worked in similar programs in another country.

I have abandoned the traditional research path to do what really matters to me now. The new path has drawn me closer to kids and has forced me to reexamine who I am and how I can contribute to their lives. At the same time, it has separated me from the research community to which I was so accustomed. However, I feel much better about what I am doing.

A second constant is a personal commitment to service learning work and providing professional programs for undergraduates and graduate students to work in programs for underserved youth. A spirit of true collaboration is at the forefront of this type of commitment. In the preface, Don Hellison suggested that the fence separating the ivory tower and community programs must be torn down for any collaboration to happen. Hal Lawson (1997) underscored the point about universities needing to change or become irrelevant. Their agenda must focus on connecting the ivory tower to its major constituents, that is, kids, leaders, and administrators in schools, social agencies, and other community programs. To make these relationships feasible and meaningful, programs must be set up by faculty who are willing to step into what Donald Schon (1987) called the "swampy lowland of practice." All of us are running and teaching in programs before and after school hours and some, like Nick Cutforth and James Kallusky, provide programs during the school day. Running these programs has required us to cultivate collaborative bonds between the university, youth agency, and school. Sometimes the needs among all three are very different, thus requiring some give and take. This means that all parties have to acquire a shared understanding of what needs to be done to make these programs work. Listening ears and sensitivity to cultural differences of each other's setting are important requisites to make the collaborative process successful.

A third constant is time. This work is labor intensive, not only daily but for the long term. That is why this commitment to youth development involves long-term involvement in programs. There is emotional cost as well. You will encounter low points that sometimes cause you to doubt what you are doing. Therefore, persistence and "endurance" are needed; you have to outlast the kids. Programs and staff that have short-term involvement, a narrow research perspective, and restrictive funding guidelines will struggle to make any impact on kids' lives.

A final constant is peer, faculty, and institutional support. If professors are to willfully and effectively engage in service learning work and contribute positively to kids' lives as well as to professional development and community programs, institutional support must in be place. That is, all parties must commit to connecting community resources and programs to the professional activities of the university. This will not be easy, given the economic and political reliance on obtaining grants and the university's strong historical connection to its research mission. However, if the helping fields such as ours are to gain public trust, we must respond to the cries for help from community agencies and schools.

Institutional support will also mean that the "research" products of service work must be viewed in different ways (Martinek & Hellison, 1997b). The boundaries of traditional research paradigms must be stretched so that creativity and application become possibilities in the research process. For many traditionalists, research conjures up images of controlled quantitative and qualitative methods, sophisticated statistics, publications in the best scholarly journals, and ultimately recognition by a prestigious academy. When we research programs that focus on values, relationships, feelings, and other virtues of life, the characterization of research takes on new and different meanings. Attempting to better understand kids' struggles often requires that we be creative inquirers. Creating also requires work and perseverance. We are reminded of this by Clarence Day's claim:

> The creative impulse seems not to wish to produce finished work. It certainly deserts us halfway after the idea is born; and if we go on, creating becomes work (Patton, 1987, p. 50).

This will probably require that the products of service-bonded research (i.e., workshops, applied articles, position papers, program development, and personal involvement) be placed on equal footing with its traditional research counterparts. It means that the institutional reward system must embrace the notion that community-bonded work is valued. This means that both peers in professional development programs and other colleagues in the science disciplines view what we do as an important and scholarly contribution to our field. If this doesn't happen, few, if any, young assistant professors will venture into community programs.

A question we are often asked is, Do our programs and what we do make a difference? Those who choose this type of work will deal with this question daily. Throughout this text we have given tidbits of what we have found. In chapter 12, for example, we described the favorable products of our work that have been derived from systematic evaluation. It will be difficult to determine how much impact you really make. We often use the analogy of planting seeds to answer this question. The ideas about learning to take responsibility are seeds that you will try to plant in your own programs. Using the responsibility goals helps these seeds germinate into ways of being more sensitive and responsive to the well-being of others. The model that we all use is not a "magic bullet" for curing the social problems that plague kids—you have no control over these problems.

The sprouting of these seeds is often found in the small victories that we see and hear from kids. We think these are great indicators of success; they tell us if we are on the right path. Although our nation's poor continue to be marginalized from mainstream society, and the jail incarceration rate continues to escalate, we somehow manage to find nuggets of hope in the kids we work with. Not everything we do is successful. We have had plenty of bad days filled with confrontation and indifference. We have shared moments of joy from struggling together to get things right. And yet in the midst of all this I am personally reminded of the valuable contribution kids can make when I see one of our fifth-grade club members showing a younger club member how to shoot a set shot. Or when Darren, one of our club members who just got suspended for bringing a weapon to school, calls me to tell me he's "sorry for letting the club down." Or when I urge Calvin, one of our apprentice teachers, to start a reflection session during a club session and he places both his hands on my shoulder and says "Don't worry, Tom. You don't have to tell me—I know the routine." And there is Darnel, a middle school club member who hated basketball and continually shied away from most sports in the early grades. One day she said to me, "Tom, I think I am going out for the basketball team at school—I am getting the hang of it." Or when Shronda, during a group discussion, talks about being committed to the club, "Once you decide to be a part of this club you stay with it. If someone drops out that doesn't matter to me—one monkey doesn't stop the show. Regardless of whether that person comes or not, the program will roll on." Or when a youth corps member, after working with some difficult nine- and ten-year-olds, announces, "Now I know what my teachers put up with when they had me."

So, do you think you want to do this type of work? Taking up the challenge of making a difference in kids' lives will require an understanding of the culture of kids and their values. Understanding their view of schooling and school, their neighborhood, adults, and life in general are all part of the agenda. Without this backdrop, efforts to connect with youngsters and provide worthwhile experiences will fall short. And yes, it helps to have peer, faculty, and institutional support. But the most important ingredients for success are your commitment, your preparation, and your persistence. We need leaders in the youth development fields, people willing to accept the challenges and take risks. We invite you to join us on this wonderful journey!

References

Allen, W. (Producer & Director, Orion films) (1989). *Crimes and misdemeanors* [Film].

Bellah, R.N., Madsen, R., Sullivan, W.M., Swidler, A., & Tipton, S.M. (1996). *Habits of the heart: Individualism and commitment in American life* (2nd ed.). Berkeley: University of California Press.

Benson, P.L. (1997). *All kids are our kids: What communities must do to raise caring and responsible children and adolescents.* San Francisco: Jossey-Bass.

Carson, R. (1984). *The sense of wonder.* New York: Harper & Row. (Original work published 1956)

Coles, R. (1997). *The moral intelligence of children.* New York: Random House.

Compagnone, N. (1995). Teaching responsibility to rural elementary youth: Going beyond the urban at-risk boundaries. *Journal of Physical Education, Recreation and Dance, 66*(8), 58-63.

Covey, S.R. (1991). *Principle-centered leadership.* New York: Simon & Schuster.

Creighton, B., & Lee, G. (no date). *Teaching personal and social responsibility through physical education: A teacher resource.* Te Kura Akau Taitoka, New Zealand: Dunedin College of Education.

Cummings, T. (1997). *Testing the effectiveness of Hellison's personal and social responsibility model: A dropout, repeated grade, and absentee rate comparison.* Unpublished master's thesis, California State University, Chico.

Cutforth, N.J. (1997). "What's worth doing": A university professor reflects on an after-school program in a Denver elementary school. *Quest, 49,* 130-139.

Cutforth, N.J. (2000). Connecting school physical education to the community through service learning. *Journal of Physical Education, Recreation and Dance, 1* (2), 39-45.

Cutforth, N., & Parker, M. (1996). Promoting affective development in physical education: The value of journal-writing. *Journal of Physical Education, Recreation and Dance, 67*(7), 19-23.

Cutforth, N.J., & Puckett, K.M. (1999). An investigation into the organization, challenges, and impact of an urban apprentice teacher program. *The Urban Review, 31*(2), 153-172.

Danish, S., & Howard, C. (1991). *Going for the goal.* Unpublished document, Virginia Commonwealth University, Richmond.

Debusk, M., & Hellison, D. (1987). Implementing a physical education self-responsibility model for delinquency prone youth. *Journal of Teaching Physical Education, 8,* 104-112.

deCharms, R. (1976). *Enhancing motivation: Change in the classroom.* New York: Irvington.

Demos, E.V. (1989). Resiliency in infancy. In T. Dugan & R. Coles (Eds.), *The child in our times—Studies in the development of resiliency* (pp. 3-22). New York: Brunner/Mazel.

Dewey, J. (1900). *The school and society.* Chicago: University of Chicago Press.

Dickens, C. (1952). *A Christmas carol.* Philadelphia: Lippincott. (Original work published 1868)

Eddy, M. (1998). *The role of physical activity in educational violence prevention programs.* Doctoral dissertation, UMI dissertation services, Ann Arbor, Michigan.

Erickson, J., & Anderson, J. (Eds.) (1997). *Learning with the community: Concepts and models for service learning in teacher education.* Washington, DC: American Association of Higher Education.

Field, T., Nolin, M., & Cort, R. (Producers), & Herek, S. (Director). (1995). *Mr. Holland's opus* [Film].

Gatto, J.T. (1992). *Dumbing us down: The hidden curriculum of compulsory schooling.* Philadelphia: New Society.

Gatto. J.T. (1998). In defense of the original sin: The neglected genius of American spirituality. *The Sun, 265,* 10-14.

Georgiadis, N. (1992). *Practical inquiry in physical education: The case of Hellison's personal and social responsibility model.* Unpublished dissertation, University of Illinois at Chicago.

Gold, M., & Mann, D.W. (1984). *Expelled to a friendlier place: A study of effective alternative schools.* Ann Arbor: University of Michigan Press.

Good, T., & Brophy, J. (1990). *Educational psychology* (2nd ed.). New York: Longman.

Griffin, L., Mitchell, S., & Oslin, J. (1997). *Teaching sport concepts and skills: A tactical games approach.* Champaign, IL: Human Kinetics.

Haas, T., & Lambert, T. (1995). To establish the bonds of common purpose and mutual enjoyment. *Phi Delta Kappan, 76,* 136-142.

Hellison, D. (1978). *Beyond balls and bats: Alienated (and other) youth in the gym.* Washington, DC: AAHPER.

Hellison, D. (1993). The Coaching Club—Teaching responsibility to inner-city students. *Journal of Physical Education, Recreation and Dance, 64* (5), 66-70.

Hellison, D. (1995). *Teaching responsibility through physical activity.* Champaign, IL: Human Kinetics.

Hellison, D. (1996). Teaching personal and social responsibility in physical education. In S.J. Silverman & C.D. Ennis (Eds.), *Student learning in physical education: Applying research to enhance instruction* (pp. 269-286). Champaign, IL: Human Kinetics.

Hellison, D. (1999). Promoting character development through sport: Rhetoric or reality? *New Designs for Youth Development, 15,* 23-27.

Hellison, D., & Cutforth, N. (1997). Extended day programs for urban children and youth: From theory to practice. In H. Walberg, O. Reyes, & R. Weissberg (Eds.), *Children and youth: Interdisciplinary perspectives* (pp. 223-249). San Francisco: Jossey-Bass.

Hellison, D., & Kallusky, J. (1999). The Youth Leader Project Partnership in physical education in higher education. *Chronicle of the National Association for Physical Education in Higher Education, 10*(2), 6, 14.

Howe, Q. (1991). *Under running laughter.* New York: Free Press.

Ianni, F.A.J. (1989). *The search for structure: A report on American youth today.* New York: The Free Press.

Jeneid, M. (1967). *Adventuring outward bound.* Melbourne, Australia: Lansdowne Press.

Joyce, B., & Weil, M. (1986). *Models of teaching* (3rd ed.). Englewood Cliffs, NJ: Prentice-Hall.

Kierkegaard, S. (1987). *Either/or (Part I)* (H. Hong & E. Hong, Trans.). Princeton, NJ: Princeton University Press. (Original work published 1843)

Koering, T. (1999). *The effects of positive coaching.* Unpublished master's thesis, University of North Dakota, Grand Forks.

Kohn, A. (1991). Caring kids. *Phi Delta Kappan, 72,* 496-506.

Komives, S.R., Lucas, N., & McMahon, T.R. (1998). *Exploring leadership: For college students who want to make a difference.* San Francisco: Jossey-Bass.

Kounin, J. (1970). *Discipline and group management in classrooms.* New York: Holt, Rinehart, & Winston.

Lawson, H.A. (1997). Children in crisis, the helping professions, and the social responsibilities of universities. *Quest, 49,* 8-33.

Lewis, M. (1997). *Poisoning the ivy.* Armonk, NY: Sharpe.

Martinek, T., & Hellison, D. (1997a). Fostering resiliency in underserved youth through physical activity. *Quest, 49,* 34-49.

Martinek, T., & Hellison, D. (1997b). Service-bonded inquiry: The road less traveled. *Journal of Teaching in Physical Education, 17,* 107-121.

Martinek, T., & Hellison, D. (1998). Values and goal setting with underserved youth. *Journal of Physical Education, Recreation and Dance, 69*(7), 47-52.

Martinek, T., & Karper, W. (1984). Motor ability and instructional contexts: Effects on teacher expectations and dyadic interactions in elementary physical education classes. *Research Quarterly for Exercise and Sport, 55,* 32-40.

Martinek, T., McLaughlin, D., & Schilling, T. (1999). Project Effort: Teaching responsibility beyond the gym. *Journal of Physical Education, Recreation and Dance, 70*(6), 12-25.

Martinek, T., Schilling, T., & Johnson, D. (1999). *Evaluation of a sport and mentoring program designed to foster personal and social responsibility in underserved youth.* Unpublished report from Project Effort, University of North Carolina at Greensboro.

McBride, D.L (1984). *The behaviors of adolescent boys in a residential treatment center during high ropes course experiences.* Unpublished doctoral dissertation, The Ohio State University, Columbus.

McLaughlin, M.W., & Heath, S.B. (1993). Casting the self: Frames for identity and dilemmas for policy. In S.B. Heath & M.W. McLaughlin (Eds.), *Identity and inner-city youth: Beyond ethnicity and gender* (pp. 210-239). New York: Teachers College Press.

McLaughlin, M.W., Irby, M.A, & Langman, J. (1994). *Urban sanctuaries: Neighborhood organizations in the lives and futures of inner-city youth.* San Francisco: Jossey-Bass.

Meier, D. (1995). *The power of their ideas: Lessons from a small school in Harlem.* Boston: Beacon Press.

Millikan, W.E. (1994). Youth at risk and dropout prevention: A working program. In B. Cato, H. Gray, D. Nelson, & P.R. Varnes (Eds.), *Youth at risk: Targeting in on prevention.* Dubuque, IA: Brown.

Morris, G.S.D., & Stiehl, J. (1999). *Changing kids' games* (2nd ed.). Champaign, IL: Human Kinetics.

Mosston, M. & Ashworth, S. (1986). *Physical education: From intent to action.* Columbus, OH: Merrill.

Mulaudzi, L. (1995). *Program evaluation of an implementation of a responsibility model for inner-city youth.* Unpublished master's project, University of Illinois at Chicago.

Noddings, N. (1992). *The challenge to care in schools.* New York: Teachers College Press.

Palmer, P.J. (1998). The grace of great things: Reclaiming the sacred in knowing, teaching, and learning. *The Sun, 273,* 24-28.

Patton, M. (1987). *Creative evaluation.* Newbury Park, CA: Sage.

Payson, P. (1995). *Great American speeches: 80 years of political oratory* [Videorecording]. Alexandria, VA: Pieri and Spring Productions.

Perrone, V. (1991). *A letter to teachers: Reflections on schooling and the art of teaching.* San Francisco: Jossey-Bass.

Postman, N., & Weingartner, C. (1969). *Teaching as a subversive activity.* New York: Dell.

Raywid, M.A. (1994). Alternative schools: The state of the art. *Educational Leadership, 52,* 26-31.

Reyhner, J. (1992). *Teaching American Indian students.* Norman: University of Oklahoma Press.

Rogers, C. (1969). *Freedom to learn.* Columbus, OH: Merrill.

Rohnke, K. (1989). *Cowstails and cobras II*. Dubuque, IA: Kendall/Hunt.

Rose, M. (1995). *Possible lives: The promise of public education in America*. Boston: Houghton Mifflin.

Schilling, T. (1999). *An investigation of commitment among participants in an extended day physical activity program*. Unpublished doctoral dissertation, University of North Carolina at Greensboro.

Schon, D. (1987). *Educating the reflective practitioner*. San Francisco: Jossey-Bass.

Shelley, M. (1984). *Frankenstein*. New York: Random House. (Original work published 1831).

Silverstein, S. (1976). *The missing piece*. New York: Harper & Row.

Smedes, L.B. (1990). *A pretty good person*. New York: Harper & Row.

Smink, J. (1990). *Mentoring programs for at-risk youth: A dropout prevention research report*. (National Dropout Center Rep. No. CG 022476). Clemson, SC.

Smith, M. (1990). Enhancing self-responsibility through a humanistic approach to PE. *The Bulletin of Physical Education, 26*(3), 27-31.

St. Exupery, A. de. (1943). *The little prince*. New York: Harcourt, Brace, & World.

Stiehl, J. (1993). Becoming responsible—Theoretical and practical considerations. *Journal of Physical Education, Recreation and Dance, 64*(5), 38-41.

Testerman, J. (1996). Holding at-risk students: The secret is one-on-one. *Phi Delta Kappan, 51*, 364-365.

Turnbull, W. (1995, November 17-19). Integrity. *Grand Forks (ND) Herald*, USA Weekend, p. 10.

Van Tulder, M., Van der Vegt, R., & Veenman, S. (1993). Inservice education in innovative schools: A multi-case study. *Qualitative Studies in Education, 6*, 129-142.

Wang, M.C., Haertel, G.D., & Walberg, H.J. (1994). Educational resilience in inner cities. In M.C. Wang & E.W. Gordon (Eds.), *Educational resilience in inner-city America: Challenges and prospects* (pp.45-72). Hillsdale, NJ: Lawrence Erlbaum Associates.

Witmer, J.T., & Anderson, C.T. (1994). *How to establish a high school service learning program*. Alexandria, VA: Association for Supervision and Curriculum Development.

Wright, P. (1998). *The impact of a responsibility model based martial arts program on violence prevention*. Unpublished master's thesis, University of Illinois at Chicago.

Youth on an Upward Roll Program. (1997, October). *Quarterly report*. St. Paul: State of Minnesota Department of Children and Learning Services.

Index

About the Authors

Don Hellison, PhD, is best known for his work with underserved youth. He is a professor of kinesiology at the University of Illinois at Chicago, where he is also the director of the Urban Youth Leader Project. He is the author of numerous books, including *Teaching Responsibility through Physical Education.* Among the awards Dr. Hellison has received are the National Association of Sport and Physical Education (NASPE) Hall of Fame Award in 1999 and the International Olympic Committee President s Prize in 1995. He earned his doctorate in physical education from The Ohio State University.

Nick Cutforth, PhD, is a noted educator, author, and researcher in the field of service learning and underserved youth. As associate professor in the college of education at the University of Denver, his duties include teaching courses in urban education. Dr. Cutforth received the Latin American Research and Service Agency s Bernie Valdez Education Award in 1997. He earned his doctorate in curriculum, instruction, and evaluation from the University of Illinois at Chicago.

James Kallusky, EdD, has earned a strong reputation for his efforts teaching, directing, and researching physical activity programs for underserved youth. In addition to his duties as assistant professor in kinesiology and physical education at California State University at Los Angeles, he is the executive director for Youth Agency Administration Studies. He earned his doctorate in physical education from the University of Northern Colorado.

Tom Martinek, EdD, is a well-known scholar in the psychology of physical education and director of Project Effort for Underserved Youth. A professor of exercise and sport science at the University of North Carolina at Greensboro, he has developed youth programming and worked directly with underserved kids in the community. He is the 1999 recipient of the Arthur Wilde Distinguished Alumni Award from Boston University, where he earned his doctoral degree. Dr. Martinek also was named University Teacher of the Year by the North Carolina Alliance for Health, Physical Education, Recreation and Dance in 1993.

Melissa Parker, PhD, is an associate professor of kinesiology and physical education at the University of Northern Colorado and a prominent voice in the field of physical education. She has developed service learning programs at several universities and worked with children in a wide range of program settings, from in-school physical education classes to before- and after-school programs, outdoor adventure, and sports. She is also a coauthor of *Children Moving*. Dr. Parker earned her doctorate in curriculum and instruction from The Ohio State University.

Jim Stiehl, PhD, has dedicated the past 30 years to bringing the needs of alternative kids to the forefront. A professor and director of the school of kinesiology and physical education at the University of Northern Colorado, he was named the Central District Alliance for Health, Physical Education, Recreation and Dance Scholar of the Year in 1993. Dr. Stiehl is also coauthor of the book *Changing Kids Games.* He earned his doctorate from the University of California at Los Angeles.